THE COMMONS
UNDER SCRUTINY

THE COMMONS UNDER SCRUTINY

Edited by

MICHAEL RYLE

and

PETER G. RICHARDS
for the Study of Parliament Group

ROUTLEDGE

First published in 1977 by Fontana
as *The Commons in the Seventies*
Revised edition published in 1981 by Fontana as *The Commons Today*

Third revised edition first published in 1988 by Routledge
11 New Fetter Lane, London EC4P 4EE

© 1977, 1981, and 1988 The Study of Parliament Group

Typeset in 10/12pt Baskerville Linotron 202
by Hope Services, Abingdon, Oxon
Printed in the British Isles
by The Guernsey Press Co Ltd, Guernsey, Channel Islands

British Library Cataloguing in Publication Data
The Commons under scrutiny.—New ed.
1. Great Britain. Parliament. House of
Commons
I. Ryle, Michael   II. Richards, Peter G.
(Peter Godfrey), 1923–1987
328.41′072

ISBN 0-415-01147-7

IN MEMORY OF
PETER G. RICHARDS

On 22 September 1987 Peter Richards completed his part of the editorial work on the manuscript he had then received. On 23 September he died immediately after attending a meeting of the Hansard Society. It was typical of both his total reliability and his love of Parliament that Peter should have completed these tasks before his death.

In his inaugural lecture at Southampton University in 1972, Peter Richards said 'Support for Parliament . . . depends necessarily on fuller public understanding of the nature and purpose of parliamentary institutions.' In this book we have all been seeking to further that understanding. For these reasons his fellow contributors wish to dedicate *The Commons Under Scrutiny* to the memory of Professor Peter G. Richards.

MICHAEL RYLE

March 1988

v

CONTENTS

CONTENTS

PREFACE

The Study of Parliament Group is an association of some members of the staff of Parliament and academics who have undertaken research in the area of parliamentary studies. The group was formed in 1964 and, over the years, has published a range of books and articles and presented evidence to parliamentary committees, mainly on questions of procedural reform. In 1970 the group published a volume of essays entitled *The Commons in Transition* at a time when arguments on the need to change procedures were widely discussed. The volume was well received and a fresh volume, *The Commons in the Seventies*, appeared in 1977; this book provided an opportunity to reflect on the experience of the reforms and attempts at reform that had taken place in the 1960s. A revised edition, *The Commons Today*, was published in 1981. By then the new system of select committees had just become established and so a major objective of the group at the time of its foundation had been achieved. Strangely enough at this period much of the optimism about the value of such changes had begun to fade.

The Commons under Scrutiny is thus the fourth volume of essays in this series. It reflects the experience of the 1980s, a period of remarkable political stability. The Conservative Government has enjoyed a dominant and secure position. Yet the vigour of the House of Commons has increased. Its ability to examine and challenge government actions has never been of greater value.

Compared with its predecessors, the present volume shows some similarities and some alterations. The innovations include a chapter on sources of information available to MPs – an important topic unjustly neglected in the past – and a discussion of recent developments in parliamentary privilege. Chapter 6, Opposition to Government, examines the vital role of party organizations in the work of the Commons. Our readers will be aware of some variation in the character of the essays: no apology is made for the lack of uniformity. The contributions vary in subject matter. Some are broadly descriptive; some are more specialized; some tend to be more analytical. The authors also have dissimilar experience obtained either from official duties at Westminster or alternatively from academic life.

It must be stressed that the essays, including those by the editors, must be regarded simply as expressions of individual opinion. The Study of Parliament Group has no collective view on the issues raised in the book and accepts no responsibility for the views expressed. But the Group is deeply committed to the values of representative, democratic government. The strength of such a system depends upon public appreciation and support. The purpose of the essays is to promote critical understanding of the pattern of activity at Westminster.

Michael Ryle
Peter G. Richards
September 1987

Chapter One

THE ROLE OF
THE COMMONS

PETER G. RICHARDS

The House of Commons is a form of theatre. There is a stage, there are actors; there is a play and an audience. But the theatre has many abnormal features. The way the play develops can have a significant impact on the whole of the community. While there can be an element of drama or even fantasy in the proceedings, what happens is always related to harsh facts from the world outside. The stage is rectangular. The scenery never changes. The actors portray themselves. The subject of the play alters frequently. The theatre is sometimes crowded; more often it is virtually empty. Sometimes there are minor studio productions elsewhere in the building. The actors are paid. Leading ladies and gentlemen get higher salaries but some well-known performers only get the basic wage.

A group of the actors decides the nature of the performance but it does take some notice of what the company as a whole would like to do. Indeed, the group does not decide the whole of the programme and some time is left free so that initiative can pass to other members of the company. Yet when there is dispute about the programme or, more often, about the conclusion of a play, the controlling group almost always gets its way for the actors divide themselves into factions and it usually has the support of the largest faction.

Our theatre has an unusual shape. There is no proscenium arch, nor even a stage in the normal sense. The setting is a rectangular arena where the actors sit on benches facing each other (see figure 1.1). They are forced to divide themselves between the two sides; each one must either line up behind the governing group or confront and oppose it from the seats opposite. The design is fashioned for verbal jousting and, to prevent any possibility of physical aggression during a performance, it is forbidden to cross the floor from one set

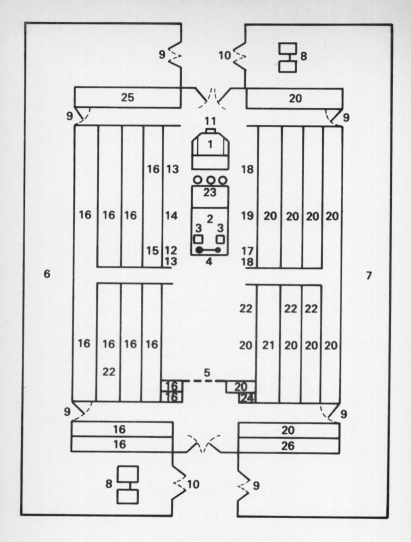

Figure 1.1 Plan of the Commons Chamber
(slightly simplified)

KEY

1 Speaker's Chair

2 Table of the House

3 Dispatch boxes

4 The Mace

5 The bar of the House

6 Aye division lobby

7 No division lobby

8 Division clerks' desks

9 Entrances to lobbies

10 Exits from lobbies

11 Petition bag

12 Prime Minister

13 Government whips

14 Other ministers

15 Parliamentary private secretaries

16 Government backbenches

17 Leader of opposition

18 Opposition whips

19 Shadow ministers

20 Opposition backbenches

21 Social and Liberal Democrats

22 Other smaller parties

23 Clerks at the table

24 Serjeant at Arms

25 Civil servants

26 Strangers

of benches to the other. Order is maintained by an impartial master of ceremonies, Mr Speaker. The architecture symbolizes a two-party system. It is quite different from the semi-circular or horseshoe pattern common in European assemblies.

The analogy between the House of Commons and a theatre cannot be pressed too far. Unlike a theatre, the Commons has a dual audience. The smaller, internal audience, the members of the theatre club, are the 650 Members of Parliament. This audience also provides the actors, some of which have major roles while others are rarely heard. The wider audience is represented in token form by the people in the public gallery. Seats are free, and tickets may be obtained from the actors or by queuing on the day. The presence of reporters from the mass media, combined with a sound recording, enable the whole community to know what takes place.

The House of Commons is important because of events that take place beyond its walls. At irregular intervals the members are elected to represent people from different localities. These elections give authority and legitimacy to the theatre club. Our system of government is based on the principle of parliamentary sovereignty which means that Parliament can do as it chooses and cannot be lawfully challenged. To quote the more formal language of Professor Dicey;

> The principle of Parliamentary sovereignty means . . . that Parliament . . . has . . . the right to make or unmake any law whatsoever; and further, that no person or body is recognised by the law of England as having a right to override or set aside the legislation of Parliament. [1]

As the powers of the House of Lords were restricted by the Parliament Acts of 1911 and 1949 and are further inhibited by the strength of democratic sentiment, the sovereignty of Parliament has almost become the sovereignty of the Commons.

While the Commons has great power there is a severe limitation on what, in practice, it can achieve. A theatre cannot lay down comprehensive and consistent policies. It cannot control the vast bureaucracy required to run a modern welfare state. So the Commons cannot govern: it can only call to account those who do govern. John Stuart Mill described the role of the Commons as follows:

> Their part is to indicate wants, to be an organ of popular demands, and a place of adverse discussion for all opinions

4

relating to public matters, both great and small; and, along with this, to check by criticism, and eventually by with-drawing their support, those high officers who really conduct the public business, or appoint those by whom it is conducted.[2]

So the theatre club can express no confidence in the performance of its guiding group, the Cabinet, but it cannot do that work itself.

Much of the time of the Commons, in the Chamber and in committee, is devoted to legislation. The public see the passage of legislation as a major task of the Commons but, even here, the initiative comes almost entirely from the Cabinet. A body of 650 people cannot draft complex legal clauses. Initial spadework must always be done by small groups of people with specialized knowledge or skills. Mill argued that 'a numerous assembly is as little fitted for the direct business of legislation as for that of administration'.[3] Ninety years later Professor Griffith regarded the task of Parliament in legislation as 'examination, criticism, approval'.[4] The existence of private members' legislation does not invalidate this conclusion: in this case the initiative moves from ministers supported by civil servants to an individual backbencher often supported by a pressure group.

The Commons is held back not only by the limitations of its organization but also by adherence to political parties. In a sense, this inhibition is self-imposed. At any time a Member could break free from political ties, and it is always possible to speak and vote as you wish in the theatre of the Commons' Chamber. But the restraints are severe. It is commonly said that Members accept party discipline because to defy the party damages the prospect of joining the political ladder that leads to the Cabinet. However, sometimes rebels are forgiven. Much depends on the nature and extent of any transgression. The pressures from outside Parliament are even stronger. Members enter the Commons as a result of active support from their party. They sacrifice time, money, privacy, and perhaps a career, to promote a cause. It is not easy to turn away from such a commitment through disagreement on a particular policy. Loyalty has a strong pull. Local supporters will be dismayed if you fail to uphold accepted party attitudes. Ultimately local hostility becomes unpleasant and makes renomination as a candidate for the next election either difficult or impossible.

Of course, a Member can fight the next election with a different party label. Such a move is usually unsuccessful. The biggest defection of recent times came in 1981–2 when twenty-eight Labour Members moved across to the new Social Democratic Party, but only four of them survived the 1983 general election. There is a school of thought which asserts that a seat in the Commons belongs morally to a party, not to an individual; people, most people, vote for a party not a person. The implication of this argument is that a Member who changes party should resign and contest the ensuing by-election. Bruce Douglas-Mann (Merton and Morden) was the sole SDP recruit to take this course and lost his seat in the process.

Thus party is powerful in Parliament and this power is reinforced outside Westminster by the wider audience – the electorate. Within Parliament, party organization helps business to proceed smoothly. Representatives of the parties, the whips, hold regular negotiations over the timetable for future debates. An element of give and take in these matters is traditional but the government will always have the last word as it has the majority in the House. Yet the ultimate authority of the Commons always remains: a Cabinet is doomed if it loses its majority in any division amounting to a vote of confidence. Thus the effect of a breakdown of party loyalty is greatest when the disturbance is among government supporters. Normally when Members stray from the party line, the numbers involved are limited and there is no consequence for public policy. The larger the ministerial majority, the more difficult is it for dissidents to have influence. If the majority is slim or non-existent, as between 1974 and 1979, the position is far more tense. It becomes much easier for the discontented to defeat the government but they become more reluctant to do so. In this situation the Cabinet is shaky; any defeat makes a weak situation even worse. With an issue of major importance the Prime Minister may feel that a defeat would so undermine the credibility of the government as to make it impossible to continue: if so, an immediate general election is inevitable. So when Members have greater power to wound they are more afraid to strike.

To stress that the Commons does not govern and that it is restrained by party membership can give a misleading impression of impotence and inertia. The House of Commons still plays a vital role in our system of government, although some of its functions are recognized inadequately. Walter Bagehot started his review of the tasks of the Commons by describing the elective function[5] – the Commons was an electoral college that chose the nation's leaders.

However, at this time the strength of modern party organization was unknown. Now a general election decides the party composition of the Commons, so it is the voters who determine who shall direct the nation's affairs. Of course, if the voters fail to deliver a clear verdict, if no party has an overall majority in the Commons, then it is the elected Members rather than the voters who decide the party composition of the Cabinet. (To return to the opening analogy of the dual audience, it is the people inside the theatre, not those outside, who are in charge.) Thus after the election in February 1974 it was the Commons, in particular the small group of Liberal MPs, that insisted that a Labour government should replace the Conservative administration.

Bagehot then argued that an important task of the Commons was to maintain the government: by providing consistent support for ministers, it enabled the business of the state to carry on. Alternatively, it could fail to provide support in which case either the Cabinet must resign or Parliament is dissolved. That choice rests with the Prime Minister. Whether the Monarch should always accept the advice of a Prime Minister to dissolve is a matter of controversy,[6] but in all normal circumstances such advice will be accepted. Thus, except immediately after a general election, if the Commons fails to maintain the government, as in 1979, the strong probability is that the electorate will be consulted about the future course of events.

In terms of individuals, as opposed to party, the Commons plays a dominant role in deciding who shall govern. With rare exceptions, the Prime Minister is a party leader. Party leaders are elected by their supporters. Conservative MPs vote to choose their leader. Other parties, in differing ways, bring the party as a whole into the electoral process. In the Labour Party the trade unions have a powerful voice. But in all parties the choice is between leading party spokesmen in the Commons. The quality of the reputation built up in Westminster is a major factor in deciding who is chosen. Parties which open up their electoral process to supporters outside Parliament run a risk of ending up with a leader not well respected by the Westminster players.

It is a long climb up the political ladder to a position where a politician becomes a credible candidate for party leadership. During this climb Members are constantly judged by their colleagues. As Harold Laski noted, 'the selective function of the House of Commons is the most mysterious of its habits'.[7] He also argued that 'the selective function has been amazingly well done. It has proved character as well as talent. It has measured the hinterland between oratorical quality and administrative insight with much shrewdness'.[8] It may be that this view is a little optimistic: some people seem to obtain advancement because they are good performers in the Chamber or on the mass media rather than because they are, or are expected to be, able to give effective direction to a Whitehall department. Further, in the case of the Conservative Party, promotion depends upon the favour of the party leader and his or her close associates. Elevation may depend not only on parliamentary reputation but on the shade of an individual's political opinions. There is a considerable array of talent on the Conservative benches that Mrs Thatcher has chosen to ignore.

The Labour leader is more restricted. When in opposition, Labour MPs hold an annual election for fifteen frontbench spokesmen. These form the Shadow Cabinet, together with the leader and deputy leader, elected on a wider franchise, the chief whip, elected by Labour MPs, and representatives of the Labour peers. When Labour wins power the Shadow Cabinet becomes the real Cabinet, possibly with some changes of portfolio. Those who came close to winning a place in the Shadow Cabinet have a strong claim to be picked by the leader as a junior party spokesman and later, if all goes well, to a ministerial position below Cabinet level. Under this system backbench opinion has a significant influence over the selection of ministers in a Labour government. Elections to the Shadow Cabinet are contested on the basis of opinion on policy as well as on a judgement of personal qualities. Left and right wings of the Parliamentary Labour Party nominate informal lists of candidates which they hope MPs of their persuasion will support. Even so, those who win in the ballot do so because both their views and their talents command respect.

So the Commons is a theatre or arena in which the Members struggle for recognition. Iain Macleod, as a young backbencher, won a debating duel with Aneurin Bevan, then regarded as Labour's formidable orator:[9] MacLeod's appointment as Minister of Health followed shortly after. Certainly promotion is not usually so rapid or dramatic. But many MPs advance their chances of junior ministerial office or promotion in opposition by their performance in the Chamber, for example at Question Time, or by competent work in committees.

Another major task of the Commons is to ventilate public opinion.

Bagehot described this role as the expressive function. The nature of the process varies with the scale of the debate. Sometimes Members express a party view; occasionally they put forward a personal view that may be critical of their party's policy; sometimes they press a local cause; sometimes they are advocates for some particular interest. Much of this discussion, although faithfully recorded in Hansard, is little noticed. Just occasionally the Commons becomes the forum for a debate which excites the nation or reflects the excitement of the nation. These events are commonly associated with military action, such as the debates before the outbreak of war in 1939, the debate on the conduct of the war which led to the resignation of the Chamberlain government in May 1940, a series of discussions at the time of the Suez invasion of 1956, and the Saturday debate in 1982 following the Argentine invasion of the Falkland Islands.

The very name Parliament indicates that it is a place for talking. But who should do the talking? The traditional answer is the peers and the elected members in the Commons. Today the situation is a little more flexible. Only Members and peers can vote and speak in their respective chambers, but elsewhere in the parliament building other people can be brought into the discussion. In the select committee rooms members of the public and civil servants appear as witnesses and present evidence to committees. Such activity is not entirely new but its extent has increased greatly since the establishment of a comprehensive range of subject select committees in 1979. This development certainly broadens the nature of the 'expressive function' because opinion can now be voiced not only by members of the 'theatre club' but also by people with specialized contributions to offer who are drawn from the wider audience outside. In addition some speeches made by Members depend on 'briefings' from organizations with which they are sympathetic, so interest groups can often secure a hearing for their views in the Commons.

There is a further important qualification to be made about the speeches made by Members in the Commons. No doubt they reflect opinion, but in quantitative terms they may not reflect it accurately. Capital punishment is the leading example of an issue where the views of Members do not correspond with those of electors as reported in opinion polls. But the concept of representative government does not demand an equation between the attitudes of Members and those who elect them. On this matter the task of the Member was set out by Edmund Burke in 1776: 'Your representative owes you, not his industry only, but his judgement; and he betrays, instead of serving you, if he sacrifices it to your opinion.'[10] The principle of democracy is preserved, not by telling a Member how to vote, but through the right to replace him at the next election if dissatisfied with the way in which he has carried out his duties.

If Members help to keep ministers in touch with public opinion, albeit imperfectly, they also assist in public understanding of current political issues. Parliament has an educational role to play. Sadly this role has declined. The press devote less space to reporting parliamentary debates than was done in the past. Only the 'quality' daily press carries regular reports; the popular papers are most interested at moments of high tension or when something unusual or slightly sensational occurs. A party split is good copy; uproar in the House is even better. For most of the papers, ordinary but not unimportant parliamentary business passes with little notice. However, the volume of political information available to the public is greater than ever before. It is conveyed through television and radio as well as through the press; increasingly the sources are news conferences, lobby briefings, and specialized articles rather than coverage of parliamentary proceedings. Of course, it is not necessary to rely on the mass media to follow parliamentary activity; the full verbatim record is available in Hansard. Yet the use made of Hansard has dropped. In 1946 the circulation of the daily edition was 22,000 but in 1986 the figure had fallen to 5,000. Yet to stress the decline in the direct reporting of the Commons can give a misleading impression. The Commons still plays a significant role in stimulating the interest of the media in particular issues and so helps to frame the contemporary political agenda. Much less attention would have been paid to the circumstances surrounding the sinking of the *Belgrano* without the activity of Tam Dalyell.

Large commercial and industrial organizations, together with a wide variety of pressure groups, are highly concerned with affairs at Westminster. Sometimes their motive is to learn, simply to keep in touch with what is happening, or when relevant legislation is under discussion their concern may be to influence the shape of a bill. The Commons itself makes no great effort to promote its educational role, and television in the Chamber, for example, was long resisted. However, in 1978 the Study of Parliament Group proposed that a public information office be established to provide material both about Parliament and the business currently before it. Action has now been taken on these lines and a parliamentary bookshop is included in the building in Bridge Street due to be completed in 1990.

The educational function of the Commons can be approached in a narrow, partisan way. The major parties like to see the Commons arena used to advance the party cause. It is good for morale and good publicity for your side to be on top in controversial debates. However, to argue that the Commons performs a continuous election campaign is an exaggeration. The element of party tension in the Chamber depends upon the nature of business and the proximity of an election. Many people feel that when party friction is high – as at Prime Minister's questions – the House is least attractive. Attempts to score party debating points are trivial and time-wasting. Perhaps Members engage in political jousting because it is customary and may advance a personal reputation. Certainly, the House in a partisan mood is least able to exercise effective scrutiny over ministerial action. The public at large may be little interested in an issue that arouses great party excitement. Indeed, the Commons is not the best venue for parties to seek public support: policy can be displayed more effectively at news conferences, press briefings, and at the annual party conference.

The legislative function of the Commons was discussed above and stress was laid on the fact that a large assembly cannot itself frame the details of legislation. Its task is to accept, reject, or perhaps make improvements to proposals presented by ministers or individual backbenchers. This process helps to keep Members in touch with the public because controversial measures will stimulate lobbying and swell the volume of mail: non-party issues, such as abortion, often stir the greatest activity. Gavin Drewry (chapter 7) reviews the legislative process in detail. Here it is sufficient to note that ministers, backed by a secure majority, normally get bills passed in the form they want, although sometimes they retreat in the face of objections. In 1981 all-party criticism of the idea that local referenda should be held to authorize rate rises above a norm set by Whitehall caused the scheme to be dropped. In 1986 pressure from a group of government backbenchers led to a change in government policy on sex education.

The House of Lords in the 1980s developed an increasingly independent attitude and has not infrequently amended government legislation. Ministers are placed in an awkward situation when the objections in the Lords are widely shared by their own supporters in the Commons. Such circumstances can lead to a ministerial retreat, as in 1980 when the proposal to introduce charges for school transport was dropped; both rural communities and the Roman Catholic Church opposed the suggestion with vigour. So the Lords can reinforce government critics in the Commons. The Lords are most influential when the Cabinet is in a weak position, as between 1974 and 1979, or when they echo the doubts of government backbenchers.

During recent years the Commons has spent an increasing amount of energy on the scrutiny of policy and administration. In the nineteenth century and before, little attention was paid to the routine business of central government because there was far less of it. The twentieth century has seen the steady advance of activities connected to the provision of welfare; the civil service has had a growing impact on the lives of everyone; those who feel they have been badly treated learn to complain. So Members get more reaction from irritated constituents and are expected to take an active interest in local and individual problems. The custom now is to hold local 'surgeries' and become, to a limited extent, an alternative to a Citizen's Advice Bureau.

This activity has greatly affected the work of the Commons. Much more use is made of Question Time and the motion for the adjournment (see p. 86–7) to raise constituency matters. Correspondence between backbenchers and ministers has increased and is perhaps more likely to promote satisfaction than intervention in the Chamber. The impossibility of any effective supervision of executive action by the question or debate on the floor of the House has led to the extension of committee work. Concern about public expenditure led to the appointment of a Public Accounts Committee as early as 1861. Stronger demands to review proposed spending produced the Select Committee on Estimates in 1912. Uneasiness over the power of ministers to authorize subordinate legislation led to the establishment in 1944 of a Select Committee on Delegated Legislation – later renamed the Committee on Statutory Instruments. The demand to achieve some accountability of nationalized industries produced a further select committee in 1956. Complaints over the quality of civil service administration led to the appointment of a Parliamentary Commissioner for Administration in 1967 together with a select committee to supervise his work. Meanwhile the Estimates Committee had been inquiring into aspects of central administration through a series of sub-committees which, after a complex process of evolution, produced the present system of departmental select committees in 1979. The value of committee work is discussed below by Nevil Johnson and St John Bates.

All this committee activity would be ineffective unless Members had information about matters they wished to challenge. Members know they must be well briefed if criticism is to achieve success. Parliamentary pressure has resulted in the allocation of limited funds which enable each Member to appoint a personal assistant and secretary. It has also helped the Commons Library to get more resources to enable it to provide Members with more material. The reports of select committees, including the evidence of witnesses, contain a mass of fact and opinion. Parliament has experienced an explosion of information. Yet there are still problems in this area. Ministers can resist the publication of material that is politically damaging and it is not easy to put the available information to effective use.

The principle that lies behind all attempts to review policy and administration is that ministers are accountable for the actions of their departments. Accountability is essential if a bureaucracy is not to be remote, arbitrary, and irresponsible; but the burden of it must fall on an individual, not an institution, for an institution cannot suffer punishment. A party can suffer retribution at an election, for a party is composed of a collection of individuals. But an election is determined by the general perception the public has of the government or perhaps the opposition. Accountability for the countless actions of government departments cannot be imposed by an occasional general election. So Parliament does what it can to make accountability a reality. But what does the word imply?[12] Does it mean answerable, responsible, or blameworthy and subject to penalty? A practical difficulty is that government departments are now so vast that ministers cannot know anything about most of the things that are done in their name: all they can do is to establish systems designed to ensure that actions by civil servants conform to government policy. So when challenged about a departmental action a minister is expected to explain what has been done. He is also expected to provide justification unless a civil servant has made a mistake, acted improperly, or done something of which his political master disapproves and had no prior knowledge. An inquiry started by a Member may lead to disciplinary action being taken against a

13

civil servant. So the ability of Members to challenge executive action, either in public or in private correspondence, is a spur, although it may be a spur to caution rather than speedy decision. But while the spur may occasionally produce penalties for civil servants, it rarely produces a sanction against a minister. A minister called on to answer for a personal misjudgement may fail to satisfy the parliamentary audience, with even his own party being unhappy. But he rarely suffers an immediate penalty. Ministerial colleagues are normally loyal, very loyal – 'there, but for the grace of God, go I'. So any minister under heavy fire, who wishes to stay in office, generally does so. (Mr Leon Brittan's resignation in 1986 provides an exception to this rule.) In this sense the effect of the accountability of ministers to the Commons is restricted. Even so, no minister enjoys having a bad time in the Commons or the damage caused to his reputation.

The final and perhaps fundamental task of the Commons is to furnish the actions of the state with legitimacy. Unlike the functions already discussed, this process depends not on how the Commons acts, but on how the wider audience responds to its actions.

There are two answers to the question as to why I should obey the law. The first is prudential: if I break the law and am found out, I shall be punished. The second answer is moral: the law should be obeyed because it has been accepted by freely elected representatives of the people. It is not claimed that each law is supported by majority opinion. In the days before universal suffrage and modern party organization the concept of majority opinion would have been impossible to apply. There was felt to be a responsible relationship between the law-makers and the whole community. The justification for law thus provided then forms a basic social cement which is essential for the successful operation of a complex economic and social system. In Northern Ireland not everyone accepts that the method of making law is justified; the social cement is weak and the result is dangerous and highly damaging.

In Great Britain people do accept the validity of the law – with the exception of a few minor, extremist groups. However, this attitude must also depend upon acceptance of an electoral system that can give peculiar results. For example, in 1951 the Conservatives obtained fewer votes than the Labour Party but still gained a narrow overall majority in the Commons. It was essentially a two-horse race as between them the two major parties secured nearly 97 per cent of the total poll. The result caused no protest in Labour circles. Both main parties accept the electoral system in the hope that its eccentricities will, in the long run, work to their own advantage. The Liberal–SDP Alliance claimed that the electoral system was unfair but their objection did not go so far as to claim it produces unjust law devoid of validity. The supporters of the former Alliance parties are people of moderate opinions who would not easily reject the moral basis of law.

Yet if elections produce sufficiently peculiar results it is inevitable that public disquiet will emerge about the moral validity of new law. A three-party situation increases this possibility. Suppose a party wins an overall majority in the Commons with, say, less than 40 per cent of the total poll and also with fewer votes than another party, what is the moral basis for controversial laws imposed by the new government? The justification can be that our system is successful, but that claim is unlikely to be persuasive. Some will deny that the outcome of state action in this country is particularly successful. Others will argue that success is inadequate excuse for the denial of democracy: that the idea merely resurrects the long-discredited defence for the fascist regime in Italy – that Mussolini made the trains run on time. An alternative justification would be to fall back on an appeal to tradition: that this is the way public decisions are effected in Britain and we respect the outcome of elections. But the medieval idea that each part of the country should send someone to London to represent them assumed the independence of Members, not that they should be marshalled into disciplined groups. We now live in an era of more precise measurement. People may ask about the validity of a system if it manifestly fails to reflect opinion.

As things stand there is no serious challenge to the consensus that the Commons confers legitimacy on government measures by voting for them. It is of central importance to society that this consensus is retained. Whether the Commons continues to be able to provide a mantle of legitimacy must depend upon the chance of election results and public reaction to them.

Opinion polls explore the popularity of politicians, parties, and policies. They do not, however, enquire about the standing of institutions. So it is difficult to judge the public's view of Parliament; it is probably ambivalent. On the one hand there is respect for the traditions of British political life and the sense that Westminster embodies our democratic rights. Such sentiments provide a basis for coherence and security in our society. Yet on the other hand it may be argued that the House of Commons is a place where elected representatives go to advance personal ambition or the interests of their party or their class. Parliament is also a natural focus for discontent. People go there to lobby against a particular policy or proposed legislation, or to try to resolve some local or personal problem. It was noted above that Parliament does not govern, but there is a widespread belief that it ought to be able to put things right. When Members, individually or collectively, do not deliver what is expected of them, when the economy does not prosper, when welfare administration stumbles, then Parliament becomes associated with failure and inadequacy.

So the general perception of Parliament is uncertain, perhaps a little blurred. Often Parliament fails to provide satisfaction but few would dispute the claim that without it we should be much worse off.

The essays which follow explain and analyse in some detail how the House of Commons undertakes its varied functions. There can be no tidy relationship between particular functions and the different sectors of parliamentary activity. In the case of legislation there are set times and specific procedures to deal with this business. But the task of assessing individual ability in the context of choosing future leaders goes on all the time at Westminster, in the Chamber, the committee rooms, the bars, and the lobbies; indeed, the process continues outside Parliament as MPs observe the performance of their colleagues on television and radio and also in the press. Even the more specialized of the activities described below can be said to make an indirect contribution to the general purposes of a legislature.

Michael Rush deals with the initial question about what sort of people the actors are who perform in the parliamentary theatre. Actors cannot do well without a good script, so they need help to organize their material. Ministers are briefed by civil servants; leading members of the opposition have personal assistants; backbenchers make what arrangements they can but they do get support from the Commons Library which provides them with an increasingly sophisticated information system which is described by Geoffrey Lock.

The behaviour of actors in the main theatre – the Chamber – is guided by many rules and conventions; Robert Borthwick paints a picture of how proceedings are conducted. Debates provide a major opportunity to exercise expressive functions by giving vent to public opinion, while those who study the debates will learn more about the subjects under discussion. Helen Irwin shows that backbenchers are increasingly keen to make use of the opportunities that Commons procedure makes available for them. The legislative process discussed by Gavin Drewry combines the functions of debates with scrutiny of specific proposals for fresh law and also provides a cover of legitimacy for what is decided.

Ultimately, the objective of opposition Members is to damage the reputation of the government amongst the electors. They also try to persuade the Commons to withdraw support from the Cabinet but, due to party loyalty, this goal is rarely achieved. Philip Norton shows how the opposition uses the opportunities offered by parliamentary procedure to campaign against ministers in the hope that their efforts will both influence policy and make an impact on public opinion. Three chapters study separate aspects of the substantial amount of time and effort devoted to review of executive action: Ann Robinson examines the attempts to supervise control of national expenditure; Nevil Johnson comments on the select committee system established in 1979; St John Bates looks at other aspects of the process including the scrutiny of statutory instruments and the work of the Parliamentary Commissioner for Administration.

It is of vital importance that the House of Commons should undertake its duties free from threats and improper pressures. A variety of awkward issues can arise about the proper relationship between the Commons and the world outside. Geoffrey Marshall explains the somewhat abstruse concept of parliamentary privilege which is designed to preserve the dignity of Parliament and the ability of Members to carry out their duties without fear of hindrance.

Finally, Michael Ryle discusses where the House of Commons stands today, refers to some of the problems it now faces, and speculates a little about the future.

Chapter Two

THE MEMBERS OF PARLIAMENT

MICHAEL RUSH

INTRODUCTION

The avowed intent of the Council for Social Democracy – the pre-cursor of the Social Democratic Party – at its inception in January 1981 was 'to break the mould' of British party politics. The general election of 1987, however, will not be remembered for any breaking of the mould, but for other features – for the election of a record number of women MPs, for the election of the first black MPs for more than sixty years and the first ever black woman MP, for the Labour Party's third electoral defeat in a row, and, perhaps above all, for the re-election of Margaret Thatcher for an almost unheard of third successive term as Prime Minister. Indeed, her feat is unprecedented in modern times: it is necessary to go back before the Reform Act of 1832 to Lord Liverpool to find a precedent.

Yet, if the mould is unbroken, it has been partly remoulded. The post-war period has been characterized by two-party dominance, a historic feature of British party politics which reached its zenith in the 1950s when the Conservatives and Labour parties consistently captured well over 90 per cent of the popular vote and more than 98 per cent of the seats in the House of Commons. Even now the Commons remains dominated by these two parties, as table 2.1 shows, sharing between them no less than 92.9 per cent of the seats following the 1987 election. What has changed, however, is that their share of the popular vote has fallen to 75 per cent – indeed, it was only 70 per cent in 1983. Of course, a very different picture would emerge under a system of proportional representation, which would deny the Conservatives an absolute majority in the Commons and result in rather fewer Labour and considerably more Liberal–

18

Table 2.1   Party affiliation of MPs elected at the General Election of 1987

Party affiliation	Number		%	
Conservative	375		57.7	
Labour	229		35.2	
Liberal	17⎱ 22[a]		2.6⎱ 3.4[a]	
Social Democratic Party	5⎰		0.8⎰	
Scottish National Party	3			
Plaid Cymru	3			
Official Unionist Party	9			
Democratic Unionist Party	3		3.6	
Ulster Popular Unionst Party	1			
Social Democratic and Labour Party	3			
Provisional Sinn Fein[b]	1			
Mr Speaker[c]	1			
Total	650		99.9	

Notes: *a* Liberal–SDP Alliance.

   b Gerry Adams, first elected in 1983, has never taken his seat at Westminster.

   c Bernard Weatherill, former Conservative MP for Croydon NE, 1964–83, elected Speaker after the general election of 1983.

SDP Alliance Members*, but such matters lie beyond the scope of this chapter, except perhaps to note that a House of Commons in which the norm were that no single party had an absolute majority might well operate rather differently under the circumstances of minority or coalition governments. The significance of recent elections for the composition and operation of the House of Commons is that there has been an important change in the nature of the party system. Again, whether that change is of a temporary or longer-lasting nature is not of immediate concern, but its existence should be noted.

What has also changed is that, from a situation of two-party dominance in which the two major parties – Conservative and Labour – were, over a period of time, evenly balanced, there has been a shift to a situation in which one party has been in office and the other in opposition continually since 1979. It might be argued that a not dissimilar situation occurred between 1951 and 1964, when Labour lost three elections in succession and spent thirteen years in opposition, but that period differed from the current situation

* Following the breakup of the Alliance and the formation of the Social and Liberal Democratic Party, all the Liberal and two of the five SDP MPs elected in 1987 have joined the SLD. The remaining three Social Democrats remain SDP MPs.

in that between each general election Labour could be said to have had a reasonable expectation of office at the next election and, in any case, thirteen years of Conservative government were partially and subsequently offset by six years of Labour government. The principal impact of the founding of the SDP, therefore, and more particularly of the Liberal–SDP Alliance, was to split the anti-Conservative opposition, though it is an over-simplistic interpretation of recent electoral behaviour to assume that this alone explains two of the three Conservative victories.[1]

The mould has, for the time being, been reshaped; it may at some future date be broken or restored to its former state, but that too remains beyond the scope of this chapter. What is immediately relevant is that changes in the party system affect the composition of the House of Commons not only in terms of party representation but in socio-economic terms as well, since the parliamentary parties differ significantly in socio-economic composition. However, the composition of the House is affected by other factors, of which one of the most important is the electoral system.

The present first-past-the-post or simple plurality electoral system is responsible for a disproportionate relationship between electoral support for the parties and the number of seats each party wins in the House of Commons. Thus, in only one of the thirteen general elections held between 1945 and 1987 (that of February 1974) has one or other of the two major parties failed to win an absolute or overall majority of seats in the Commons, yet in none of these elections has the winning party won an absolute majority of the votes cast. So-called 'third parties' and minor parties tend to be electorally squeezed by the two major parties: for example, in 1987 the Conservatives won 57.7 per cent of the seats with 42.4 per cent of the votes, Labour 35.2 per cent with 30.8 per cent of the votes, and the Alliance a mere 3.4 per cent of the seats for 22.6 per cent of the votes. Moreover, relatively small shifts in electoral support from one election to another produce more substantial changes than would be the case under proportional representation. In addition, two other factors affect the turnover of the House of Commons – the retirement of sitting Members and by-elections.

The average turnover of MPs from one Parliament to another since 1945 is 22 per cent, although the proportion is usually low when elections follow swiftly in succession, as they did in 1950 and 1951 and February and October 1974, when the turnover was 12 per cent and 7 per cent respectively. Turnover between 1983 and 1987 was exactly the average of 22 per cent, of which 12.8 per cent was due to the retirement of replacement of sitting MPs, 7.4 per cent to electoral losses (mostly the defeat of sitting Members) and 1.8 per cent to by-elections. In most earlier Parliaments the proportion due to by-elections has been higher (averaging 6 per cent), but the present government has shown a marked reluctance to create by-election vacancies by appointing MPs to posts incompatible with continued membership of the Commons, such as judgeships, or elevating Members to the House of Lords for fear of giving hostages to electoral misfortune.

Ultimately, the most important factor in determining the socio-economic composition of the Commons is the process by which candidates are selected. This is, of course, the responsibility of the political parties, but in practice selection is largely in the hands of local constituency parties rather than the national party organizations or the national leadership. The national parties can usually do no more than veto candidates they do not approve of, though such vetoes are rare, and can seldom ensure the choice of particular candidates they favour. The Labour Party constitution gives the party's National Executive Committee the power to impose a candidate for a by-election, a power which was used as recently as 1986 when George Howarth was chosen by the NEC as candidate for Knowsley North against the will of the local party. Similarly, the NEC may withhold or withdraw its endorsement or approval of a candidate chosen by a local party, a power it used shortly before the 1987 election when it withdrew approval of Sharon Atkin as candidate for Nottingham East following remarks she made about racist attitudes in the Labour Party. Both these cases, however, were rare examples of the use of these powers and are therefore exceptions to the general rule of local autonomy in selection. Basically, the selection of candidates is a closed rather than an open process, limited to a small number of local party activists, although there have been moves in recent years to widen local party participation in selection. There have also been moves to make it easier for local parties to replace sitting MPs, though they have been of greater significance in the Labour Party, where in 1987 seven, possibly eight, sitting MPs were refused readoption or 'deselected' by their local parties.[2] Moreover, given that independent or non-party candidates seldom find favour with the electorate, the choice of candidates by the parties

21

remains crucial and, even with the relative increase in the proportion of successful third-party candidates from 1.2 per cent in 1970 to as many as 6.1 per cent in October 1974, party choice remains paramount.

Selection, however, is subject to supply as well as demand, although it is by no means clear in what proportions. On the one hand, there is little doubt that prejudice against women candidates and MPs exists in local parties, but there is also little doubt that fewer women than men seek selection as parliamentary candidates. Similarly, certain occupations lend themselves more readily to embarking on a political career than others, usually because they provide a degree of financial security, or can be pursued on a part-time basis, or can be resumed if a political career is interrupted or terminated. The classic case is that of the lawyer, but other occupations such as journalism and many business careers can provide similar opportunities. Private wealth or income, often so important in the past, is generally less important than the availability of time to develop the necessary skills, experience, and contacts, first to secure election and then to 'nurse' the constituency prior to election. For many Labour MPs, past and present, the trade union movement has provided a route to Parliament and in all parties local-government experience has provided another avenue. However, what impels the undoubtedly small minority of individuals who seek political careers remains relatively unresearched, although such evidence as exists suggests not only that the answer is complex rather than simple, but that it involves psychological factors – an area into which few political scientists choose or dare to stray.[3]

THE AGE AND SOCIO-ECONOMIC BACKGROUNDS OF MEMBERS OF PARLIAMENT

That the House of Commons is socio-economically unrepresentative is well-known and well-documented, but what is less clear is whether this has any significance. In short, does it matter? Further discussion of this question, however, is best left until after the socio-economic composition of the House of Commons has been examined.

The general election of 1987 resulted in the election of a record number of women MPs – forty-one or 6.3 per cent of the total, a marked increase on the twenty-three elected in 1983, but far short of the target of the 300 Group, the all-party pressure group which seeks parity of male and female representation in the Commons. More often than not there have been more Labour than Conservative women MPs and 1987 was no exception, with twenty-one Labour and seventeen Conservative Members.[4]

The House of Commons is rather more representative in terms of its age distribution, but the correspondence with the electorate is hardly close: as table 2.2 shows, well over two-thirds of all MPs elected in 1987 were aged between 40 and 59. Compared with the adult population only two age groups (30–39 and 60–69) are represented in similar proportions among MPs. The youngest age group (under 30), consisting of 20 per cent of the adult population, accounts for less than 1 per cent of MPs, and the oldest group (70 or over) are considerably underrepresented. The two middle groups (40–49 and 50–59) are represented in twice the proportion found in the adult population. None of this should come as a surprise: would-be MPs will have had some experience in work and politics before being selected for winnable constituencies, so that the age at which most MPs are first elected to Parliament is between 30 and 49, with a considerable concentration between 35 and 45. On the other hand, most MPs now retire in their 60s, although a few septuagenarians continue to seek and secure re-election. But where a sitting Member in the mid- to late-sixties shows no inclination to retire, pressure to do so is likely to come from the MP's local party.

In contrast to the situation before 1964, when Labour MPs were on average significantly older than their Conservative colleagues, there is little or no difference amongst the parties: the median ages of Conservative, Labour, and Alliance MPs in 1987 were 49, 48, and 46 respectively. There can be little doubt that this is attributable to the introduction of the Member's pension scheme from 1964, which

Table 2.2   Age of MPs elected in 1987

Age	Conservative		Labour	Alliance	Other		Total
	%		%			%	
Under 30	0.2	(1)	—	2	—	0.5	(3)
30–39	15.2	(57)	16.6 (38)	4	4	15.8	(103)
40–49	37.9	(142)	38.9 (89)	8	9	38.2	(248)
50–59	33.1	(124)	28.8 (66)	7	7	31.4	(204)
60–69	12.0	(45)	14.8 (34)	1	4	12.9	(84)
70 or over	1.6	(6)	0.9 (2)	—	—	1.2	(8)
Total	100.0	(375)	100.0 (229)	22	24	100.0	(650)

considerably eased the financial pressures on the less well-off, mostly Labour MPs.

In most other aspects of their socio-economic backgrounds, however, the contrast between the parties is marked, quite apart from the continuing contrast with the electorate. This is clearly the case in respect of education, as table 2.3 shows:

Table 2.3 The educational backgrounds of MPs elected in 1987

	Conservative		Labour		Alliance	Other	Total	
	%		%				%	
A. *Level of full-time education*								
Elementary	—		3.5	(8)	—	2	1.5	(10)
Secondary	17.3	(65)	23.1	(53)	4	5	19.5	(127)
Elementary/secondary+[a]	9.6	(36)	15.7	(36)	2	10	12.9	(84)
Graduate	73.1	(274)	57.6	(132)	16	7	66.0	(429)
Total	100.0	(375)	99.9	(229)	22	24	99.9	(650)
B. *Graduates*								
Oxford	24.8	(93)	10.0	(23)	3	—	18.3	(119)
Cambridge	21.3	(80)	5.7	(13)	3	—	14.8	(96)
Other universities	22.1	(83)	40.2	(92)	9	6	29.2	(190)
Polytechnics	1.1	(4)	1.3	(3)	—	1	1.2	(8)
Overseas	1.6	(6)	0.4	(1)	1	—	1.2	(8)
Service colleges	2.1	(8)	—		—	—	1.2	(8)
Non-graduates	26.9	(101)	42.4	(97)	6	17	34.0	(221)
Total	99.0	(375)	100.0	(229)	22	24	99.9	(650)
C. *Type of school attended*								
Public school	62.7	(235)	12.7	(29)	10	3	42.6	(277)
Non-public school	37.3	(140)	87.3	(200)	12	21	57.4	(373)
Total	100.0	(375)	100.0	(229)	22	24	100.00	(650)

Note: a Elementary/secondary +=elementary or secondary schooling plus technical, vocational, or similar non-graduate education.

Two-thirds of the MPs elected in 1987 were graduates and a third had attended either Oxford or Cambridge. The tendency in recent elections has been for the proportion of graduates to increase and the proportion of Oxbridge graduates to show a slow decrease, but these proportions contrast markedly with the approximately 5 per cent of the population who are graduates and the 7 per cent of the *undergraduate* population who attend Oxford and Cambridge. Similarly, although the proportion of MPs who attended public schools has been declining in recent elections, at more than two-fifths this contrasts starkly with approximately 5 per cent of the adult population.

The differences between the parties are, however, marked: considerably more Conservatives are graduates, more than three-fifths of whom are Oxbridge products, whereas most Labour graduates, more than two-thirds, are the products of the University of London or provincial universities. Again, the overwhelming majority of those who attended public school are Conservatives, although the proportion of Labour MPs from public schools is still two-and-a-half times the national average. Nonetheless, there has been some convergence between the two major parties: historically the proportion of Labour MPs who are graduates has increased and this pattern of convergence is repeated in the occupational backgrounds of MPs.

Table 2.4 Occupations of MPs elected in 1987

Occupation	Conservative		Labour	Alliance	Other	Total	
	%		%			%	
Professions	33.3	(125)	41.0	(94)	12	13	37.5	(244)
Business	51.5	(193)	4.8	(11)	5	9	33.5	(218)
Workers	0.8	(3)	29.7	(68)	—	2	11.2	(73)
Miscellaneous	14.4	(54)	24.5	(56)	5	—	17.7	(115)
Total	100.0	(375)	100.0	(229)	22	24	99.9	(650)

Definitions: Professions: lawyers, doctors, dentists, school, university. and adult education teachers, retired officers of the regular forces, and all recognized professions.
Business: all employers, directors of public and private companies, business executives, stockbrokers, farmers and landowners, and small businessmen.
Workers: self-explanatory, but including all employed manual and non-manual (or 'white-collar') workers and full-time trade-union officials.
Miscellaneous: housewives, professional politicians, welfare workers, journalists, professional party organizers, and miscellaneous administrators.
These definitions are the categories used by S. E. Finer, H. B. Berrington, and D. J. Bartholomew in *Backbench Opinion in the House of Commons, 1955–59*, Oxford: Pergamon, 1961, and in the Nuffield Election series, but following the formers' practice of classifying occupations according to the MP's principal occupation prior to election. Many MPs, especially on the Conservative side of the House, accept company directorships or develop other business or journalistic interests after their election and an analysis based on such considerations would produce significantly different figures, although these would not invalidate the principal conclusions of the occupational analysis that follows.

Well over two-thirds of the MPs elected in 1987 were members of the professions or in business; a further one-fifth had miscellaneous occupations, such as journalism, social work, or professional party work; and fewer than one in eight were routine manual or non-manual workers. The contrast with the adult population is self-evident, but so also is the contrast between the two major parties. Hardly surprisingly, the vast majority of businessmen are Conservatives and all but five of the workers Labour, but both parties draw heavily on the professions, although lawyers are the main Conservative and teachers the main Labour professional groups. Historically, there is again evidence of a convergence between the parties: before 1922 nearly 90 per cent of all Labour MPs were workers; between 1922 and 1935 the proportion was 56 per cent, and since then it has tended to decline to less than 30 per cent.

The data on education and occupation suggests that the House of Commons is now largely middle class in its socio-economic composition and this is confirmed by table 2.5, which analyses MPs' backgrounds according to the Hall–Jones scale of occupational prestige:

Table 2.5 Analysis of the occupations of MPs elected in 1987 according to the Hall–Jones scale of occupational prestige

Class	Conservative	Labour	Alliance	Other	Total
	%	%			%
Class 1	40.5 (152)	24.0 (55)	12	7	34.8 (226)
Class 2	44.5 (167)	31.9 (73)	5	12	39.5 (257)
Class 3	12.8 (48)	17.0 (39)	3	3	14.3 (93)
Class 4	1.9 (7)	5.7 (13)	2	—	3.4 (22)
Class 5a	—	3.5 (8)	—	—	1.2 (8)
Class 5b	0.3 (1)	10.9 (25)	—	1	4.2 (27)
Class 6	—	7.0 (16)	—	—	2.5 (16)
Class 7	—	—	—	1	0.1 (1)
Total	100.0 (375)	100.0 (229)	22	24	100.0 (650)

Note: Short definitions of the classes on the scale are as follows:
  Class 1: professionally-qualified and high administrative.
  Class 2: managerial and executive (with some responsibility for directing and initiating policy).
  Class 3: inspectional, supervisory, and other non-manual (higher grade).
  Class 4: inspectional, supervisory, and other non-manual (lower grade).
  Class 5a: routine grades of non-manual work.
  Class 5b: routine grades of non-manual work.
  Class 6: manual, semi-skilled.
  Class 7: manual, routine.

The Hall–Jones scale of occupational prestige divides occupations into seven classes, one of which is sub-divided into two. Approximately four-fifths of the adult population are found in Classes 4–7. Compared with this 74.3 per cent of MPs are found in Classes 1 and 2, and only 11.4 per cent in Classes 4–7. Thus even a majority of Labour MPs are classified as being Classes 1 and 2, although no fewer than 85 per cent of Conservatives fall into these two categories. Conversely, only 27.1 per cent of Labour and a mere 2.2 per cent of

Conservatives are in Classes 4–7. It is basically true that Conservative and Labour MPs tend to come from different social groupings, not only in that the vast majority of working-class MPs are Labour, but also in that the two parties tend to draw upon different segments of the middle class. It is also almost certainly the case that many Labour MPs, who by most definitions of class are undoubtedly middle class and probably generally perceived as such, are first- or second-generation members of that class and, if parental or family background were taken into account, more would be classified as working class. Nevertheless, there has been a socio-economic convergence of the two major parties in which a greater shift has occurred in Labour than in Conservative ranks. There is some evidence that some local Labour parties are consciously selecting working-class candidates, but its impact on the number of working class MPs remains limited to maintaining their proportion within the Parliamentary Labour Party at rather less than one-third.

This relative socio-economic convergence of the two major parties almost certainly owes a great deal to the widening of educational opportunities since 1944 and consequent higher levels of social mobility. First- and second-generation middle-class individuals, with strong working-class antecedents, may well be attracted to the Labour Party and be attractive to local parties seeking highly articulate candidates with a knowledge and understanding of working-class attitudes and needs. Yet none of this demonstrates that the socio-economic composition of the House of Commons has any meaning in terms of political behaviour in general and legislative behaviour in particular. Of course, for élite and class theorists it is proof positive of their ideas, but such ideas generally rely too much on the existence of common characteristics and the holding of particular positions or offices without testing whether any relationship exists between the exercise of power and such characteristics. Studies of backbench behaviour in the 1940s and 1950s have shown some relationship between socio-economic characteristics and legislative behaviour in the House of Commons[5] and a study of the information sources of MPs in the late 1960s found a relationship between the backgrounds of MPs and support for procedural reform.[6] It is, of course, only too well-known that the most important determinant of political behaviour in the Commons is party, but it is a mistake simply to regard MPs as lobby fodder, not only because (as other research has shown) Members have become more prone to resist the threats and blandishments of the whips,[7] but also because the role of the backbench MP has grown considerably in the last twenty-five to thirty years. The demands made upon Members, both by constituents and by Parliament itself, have increased and have been accompanied by a growing professionalization of the role of the Member of Parliament.

THE PROFESSIONALIZATION OF THE MEMBER OF PARLIAMENT

The present Palace of Westminster was officially opened in 1852, having been built as a replacement for the building largely destroyed by fire in 1834. It was designed primarily as a meeting place for the House of Commons and the House of Lords and had many of the facilities and much of the atmosphere of a London club, both of which it largely retains. Indeed, it was described in the nineteenth century as 'the best club in London'. In no sense, however, was it designed to meet many of the needs of the modern MP for office accommodation, secretarial and research assistance, and information services. Moreover, MPs were unpaid and received no allowances to meet any of the expenses they might incur in carrying out their parliamentary duties. Private wealth or income was a virtual necessity for an MP, although constituents in the mid-nineteenth century (apart from periodic job-seekers) were not very demanding and the parliamentary demands on Members were not very great. The introduction of a £400 annual payment to MPs in 1911 arose largely out of the needs of Labour MPs, most of whom had no private means, and this was typical of the way in which services and facilities for Members developed. The pattern was and continues to be one of piecemeal and pragmatic change, but the pace quickened sharply in the 1960s and the first report of the Top Salaries Review Body (TSRB) on Members' pay and allowances in 1971 was to be crucial watershed in the professionalization of the Member's role.

In 1960 a Member of Parliament received a salary of £1,750, of which £750 was regarded as an appropriate amount to cover parliamentary expenses. In addition MPs had had free travel on parliamentary business between London and their constituencies since 1924 and later for such travel between home and the constituency and home and London. Telephone calls within the London area were also free and there was free postage for letters on parliamentary

business to ministers, government departments, nationalized industries, and some other bodies. Headed stationery within the Palace of
Westminster was free, and Members were allowed up to £8-worth of
such stationery for use outside Westminster. All other expenses
incurred in carrying out parliamentary duties had to be met from
Members' own pockets. In practice, a majority of MPs in 1960 were
allowed by the Inland Revenue expenses against tax which exceeded
the £750 included in the Member's salary to cover parliamentary
expenses. Indeed, a number of MPs were allowed expenses against
tax which exceeded their parliamentary salaries. In short, no meaningful distinction was drawn between the salary paid to MPs and the
expenses incurred in carrying out their parliamentary duties.

Quite apart from this, office accommodation in the normal sense
of the term was virtually non-existent. Since *single* rooms are still
only available to a minority of backbenchers, it has long been the
practice at Westminster to talk of 'desk spaces' – some in single
rooms, but mostly in shared rooms or in various other areas such as
the Cloisters. In 1957 hardly any desk-spaces were allocated to
backbenchers, but by 1960 105 desk-spaces were available to them.

It was in these circumstances that a committee chaired by Sir
Geoffrey Lawrence was appointed in 1963 to review the whole
question of Members' remuneration. Although the Lawrence Committee recommended an increased salary of £3,250, the blurring
between salary and expenses remained, with £1.250 being regarded
as an appropriate sum to cover parliamentary expenses. However,
the committee also recommended the introduction of a pension
scheme for MPs and this was a major step towards stabilizing the
parliamentary career structure by removing the necessity felt by
many, especially on the Labour side of the House, to continue to
seek re-election beyond the age of 65.[8] Meanwhile, the pressure for
better services and facilities had grown considerably, especially with
the influx of new MPs in 1959 and 1964. As result, in 1969 MPs were
given a secretarial allowance of £500 and free postage and telephone
calls on parliamentary business within the UK. Even more importantly, Members' pay and allowance were referred to the newly-
formed Top Salaries Review Body, chaired by former MP, Lord
Boyle. When it reported in 1971 the TSRB recommended that a
clear distinction be drawn between salaries and expenses. The Boyle
Committee also recommended the introduction of a subsistence allowance to cover the cost of living in London while Parliament was in

session, increased free travel facilities, modifications to the pension scheme, and the introduction of severance pay for defeated MPs.[9] In addition, unlimited supplies of official stationery were made available from 1972.

The acceptance of the Boyle principle on expenses was a crucial step towards the professionalization of the Member of Parliament and, although the severe inflation of the 1970s and early 1980s resulted in successive governments limiting rises in Members' salaries, the various allowances were generally allowed to rise more in line with and sometimes in excess of the rate of inflation. Furthermore, most allowances were in due course linked to various civil service allowances, as well as being reviewed regularly by the TSRB.

Thus in 1987 the Member's salary was £18,500, having been linked to the salary scale of a senior principal in the civil service, rising to £22,548 in January 1988. This increase was approved by the House of Commons in July 1987, shortly after the June election, against the wishes of the government,[10] as was an increase in the secretarial and research allowance (now renamed the office cost allowance) to £20,140 a year earlier in 1986.[11] The various other allowances, linked to civil service rates, continue to be paid, of course, and the provisions for free postage and telephone calls remain intact. The position on accommodation has been improved by making additional office space available within the Palace of Westminster, but more particularly by extending parliamentary accommodation to other buildings nearby, notably the former New Scotland Yard building, known as Norman Shaw North and Norman Shaw South. In addition further accommodation for both Members and their staffs will become available with the redevelopment of Bridge Street opposite the Houses of Parliament. In 1987 desk spaces were available for all those backbenchers who wanted them and accommodation in single rooms was available for 187 backbenchers.

The period since 1960 has also seen other important developments affecting the role of the MP, particularly the extension of information services through the House of Commons Library and the provision of additional support for select committees, especially since the establishment of the departmental select committees in 1979. In 1960 the establishment of the House of Commons Library was thirty-two; in 1972 it was sixty-six, 1982 126 and in 1987 151. The total number of staff directly employed by the House of Commons rose from 500 in 1972 to 909 in 1987.[12] Comparing the cost of operating the House of Commons, including MPs' salaries, is more complex because of changes in the form of the estimates. However, in 1973–4 the House of Commons estimates amounted to £12.7m, whereas in 1987–8 at least £69m of the £96m allocated to parliamentary expenditure in the estimates was to support the organization and operation of the House of Commons and its members,[13] a massive increase, even taking inflation into account.

These changes have also been accompanied by important developments in the organization and control of parliamentary services and facilities. Prior to 1965 control of the Palace of Westminster was vested in a royal official, the Lord Great Chamberlain, who delegated responsibility for House of Commons accommodation to the Commons Serjeant at Arms acting on behalf of the Speaker. MPs had no direct control or real say over their own accommodation, services, or facilities. In 1965, however, control over Commons accommodation and services was vested in the Speaker, advised by a House of Commons (Services) Committee, which operated through sub-committees concerned with the library, accommodation, refreshment facilities, and administration. Nonetheless, no single person or body was in charge of services and facilities and there was a substantial degree of *ad hoc* decentralization to the heads of the then five departments of the House of Commons. This situation continued until the publication of the Compton Report in 1974,[14] which recommended a unified service under a chief officer, probably to be the Clerk of the House. The report encountered strong criticism in many quarters and was not implemented, but led to the appointment of a committee under a senior backbencher and former minister, Arthur Bottomley, which recommended that services and facilities should be overseen by a House of Commons Commission, which would be the statutory employer of all Commons staff and would replace the government in giving approval to the annual House of Commons estimates.[15] The Bottomley Report was accepted and implemented by the House of Commons (Administration) Act, 1978, and the Commission came into operation in January 1979. The Commission consists of the Speaker, as chairman, the Leader of the House of Commons, the opposition shadow leader and three backbench MPs, one Conservative, one Labour, and one representing other parties. Day-to-day interdepartmental co-ordination is achieved through a Board of Management consisting of the heads of the now six departments of the House, and the Services Committee continues to advise and make recommendations about services and facilities. In addition, a liaison committee comprising select committee chairmen advises the Commission on matters relating to select committees.

CONCLUSION

The increase in Members' salaries, the provision of considerably more appropriate and adequate services and facilities, and changes in their administration, are the product, on the one hand, of increased demands made upon Members and, on the other, of demands made by Members themselves, which largely reflect their attitude towards their role as Members of Parliament. Several of the reports presented by the TSRB have included surveys of MPs and these show quite clearly that, in spite of the fact that no fewer than 72 per cent of MPs have outside earnings or occupations (according to the most recent survey in 1982), for the overwhelming majority being a member of Parliament is the main activity and is a full-time rather than a part-time job. The same survey also shows that on average backbenchers spent 67 hours per week on parliamentary business when Parliament was in session and 48 hours per week when it was not.[16] The same point can be illustrated by the staff employed by MPs. A survey conducted in 1971 found that about two-thirds of backbench MPs had part-time secretarial assistance, and about a quarter full-time secretarial assistance or its equivalent, leaving a small minority who had none at all or who used an agency that then operated in the Palace of Westminster. The same survey found that fewer than 10 per cent of backbenchers employed a research assistant.[17] The most recent survey, conducted in 1986, found that 81 per cent had at least one full-time member of staff, including research assistants, and 60 per cent specifically employed research assistants. The average number of staff employed by backbenchers was 1.23 secretaries and 0.4 research assistants.[18] But perhaps the most important statistic of all can be found in table 2.6, which examines the parliamentary service of MPs elected in 1987, Table 2.6.

Table 2.6 shows that 83.4 per cent of all MPs elected in 1987 were first elected in 1970 or later, including 83.1 per cent of Conservative and 83.4 per cent of Labour MPs. This means that more than four-fifths of the members of the House of Commons were elected shortly before or since the Boyle watershed of 1971 and are used to operating with a scale of services and facilities largely beyond the experience of

Table 2.6 Parliamentary service of MPs elected in 1987

First elected	Conservative		Labour		Alliance	Other	Total	
	%		%				%	
Prior to 1950	—		0.4	(1)	—	—	0.1	(1)
1950–59	5.9	(22)	2.2	(5)	—	—	4.2	(27)
1960–69	10.9	(41)	14.0	(32)	4	3	12.3	(80)
1970–79	45.6	(171)	38.0	(87)	5	8	41.7	(271)
1980 or later	37.6	(141)	45.4	(104)	13	13	41.7	(271)
Total	100.0	(375)	100.0	(229)	22	24	100.0	(650)

Note: In a minority of cases MPs experienced a gap in their parliamentary service, although in most cases this did not last longer than a single Parliament.

most of their predecessors. The base line from which they started is essentially that of the full-time professional Member of Parliament, and their demands for yet further improvements are likely to grow rather than diminish as the cross-party defiance of governments over both salaries and allowances demonstrates: the professional MP is here to stay.

How much the professionalization of MPs is related to the socio-economic composition of the House of Commons is unclear, except that it is unlikely that generally well-educated individuals with experience of the professions or business or as trade union officials or journalists would have been satisfied with the salaries and facilities available to MPs as recently as the 1960s. Similarly, whether Parliament of the nation or Members' constituents would be better served by a House of Commons which were more nearly a microcosm of the electorate is very much a matter of opinion, but it is difficult to resist the argument that a more representative House, particularly in relation to the proportion of women MPs but in other respects as well, would be able to draw on a broader and deeper range of knowledge and experience in performing the roles demanded of the Commons as a whole and of individual MPs, not least in scrutinizing the executive. Moreover, should the House of Commons ever be widely *perceived* as unrepresentative by the electorate, its legislative and political legitimacy could be severely undermined. Nor should it be forgotten that it is, for the most part, from among MPs that ministers are chosen: constitutionally and in practice ministers are expected to be in and of Parliament and the most senior positions are normally held by members of the Commons (as opposed to the Lords). Who, then, is elected to Parliament determines not only which party or parties form the government of the day, but which members of those parties govern those who elect them.

Chapter Three

INFORMATION FOR PARLIAMENT

GEOFFREY LOCK

Members of Parliament fulfil a number of roles: they sustain or oppose the government; they scrutinize the activities of the government; they defend the collective interests of their constituents and take up their constituents' individual grievances; they legislate; they influence and develop the policies of their parties; and, on occasion, they act as the grand inquest of the nation. To fulfil these roles effectively they need information, and they need a mechanism which will bring order to the flood of information which might otherwise overwhelm them. Information originates in a variety of sources – the government, the press, radio, television, constituents (from correspondence and surgeries), local parties, interest groups, lobbyists, and contacts in Members' occupations outside Parliament. (This list does not claim to be exhaustive.) Mechanisms for organizing and delivering information include the party headquarters, the personal aide, and the House of Commons Library. The select committee has re-emerged to become once again, as in the nineteenth century, a major instrument for the gathering of information, and it is conceivable that one day the computer will become a major instrument for delivery, manipulated either by a Member or by his personal staff.

Members' information needs and their fulfilment constitute a large topic and this chapter has room for a brisk tour of the territory. The only major study[1] was carried out twenty years ago and its results formed a book of over 400 pages. The data were derived from an extensive programme of interviews with a large sample of Members, and the whole operation was a pioneering piece of original research. Since the research (or something similar) has not been repeated, this chapter is necessarily impressionistic and based on secondary sources.

(It would be difficult to repeat the 1967 study today as Members have become very reluctant to complete questionnaires or to grant interviews to research workers.) Contrasts with twenty years ago are instructive: in some fields there have been considerable developments, in others very little change.

INFORMATION FROM THE GOVERNMENT

The source of a large proportion of the information reaching Parliament is the central government, and it emanates predominantly from individual departments rather than from a centralized machine – although the Central Statistical Office fulfils a limited co-ordinating role with regard to government statistics. The forms that information from departments take include the following:

White Papers, some of which are statements of government policy, issued when the government has made up its mind; these often foreshadow legislation. Others are replies to reports by select committees. There are also regular White Papers, such as those appearing annually on defence and on agriculture. The policy papers are published by HMSO in the Command Paper series.

Green Papers, which are discussion papers giving background information on a topic, setting out possible options for action and inviting views from the general public.[2] Some discussion papers are in the Command Paper series, some are published by HMSO as non-parliamentary papers, and others are distributed by departments direct.

Explanatory and financial memoranda attached to bills, usually not very informative: the much fuller 'notes on clauses', which are sometimes made available, are more helpful.

Answers to parliamentary questions (see comments below), *statements by ministers, and speeches in debate*.

Press notices, put out by departments and oral briefings held by them. Press notices are very numerous: some are of a routine nature, such as those disseminating regular statistics, for example the monthly unemployment figures or the Index of Retail Prices; others are concerned with individual items of news.

Other material – a wide-ranging category embracing such publications as the annual reports still produced by one or two departments on their activities and the annual reports produced by other official bodies; the 'supply estimates' – detailed statements of government expenditure for which provision has to be made by the House by voting 'supply'; reports of committees of inquiry (other than parliamentary committees); statistical publications such as the *Annual Abstract of Statistics* and *Social Trends*; periodicals issued by government departments such as the *Employment Gazette* and *British Business*; and numerous leaflets produced for the benefit of the general public – for example, those explaining social security benefits.

A special category of information given by the government to Parliament is in the form of answers to parliamentary questions.[3] These are very numerous (49,947 questions appeared on the order paper in 1985–6), and have more than doubled in volume over the past twenty years. If one takes the average number of questions per sitting day (to remove the effect of variation in the length of the session), the figure rose from about 140 per day in the late 1960s (138 in 1966–7, 142 in 1967–8) to 290 in 1985–6. The increase is not unconnected with the rise of the Member's research assistant, as it is widely known that many questions are drafted by Members' personal staff. In 1985–6, civil service staff time needed to answer these questions cost almost £2.8 million, and printing the questions and answers on the order paper and in Hansard cost about £1.5 million.[4]

The printed indexes to parliamentary questions (included in the volumes of parliamentary debates, and cumulated into sessional volumes) formerly left a good deal to be desired, but have greatly improved since January 1984, when their compilation was taken over by the House of Commons Library. References to questions are also available in the Library's POLIS computer data base (see p. 47), and for the recent period (i.e. since the publication of the latest printed index) the on-line index is the only source of references. Members are not rationed with regard to the number of questions they can put down for a written answer. The range of information they are able to obtain in this way is considerable, but, in order to be admissible, questions must relate to matters for which ministers are responsible.

The burden of answering parliamentary questions was mentioned in several of the reports of the 'Rayner' Reviews of statistical services in individual government departments, which were carried out a few years ago. There were twenty-two of these reports[5] and they were drawn up in 1980 as part of the comprehensive review of the Government Statistical Service. Their authors were young 'high-fliers'

(mostly principals or assistant secretaries or their equivalents), and
the views they expressed contrast with the deferential attitude which
the civil service normally publicly evinces towards Parliament. If
Parliament is mentioned at all as a customer for statistics, the
general attitude towards it in the reports, with a few exceptions
(Home Office, Ministry of Defence, Lord Chancellor's Department),
was that it was a nuisance, causing a good deal of work and expense.
A cost limit applies on work for parliamentary questions, and ministerial consent has to be obtained for it to be exceeded. (In 1980 it
was £50; but in 1982 it was raised to £200.[6]) The reports differ on
whether the limit should be rigorously enforced or raised. Several
favoured the idea of referring MPs as much as possible to published
material in the House of Commons Library, though this practice
simply passes the buck to the Library staff, as Members on the
whole do not personally extract figures from sources. As long ago as
22 July 1968, a Member protested to the then Chancellor of the
Exchequer about the practice, saying that it was 'overburdening the
Library Research Unit, which was less well equipped to give this
information than his own Department'.[7]

As the 1979 restructuring of the select committee system had
taken place so recently, there was little comment in the reports
about the potential demands of the new committees. However the
study team at the Department of Health and Social Security had no
doubts that firm limits should be imposed in this field:

> The restraint imposed by true cost consciousness on both
> Ministers and officials is unquestionably rigorous. Members of
> Parliament will have to be referred repeatedly to published
> sources. Select Committees and Royal Commissions may have to
> obtain their own information, with their own budgets for the
> purpose, if the information is not available already within the
> Department. . . . The Public Accounts Committee may have to be
> prepared to accept that staff and resources are not available to
> provide certain information.[8]

The proposals in the passage seem to amount to a recipe for clashes
between Parliament and the executive. As far as I know, there has
been no attempt to implement them, but it is interesting to find this
sort of thinking, which is probably not uncommon in Whitehall, so
frankly expressed.

SELECT COMMITTEES

Select committees as a form of parliamentary activity are dealt with in chapter 9, but they are also relevant to this chapter. Select committees are important in the information field in three ways:

(a) Individual committee members have good opportunities for discussing the topics of inquiry with the witnesses appearing before them and these witnesses may be the outstanding experts on the subject. Thus members, many of whom tend to specialize, can enhance their knowledge and go into a subject in some depth.
(b) Committees corporately need information to guide the course of their inquiries and to form the basis of their reports.
(c) Committees form a mechanism for the dissemination of information in their reports and in their published evidence.

A study of the select committee system in the 1979–83 Parliament[9] quantified some of the flows of information during the first three and a half years of operation of the new departmentally-related committees. (There were fourteen such committees, plus three subcommittees.) During this period, the 148 members of these committees asked almost 100,000 questions; the committees received about 5,000 memoranda, of which about 1,300 were from government departments; appearances before the committees by Ministers totalled 230, and there were almost 1,800 by civil servants; the committees published almost 200 substantive reports consisting of about 4,400 pages. In addition, the oral evidence was published in supplementary volumes, together with many of the memoranda submitted to the committees (although, with the growing consciousness of the expense of printing, some committees decided not to print all the written evidence submitted to them, but to lodge part of it in the House of Commons Library).[10]

To marshall and augment their inflow of information, and to assist with the outflow, committees are able to call upon three forms of support, in addition to the services of their clerks who are of course the principal officers working for them:

(a) specialist advisers;
(b) committee assistants;
(c) the House of Commons Library.

Specialist advisers are part-time and are mostly recruited for work on particular inquiries on which they have expertise, although a few have a more wide-ranging brief and work for a committee for several sessions; many are academics. In the 1979–83 Parliament, 171 advisers were engaged, worked over 7,100 days (about forty-two days each on average over three and a half years), and cost £423,000. On average, therefore, each committee or sub-committee benefited from about 120 days' work annually, but the committees varied greatly in how much use they made of advisers, with the Foreign Affairs and Education Committees making substantial use of their services and the Home Affairs Committee very little. By 1985–6 specialist advisers had ceased to be used by the Home Affairs Committee at all, and their main users had become the Energy and Treasury Committees. In that year, a total of eighty-six advisers were appointed by the departmental committees as a group and £85,000 was spent on their fees and expenses.[11]

Committee assistants are full-time staff of the House, with subject-specialist experience, recruited on a temporary basis for not more than four years, and graded as either higher executive or senior executive officers. Only a minority of committees employ them,[12] and it looks unlikely at present that there will be any move to build up a permanent research staff for the select committee system.

The 1978 Report of the Procedure Committee mentioned with approval the idea that committees should use the Library's research staff to help them with information:

> The Library provides the only existing pool of full-time expert staff directly under the control of the House and although relatively small in numbers these staff can be of considerable assistance to Members in locating and analysing published material on a wide range of subjects. . . . We believe that select committees should make more use of these services, but it would not be right for such assistance to be provided at the expense of the Library's services to individual members.[13]

Unfortunately the Library is not staffed on a scale which would now permit much substantial work to be done for committees, though some work for them is still carried out. The work for individual Members, mentioned by the Procedure Committee, has risen considerably since 1978 without a commensurate increase in staff, so that the Library now does less work for committees than it did for the Crossman committees in the late 1960s.

In one way and another, however, committees have evolved means for supplying the information needs appropriate to their present stage of development; and there has been progress since the 1960s and 1970s. When in 1965 the Estimates Committee commissioned some survey work costing £85, it had to be paid for by the Acton Society Trust, as the Committee had no funds of its own;[14] and in the 1970s econometric work for the General Sub-Committee of the Expenditure Committee (the predecessor of the Treasury Committee) was for some time defrayed out of the Library's budget. However, committees now have access to their own funds to pay for research.

So much for the input of information into committees: what of the output from the committee system and the use made of reports within Parliament? Here the verdicts of the commentators (based on the experience of the 1979–83 Parliament) are mixed. Philip Giddings thought that it was an open question 'whether the increase in information and comment available to the House has improved the quality of its debates and legislation'.[15] However, Gavin Drewry held that 'the open Government implications of extended committee activity cannot lightly be dismissed. A great deal more information from the private world of Whitehall is entering the public domain . . . most observers agree that the new committees have at least intermittently enriched the quality of parliamentary debate'.[16]

OTHER SOURCES OF INFORMATION

The government as an information source has been dealt with at some length, as has the position of the select committees in the information network. Other sources are described more summarily, not because they are unimportant, but because there may be little recent comprehensive information about the use Members make of them.

Obviously, the press, television, and radio will be vital sources for Members – not only the national press, but also the local and regional newspapers to keep them informed of local matters, and the specialist press to keep them informed on the topics in which they have chosen to specialize. On local and specialist issues, Members may wish to set up their own collections of press cuttings (though lack of space is likely to be a problem), but on international and domestic issues the Commons Library operates several limited cuttings services. The importance of data bases in this field will grow (such as World Reporter and Textline, to which the Library subscribes), but it remains to be seen if they will eventually come to supplant manually compiled collections of cuttings entirely.

Organizations and individuals in the constituency are another major source. The consultants employed by the Top Salaries Review body put the matter thus:

> MPs are unanimous about the need to understand and be in constant touch with their constituencies. They must know the views and situation of local authorities, health authorities, other public bodies like the police and fire brigade, central government agencies in the constituency, local employers, trade unions and interest groups.[17]

In dealing with the individual problems of constituents, either at 'surgeries' or by correspondence, Members will see how national systems and policies operate in practice. Lord Attlee deplored the adoption by MPs of the welfare officer role,[18] but this function has evolved into one of the main aspects of the work – a change, influenced no doubt by the development of community politics by the Liberals in the early 1970s and by mandatory reselection of Labour Members by their constituency parties, that is probably now irreversible. The TSRB consultants reported that the requirement on Members to cultivate their constituencies was becoming increasingly time-consuming; they instanced housing, social security, and immigration as being among the most numerous categories of problem raised, and quoted 2,500 cases as a typical annual constituency case load; but this may vary greatly between constituencies. Although much of the detail is specific to the individual cases, similar problems recur and a broader national perspective may start to emerge from the examples derived from a local area. Feedback from constituents is now an important component of the Member's information input, even though many of the problems presented to him are really for the local councillor.

Pressure groups can form a useful source within a limited sphere and a reciprocal relationship can be built up. According to Mr Alderman, favourably-inclined Members will speak up for the interests of a pressure group 'and perhaps ask the occasional parliamentary question on their behalf. In return, a Member . . . can usually be assured of a constant source of reliable information on a particular area of government policy.'[19] Pressure groups will target their efforts on the committee stages of bills, 'where there usually lies the best chance of constructive amendment', and on 'all-party' parliamentary subject groups, for which pressure groups may 'provide the money, expertise, secretarial and research facilities of which Parliament itself has always been so short'.[20] Mr Greer makes a similar case for the services of the lobbyist 'whose job it is to provide [the MP] with background information so that he may effectively exercise his judgment on matters before the House. With the minimal resources they have at their disposal, MPs *need* to be supplied with information.'[21] Briefings from pressure groups and lobbyists obviously need to be used with care, and adjustments made for possible selectivity or bias; but some bodies have established high reputations in their subject fields, and their compilations would be usable without reservation – for example the British Road Federation's annual *Basic Road Statistics*, which is one of the most useful publications on the subject.

In this brisk *tour d'horizon* of information sources, it may also be mentioned that Members with occupations in addition to politics will continue to bring to bear on their political work information derived from their other professions or trades – farming Members in relation to agricultural policy and so on. As the proportion of full-time politicians in the House rises, this factor may eventually decline in importance, but is still significant for some subjects.

FORMS OF RESEARCH SUPPORT

Pressure groups and lobbyists are likely individually to be good at supplying briefings only over a limited range. What of agencies for research support over virtually any topic that a Member might wish to take up? Three possibilities are reviewed: party headquarters, personal research assistants, and the House of Commons Library.

Party headquarters

When Lord Houghton's committee came to review, eleven years ago, the functions of party research departments, support for back-benchers was not even mentioned. 'Providing briefs and an information service' was included among their functions but only in relation to working parties, policy committees, or the Shadow Cabinet rather than to individual Members[22]. A few years earlier, the Barker–Rush study concluded that financial constraints compelled the Labour Research Department to regard a regular information service for Labour MPs as 'a subsidiary concern', and that the Conservative Research Department made individual work for backbench MPs its lowest priority, though some work in this category was undertaken.[23] In the recent Report of the Top Salaries Review Body, the consultants dismissed the facilities furnished by party headquarters in one sentence: 'The Parties themselves provide research resources on which MPs can draw, but these appear to be in decline for financial reasons'. Some financial stability would be a prerequisite for the retention of a core of experienced researchers – and without such a core any research organization would have grave difficulty in functioning.

Official funds are not provided for national party headquarters, but *are* provided to assist with the office expenses of the opposition parliamentary parties (the so-called 'Short money', named after Mr E. Short MP, now Lord Glenamara, the Leader of the House of Commons when the scheme for assisting opposition parties was first adopted). A formula, which is varied from time to time, determines the total allocation to each opposition party, and the money is used at the discretion of the party leader.[24] Some is used to provide research support for the leader and other chief party spokesmen, but this is still not adequate for the task. As Sir Douglas Wass put it in his Reith Lectures: 'the Opposition still has precious little back-up for the development of its criticism and questioning. It also lacks the resources to make objective appraisals of the consequences of its own policy alternatives.'[25]

Personal research assistants

The role fulfilled in the information field by personal research assistants working for individual Members has greatly increased in recent years and growth in their numbers has been dramatic. The Barker–Rush study found that 'in 1967 only about six or seven Members in the whole House had even a share in the services of a personal assistant (other than a secretary or a good constituency agent); only one Member, to our knowledge, employed an aide with similar experience to that of a legislative counsel of the congressional type'.[26] It was scarcely surprising that the numbers should have been so low, since no allowance was then available from public funds for the payment of personal staff. When such an allowance was introduced (in 1969) it could be spent only on secretarial assistance, not on research assistance. Three years later the rules were changed to enable part of the staff allowance to be spent on research assistance, but the amount permitted was only £300 p.a. Later in the decade this restriction was lifted, and Members were allowed to choose for themselves how much they wished to spend, within the total allowance, on different types of staff. In consequence, and as a result of the rise in the value, in real terms, of the allowance for Members' personal staff, there has been a steep increase in the numbers of Members with at least a part-time research assistant. The proportion of MPs with research assistants has risen as follows:[27]

	%
1971	9
1975	29
1978	40
1983	58
1986	60

The estimated numbers of research assistants attached to Members rose from 100 in 1975 to 594 in late 1986.[28]

In 1975, a select committee chaired by Mr (later Sir) William Van Straubenzee was appointed to examine the support facilities available to backbenchers in carrying out their duties, in particular research assistance on matters before Parliament. The committee reported that

> in general we believe that the Library provides the best means of meeting the purely research needs of most Members . . . but where a Member wishes to employ his own assistant to carry out research for him he . . . should continue to be able to do so.[29]

The type of assistance the committee had in mind as being rendered by Members' own staff was personal assistance rather than research assistance, though some assistants would do research: their scope should be 'to assist Members in any work directly associated with their parliamentary duties', but not to do work for local party political purposes. The report was neither debated in the House nor the subject of a government statement; furthermore, the committee's task was left uncompleted as its wish that it should be set up for a further session to finish its study was not granted.

In the event, matters did not turn out at all as the committee had recommended. Their report had proposed an immediate doubling of the Library's research service, with a further expansion after three or four years following a review. The emphasis as far as research was concerned, as opposed to other forms of non-secretarial assistance, was to be on the centrally organized resource provided by the Library. In fact it is expenditure on personal staff that has boomed, with a rise in expenditure from £630,000 in 1974–5 to £14.2 million in 1987–8.[30] During the same period the number of researchers in the House of Commons Library has risen from twelve to twenty.

In its 1987 report, the Top Salaries Review Body displayed some scepticism about research assistants:

> We doubt that some of them do true research work. . . . The title 'research assistant' covers a variety of individuals with different qualifications, experience and reasons for coming to the work. . . . Many come to the job, leave after a short time and appear to do work of only an undemanding nature. Their presence makes heavy demands on the Library and limits the effectiveness of the contribution it can make.[31]

The consultants working for the TSRB used even blunter language:

> Currently too many research assistants are not 'expert' in any one area, and are given a variety of unco-ordinated tasks. . . . We, and many Members, consider their title, in many if not most cases, wildly overblown. . . . There is no doubt that much 'research assistant' activity adds to the Library's workload and could be better done there anyway. . . . Members are often unclear why they want assistants. More discipline and above all quality control needs to be introduced, so that, where Research Assistants are employed, they make a substantial contribution to the MPs' 'political' work at Westminster.[32]

The House of Commons Library

The staff of the Commons Library provides the third possibility for the provision of general information and research support to Members; we have seen that the Van Straubenzee Committee of 1975 considered the respective roles of personal assistants and the Library staff (though their views were never implemented). Barker and Rush considered the respective roles of the party headquarters and the Library, and suggested that it would be reasonable for the party 'to concentrate on policy work, the servicing of party spokesmen and the basic partisan and propagandist material which only they can produce', leaving the Library to develop an 'omnibus, individually-based information service' to be offered to all Members.[33] In the intervening twenty years the Library has evolved broadly on the lines suggested by Barker and Rush, in so far as it both attempts to cover all subjects (developing specialization as far as the size of the staff permits) and sees one of its principal strengths as being the provision of the specially-tailored answer to the individual Member's enquiry.

Until 1945, the Library of the House of Commons was like that of a West End club, with a very small staff and offering only a limited range of services (no research was undertaken). In that year, the development was started of the Library into a modern, if still modest, organization more suitable for the requirements of a legislature. It currently (1987) has a staff of about 150 and a budget of about £2.5 million.[34] Its main constituent parts are as follows:

(a) The Vote Office, which joined the Library Department in 1979. This is the documentation service for Members, and provides them with personal copies of the official printed material they need for their parliamentary work, for example the order paper (agenda, including notices of motions, questions and amendments), Hansard (official report of debates), Acts, bills, select committee reports, Command Papers and European Community documents.

(b) The Parliamentary (or Library) Division which includes, in its Oriel and Reference Rooms, the main first-port-of-call enquiry points for Members' short-term enquiries; the International Affairs Section, which not only has a substantial collection of the publications of international organizations (including the European Communities) but also undertakes written research of the type carried out by the Research Division; the Computer and Technical Services Section which includes the cataloguing unit, compiles the printed index for the volumes of Hansard (including the sessional index), and carries out indexing for the

Library's POLIS (Parliamentary On Line Indexing System) data base; and the Public Information Office, which *inter alia* answers numerous enquiries from the general public on parliamentary subjects, publishes a weekly and a sessional Information Bulletin on the House's business, and provides a small Branch Library for Members' personal staff including their research assistants.

(c) The Research Division, which deals with the more time-consuming enquiries from Members requiring written answers (almost 8,000 in 1986) and compiles research papers on current topics for the benefit of Members generally.

At present the staff of the Library is split between the Palace of Westminster and the two Norman Shaw Buildings, on the Victoria Embankment, about five minutes' walk away. In late 1990 it is planned to relocate many of the staff in a new building to be developed at the end of Whitehall. This will house all the staff from the Norman Shaw Buildings and some from the Palace of Westminster, so that after 1990 about three-quarters of the Library staff will work outside the Palace of Westminster and it will be possible to bring most members of the Research Division under one roof again.

The development of the Research Division has been a distinctive feature of the expansion of the Commons Library since 1945, in parallel with the evolution of similar services in parliamentary libraries in other countries. The reason for the existence of a parliamentary research service lies in the wish of Members for a group of politically impartial staff, dedicated to serving them alone, and independent of the executive. This staff would assemble and interpret information for Members for speeches, parliamentary questions, committee work, policy discussions and their parliamentary duties generally (including, particularly over recent years, assistance with a wide range of constituents' problems), and would compile papers on topical subjects, including much of the major legislation going through the House, for general distribution to Members. They would be available to help select committees (though, as mentioned earlier in the chapter, there are severe constraints on this type of work and it is diminishing), and would if necessary give oral briefings to Members or reseach assistants who were very pressed for time. All this adds up to a considerable task for the twenty specialist researchers (assisted by a similar number of supporting staff) working in the Research Division.

(The staff consists of people with qualifications *inter alia* in economics, statistics, the social and physical sciences, and law.)

The TSRB consultants recently reported with approval on the quality of the service given:'All the MPs interviewed praised the Library and its staff. Traditions of personal contact and mutual respect have been preserved'. However, the present level of staffing was inadequate: if the Library

> were freed from some of their present load, or had more people, they could produce more material of general interest, for example on the application of policy and not just on the implications of proposed legislation. MPs would be better informed and the requirement for 'ad hoc' research on behalf of individuals might even be reduced. Moreover, they are clearly overloaded. Each Senior Library Clerk in the Research Section produces about 400 replies annually to Members.[35]

Almost twenty years ago, Barker and Rush discussed the respective claims for expansion of research assistants and of the Commons Library: 'It is difficult to say which of these two developments ought to enjoy the higher priority. We would suggest only which of them, looking at our survey, would enjoy the greater support among Members if they were told they could choose only one of the two. We feel most Members would probably give the higher priority to a major advance of the House of Commons Library towards a fully developed parliamentary information system.'[36] Earlier we have seen that the Van Straubenzee Committee of 1975 endorsed this approach, advising that, in the development of research services, the emphasis should be placed on the expansion of the Library; but that in practice the opposite of what they recommended happened. The consequences of this situation were regarded unfavourably by the consultants used by the TSRB for their 1987 Report; they concluded: 'In short, we believe that the research and "information" needs of MPs are not well served by present arrangements. This is because the "system" has grown piecemeal. . . . Overall, there seems a strong case which we recommend for re-assessing the balance of resources devoted to research assistants and the Library in favour of the latter.'[37] The TSRB itself agreed:

> the evidence we received from all quarters, which described the high standards of the services provided by the library, leads us to

comment that, at some £2.2m annually, it is a very cost effective use of resources. Accordingly, it is in our view important that as Members' needs for research help grow, so the Library service should continue to develop in parallel to enable it to maintain and expand an effective service to Members.[38]

How has it come about that the bulk of the additional public funds available in this field has been spent on personal assistants for individual Members, rather than on the centrally organized resource provided by the Library? This pattern of expenditure may of course accord with the wishes of some Members, but the true explanation lies in the different ways in which the two types of fund are authorized. Members' allowances, including those for personal staff, are authorized by resolutions of the House, specifically debated, and the assembled backbenchers have on occasion disregarded the wishes of the government; whereas expenditure on the House departments (such as the Library) is included in supply estimates presented by the House of Commons Commission, but voted together with all other estimates without debate. Little has been done to co-ordinate the parts of the House of Commons budget that are on separate votes in order to ensure that spending priorities are balanced, and an effective mechanism is needed for planning action to take account of the repercussions of sudden drastic changes in the system – for example, the effect of a rise of over 50 per cent in Members' staff allowances on the facilities necessary to support the extra staff likely to be engaged, in terms of accomodation, refreshment facilities, security, and Branch Library services. Thus there can be no guarantee that the, to my mind, admirable views of the TSRB and of their consultants quoted earlier will be translated into practical decisions on expenditure.

COMPUTERS

Is modern technology the answer to the information problems of Parliament? Ten years ago, a joint committee called for action:

The Committee is unanimous in its belief that the introduction of computer-based systems into both Houses is essential if Parliament is to fulfil its proper constitutional role *vis-à-vis* the executive. Government is extending its control over an increasingly wide, complex and technical range of activities and

Parliament must have access to information of a correspondingly wide variety to enable it to evaluate government policies and legislation and to anticipate the needs of the future. The quantity of information needed to fulfil this role efficiently is enormous. . . . The Committee consider that Parliament's information services will be seriously impaired unless computer techniques are introduced as a matter of urgency.[39]

A report on computer-based indexing for the Commons Library followed,[40] and the Library's indexing system became operational in October 1980. This system is the largest information technology (IT) service currently in service at Westminster. As far as facilities directly available to Members and their staff are concerned, a significant number of Members now have their own microcomputers, and word processors are widely used;[41] but more comprehensive schemes are still at the discussion stage. A survey of Members' IT needs was commissioned from the Economic Intelligence Unit before the 1983 general election, and the Services Committee reported on the results and on other evidence in December 1984. The evidence convinced the committee

that Members could attain a level of service to the House and their constituents using data transmission and processing equipment that would be otherwise impossible without a wholly unrealistic increase in their staff. Indeed, as institutions outside the House are embracing this technology as a business standard, the House will need to keep up with such advances if it is to play its full political role. The growth of statistical data available and the mass of other information with which all Members must deal makes the speedy introduction of an effective information technology system of vital importance.[42]

The committee recommended the development of a local area network for the House, and the building brief for the new parliamentary building in Parliament Street included the requirement that provision should be made for greatly expanded use of IT equipment and the necessary cabling.[43] When the House came to debate the 1984 report, the then leader of the House (Mr John Biffen) expressed his doubts over the costs of the proposals – put at slightly over £5 million, excluding some costs which currently could not be accurately gauged – and concluded that these costs would have to be 'tested against available financial resources'.[44]

In April 1987, the TSRB noted that 'application of information technology to the work of MPs has been under consideration for some time',[45] and suggested that one of the proposals made by their consultants should be kept in mind for possible adoption in the future: this was for word processors to be provided centrally to link Westminster with constituency offices. The consultants were sceptical about a local area network: 'The existence of a Local Area Network would permit direct access by MPs [to Prestel and other external information services]. We doubt whether this access in itself would justify the cost involved in setting up such a network'. Furthermore, in the course of listing a number of IT systems available directly or indirectly to Members, the consultants remarked: 'But we are by no means convinced that MPs require direct access at present to all or any of these from a terminal on their desks'.[46] In 1984, two research workers considered the extent to which MPs would be willing to access data on public expenditure on their own computer terminals:

> The number [of MPs] using computer terminals will certainly increase, but it is evident . . . that most MPs will certainly not be willing to rely on electronic access to any significant extent in the foreseeable future. The major area of future developments in this area would therefore seem to be in providing still better facilities for the House of Commons Library, the excellence of whose service is an additional disincentive to MPs to invest their own time, effort and money on electronic equipment to provide access to information on government expenditure.[47]

If these authors are right, and if their view applies to other fields as well, this brings us back to the Library and to the need for the human element as well as the machine. Indeed it is clear that when the output of an IT system consists of *references*, rather than full-text or statistical tables, a library will be needed containing the actual sources; and even where the output looks directly usable, guidance may sometimes be needed – for example, by a statistician on tables of figures, or by a law librarian or lawyer on print-out from a legal data base.

PROPOSALS FOR A BRITISH OFFICE OF TECHNOLOGY ASSESSMENT

In the autumn of 1986, proposals were put forward for a British Office of Technology Assessment (OTA) which should be mentioned briefly here. An Early Day Motion (no. 1067) drew attention to the benefits derived by the Congress and the US Senate from the American OTA over the last thirteen years, and noted that analogous bodies were under consideration in five other countries. It urged the setting up at Westminster of an organization to advise parliamentarians of both Houses 'upon the implications and impact of scientific innovation . . . the correct evaluation of conflicting technical data' and so on and to 'prepare reports and advise parliamentarians on scientific matters independently of the executive'.

The cost of such a service has been estimated at £250,000 per annum, but the government has refused to provide finance. Efforts have been made to raise funds privately, and in early 1988 it was announced that some £50,000 had been raised and that the scheme would go ahead.[48]

CONCLUSION

Backbench MPs must have assistance in their confrontations with ministers who are supported by all the resources of government departments. At present they can call upon the relatively generously funded, but on occasion severely criticized, services of personal research assistants, or on the small, hard-pressed cadre of the Library's highly-regarded research and professional staff. In 1970 I wrote: 'A growing number of professional MPs feel that the House of Commons has far too long denied its Members facilities adequate to their role';[49] and the following year: 'It can perhaps hardly be expected that any government should be too eager to reinforce its critics.'[50] Perhaps a final word should rest with the *Economist* newspaper: 'In parliamentary systems, the government of the day has little to gain by giving parliaments their own source of knowledge and advice. Why spend money providing information for backbenchers, when ignorance keeps them so much more malleable?'[51] This sort of comment focuses attention on the importance of the information-providing agencies which do exist, and in particular on the range and quality of the services offered by the House of Commons Library.

Chapter Four

THE FLOOR OF THE HOUSE

ROBERT BORTHWICK

The floor of the House of Commons has a central place in any account of the workings of that institution. A great deal that is important in our national life passes across that stage and many of the beliefs about what is important to political success find expression in the Chamber of the Commons. It will be one of the concerns of this chapter to examine the manner in which present reality conforms to this traditional picture of the central importance of the floor of the House.[1]

In its narrowest sense the floor is a physical entity influenced by the confrontational architecture of the building. The rectangular arrangement of the House, with government benches facing opposition benches and without crossbenches, encourages a sense of an either/or argument. There is space for only a proportion (about two-thirds) of the membership. Thus on important occasions the House will appear extremely crowded, while on lesser occasions its emptiness may be slightly disguised.

Members do not have desks in the Chamber, nor even particular seats. Apart from those benches occupied by the leaders of government and opposition, Members may sit where they like, although some Members develop over time a prescriptive claim on particular seats. The Chamber has a sense of intimacy which is said to produce a conversational style of speaking, something encouraged by the fact that, apart from frontbenchers who have the benefit of the despatch box, speeches must be made from where a Member is sitting and without the benefit of any dais or anywhere to rest notes.[2]

THE PLACE OF THE FLOOR

The importance of the floor in British parliamentary life encompasses such things as a tradition of great debate, the clash of conflicting ideas, and the presence of dominating personalities. For much of the past century these elements have been seen as manifestations of a two-party system being the central organizing principle of Parliament. In this *the* Government was faced by *the* Opposition and the life of the Chamber organized to suit their mutual convenience. In the past fifteen years, as in certain earlier periods, these assumptions have been thrown into question by changes outside the House, to which the latter has struggled, as we shall see, to respond.

The House of Commons is often said to be a 'floor-centred' legislative body in contrast to those institutions, such as the United States Congress, which are 'committee-centred'. A number of elements contribute to this but three are particularly important. First is the idea that what happens on the floor is more important than what happens elsewhere in the institution; for example, the House itself gives committees their powers and duties, and can always overrule their decisions. Secondly, the floor of the Commons has been the arena for testing the major features of executive–legislative relations in Britain, for ultimately governments can survive only if they can maintain support there. The events of May 1940 or March 1979 show that this is not as inevitable as has often been assumed and, to survive, they must heed and respond to opinions expressed in debate. Most of the time governments get their way, but it is deemed important that they have to come to the Commons to explain their policies, defend their proposals, and ultimately in some sense to be accountable.

The third element in the importance of the Chamber is that in the village society of Westminster it acts as an important stage on which to build or destroy political reputations, or, equally important, on which it is believed that reputations are so made and unmade. However irrational such a process may seem as a way of discerning administrative ability, to be able to 'handle the House' is widely regarded as important. For the aspiring backbencher, as for the junior minister, the House is believed to be important as a source of reputation making. This view is reinforced by stories of politicians pitched in at the highest level who proved unable to handle the House (Frank Cousins and John Davies, who came from the two sides of industry, are the most quoted examples of this from the recent past). Apart from the effect on individual careers of what happens on the floor, there is also the effect on party morale: a succession of good or bad performances from leaders has an impact on a party's fortunes beyond the House itself. Morale both inside and outside the House depends in part on how good the performances are on the floor of the Commons.

THE PARLIAMENTARY YEAR AND THE PARLIAMENTARY DAY

The House continues to adhere to an annual cycle which begins and ends in the autumn, except when proceedings are abbreviated by the calling of a general election at some other point in the year. In that situation (as in 1979, 1983, and 1987) it is usual to follow the election with a session lasting about eighteen months.

Within a normal session there are recesses of three or four weeks at Christmas, a week at Easter, another week at Whitsun, and about ten weeks in the summer. This means that a normal session lasts for about thirty-six weeks. However, there is a measure of uncertainty over the exact timing of the recesses, particularly in the case of the start of the summer recess which varies from late July to early August. This unpredictability is defended as a necessary part of the government versus opposition struggle to secure/delay business. For many Members however it must be a source of irritation. The lateness of rising for the summer recess is a bone of contention particularly for Scottish Members, who find little overlap with Scottish school holidays.

The Procedure Committee addressed this question in a report published in early 1987.[3] It suggested making life rather more predictable for Members and pointed out that other Parliaments such as Canada's managed to live with a pre-arranged parliamentary calendar. To this end they recommended various changes to make the duration of recesses more predictable. At the time of writing the House has taken no action on this suggestion: in this, as in other areas, there is a certain conservatism in the House's reaction to suggestions for change in its traditional way of doing things.

One area where change has occurred is in the timing of the parliamentary day on Fridays. Since 1979 the House has met at 9.30 a.m. on Fridays instead of 11 a.m., with the adjournment scheduled for 3 p.m. rather than 4.30 p.m. So far, however, the House has shown a marked lack of enthusiasm for altering the times of sittings on other days of the week. Leaving aside the ill-fated experiment with morning sittings in the late 1960s, the House's basic day of a 2.30 p.m. start and a notional finish at 10.30 p.m. has remained unchanged for a very long time. In practice, as is discussed below, the notional eight-hour day on the floor is regularly exceeded and rarely does the House achieve a rising time earlier than planned. (In part this is because considerable efforts are made to ensure that debates run their allotted span so as not to upset the plans of party whips and particularly to ensure that divisions are held at predictable times.) During the 1985–6 session, excluding Fridays and one Thursday immediately before Easter when the House began at 9.30 a.m. with Question Time, the House rose between 10.25 p.m. and 10.45 p.m. on twenty-eight occasions, before 10.25 p.m. on three occasions, and after 10.45 p.m. on no less than 106 days. Of course in this last category there were occasions when rising was not much after 10.45 p.m., but there were also times when the end of the parliamentary day came much later.[4]

The House of Commons is rightly regarded as sitting for longer each day and for more days each year than most legislative bodies. In each of the most recent full sessions, 1984–5 and 1985–6, the House sat for 172 days, which makes them representative of recent sessions unaffected by the timing of a general election.[5] Each of these sessions ran for almost exactly a year (6 November 1984 – 30 October 1985 and 6 November 1985 – 7 November 1986).

In each of these sessions the House sat for a total of over 1,500 hours with an average working day of around nine hours (9 hours 6 minutes and 8 hours 57 minutes). Since these figures includes Friday sittings which rarely exceed by much the projected 5 hours 30 minutes, the average sitting from Mondays to Thursdays was well in excess of 9 hours. To put the matter another way, of the Monday to Thursday sittings during 1985–6 (and excluding the one which began at 9.30 a.m. just before a recess), sixty-two finished before midnight and seventy-five after. Among the latter were some substantial sittings including four longer than seventeen hours, the longest of which, on 5 June 1986, lasted over nineteen hours and resulted in the loss of the following day's sitting, as it extended beyond the time the next sitting was due to begin. Even this, however, pales alongside a sitting in 1984–5 which lasted over thirty hours[6] and which also resulted in the following day's sitting being lost.

WHAT HAPPENS ON THE FLOOR OF THE HOUSE

In order to give some overall picture of how the House occupies its time on the floor, table 4.1 presents details of how that time was distributed in 1984–5 and 1985–6.

Perhaps the most striking feature of these figures is the substantial place occupied by government legislation, just over 28 per cent of the total in each of the sessions. Even so this is less than it was a decade earlier when, in at least some sessions, it accounted for over

Table 4.1 Time spent on floor of the House, sessions 1984–5 and 1985–6

Category of business	1984–5 Time hrs–mins	%	1985–6 Time hrs–mins	%
Debate on Queen's Speech	38–13	2.4	36–42	2.4
Government bills	443–51	28.3	437–59	28.5
Private Members' bills	59–01	3.8	57–15	3.7
Motions in government time	176–14	11.2	169–48	11.1
Opposition days	117–33	7.5	105–21	6.9
Private Members notions	49–14	3.1	57–42	3.7
Daily adjournment	84–40	5.4	81–08	5.3
Recess adjournment[a]	30–56	2.0	30–11	2.0
Emergency adjournment (SO No. 10)[b]	3–15	0.2	3–12	0.2
Adj. debates after consolidated fund bill	35–49	2.3	37–26	2.4
Questions	124–07	7.9	127–16	8.3
Private notice questions	7–44	0.5	12–13	0.8
Statements (inc. business statements)	84–55	5.4	89–53	5.8
SO No. 10 applications[b]	5–56	0.4	5–19	0.3
Ten-minute rule bill motions	12–57	0.8	11–15	0.7
Points of order and Speaker's rulings	14–12	0.9	14–21	0.9
Statutory instruments & measures[c]	156–30	10.0	106–01	6.9
European documents	22–00	1.4	42–18	2.8
Ways and Means resolutions (Budget)	22–27	1.4	21–04	1.4
Estimates days	21–14	1.4	17–13	1.1
Private legislation	18–56	1.2	42–16	2.8
Miscellaneous	37–08	2.4	30–32	2.0
Total	1566–52	99.9	1536–25	100.0

Notes: *a* Includes time spent on motions fixing recess dates.
   b Now SO No. 20.
   c Includes time spent on orders relating to Northern Ireland.
Sources: figures compiled from the *Sessional Digest 1984–85* and *1985–86* prepared by the Public Information Office, Department of the Library, from figures supplied by the Journal Office, House of Commons.

30 per cent of the total.[7] In addition to the time spent on primary legislation, the House spends a smaller and more variable amount on secondary legislation, including matters relating to Northern Ireland and the European Community. In total these were responsible for 178 and 148 hours respectively in the years examined. Of this Northern Ireland was responsible for thirty-seven and fifteen hours and Europe twenty-two and forty-two hours. Another substantial block of time is taken by non-legislative debates in government time: 11 per cent of the total in each of these sessions, a percentage relatively unchanged from a decade earlier. Together these three categories of business, which could be said to represent the core of 'government time' on the floor, account for very nearly half the time spent there in a normal session. Even so this is slightly less than in the early 1970s when the share was over 50 per cent.

Other time that could be regarded as government time includes that spent on statements and the Budget debates. These are sufficient to take the government share to over 50 per cent. However this is perhaps a misleading way of expressing matters for, as is pointed out in Erskine May,

> although it is for the Government to initiate most of the different items of business, the manner in which they are debated and the time taken to complete the necessary proceedings are to a large extent influenced by the actions of the Opposition. . . . In a sense all Government time is equally Opposition time.[8]

Viewed in that light, it is perhaps slightly misleading to note that opposition time as such in table 4.1 amounts to around 7 per cent of the total. Erskine May goes on to put the point more sternly, 'No valid purpose is . . . served by the computation, based (as it inevitably would be) on a number of highly artificial assumptions, of a figure showing the total amount of "Opposition time" in a session.'[9]

A similar stricture applies to attempts to calculate the share of the time on the floor which belongs to backbenchers. If one takes the categories of business covered by Helen Irwin in chapter 5, on opportunities for backbenchers, then these, together with time spent on private members' bills (discussed in Gavin Drewry's chapter), account for over a quarter of the time in each of the sessions examined (27 per cent and 28 per cent respectively).[10] This may seem a surprisingly large share of the total, but for some of these items of business, notably private notice questions and oral questions to the

Prime Minister, as Helen Irwin points out, the opposition front bench has a substantial share in the proceedings.

The time that questions occupy is, of course, strictly limited by the rule ending that business each day at 3.30 p.m.; the total over the session varies therefore only according to the number of days the House sits. What has shown an increase in recent years is the time occupied by the items of business which come immediately after Question Time: private notice questions, statements, applications for emergency adjournment debates[11] and motions for 'ten-minute rule' bills. (Some evidence for this increase appears in table 4.2 below.) These opportunities are considered more fully by Helen Irwin in her chapter. However, as table 4.1 indicates, in 1984–5 and 1985–6 these items taken together occupied almost as much time as questions (111 and 118 hours compared with 124 and 127 hours on questions); and rather more if the general free-for-all of points of order is included. In each of these sessions the House spent about one-sixth of its time on what Helen Irwin calls 'prime time' business.

It is not now unusual to find these items taking at least another hour after the end of Question Time. This means that the House may well not begin its 'main' business until 4.30 p.m. or even 5 p.m. Excluding Fridays, there were in 1984–5 eighty-four days on which this business was completed by 4.30 p.m. and fifty-two on which it was not; while in 1985–6 the comparable figures were eighty and fifty-seven. In 1984–5 there were twenty-eight, and in 1985–6 twenty-five occasions when the House did not reach its main business until at least 5.00 p.m. On a number of occasions the main business did not start until after 5.30 p.m. or even 6.00 p.m. All this raises a question about what should be designated 'main' business and whether the business immediately after Question Time is not now the high point of the House's working day. It was not always thus: table 4.2 gives an indication of the way in which the expansion of the 'post-3.30' slot is very much a phenomenon of the past twenty years and particularly of the past ten. The figures in table 4.2 show the average number of minutes after the earliest possible starting time (3.15 p.m. in 1946, 3.30 p.m. for the other years) that the House began its main business on Monday to Thursdays.

In effect the ability to raise topical issues by these various 'prime-time' devices has virtually doubled the length of time available to do this purely through questions. The House is often now better attended for the business after 3.30 then before that time (except on Tuesdays

Table 4.2 Average length of time between the end of Question Time and start of main business Mondays–Thursdays

Year	No. of minutes
1946	12
1956	11
1966	22
1976	38
1986	55

Source: Figures derived from House of Commons *Hansard* and based on a sample of four weeks in February of each of the selected years.

and Thursdays when Prime Minister's Questions draw large numbers for 3.15). The period after 3.30 is ideally timed to obtain maximum publicity for whatever (or whoever) it is desired to attract attention. In that respect it stands in marked contrast to things like the daily adjournment debate which occurs often at the least useful time to gain any audience.

In addition to these informal or unofficial changes in the way that time is spent on the floor, there have been a number of explicit changes in recent years. European business is now an established category with regular late-night debates on documents emanating from the Community and longer debates on more general themes. Northern Ireland too has settled into place as a normal piece of the furniture over the past fifteen years in the shape of debates on orders relating to the province.

More recently supply days have been replaced by opposition days. Under changes introduced in July 1982 the notion of supply days was abandoned and they were replaced by nineteen opposition days with, in addition, some business previously taken on supply days being moved to government time and the provision of three estimates days. In May 1985 the number of opposition days was increased to twenty with control of three of those days being given to the second largest opposition party. It is perhaps worth observing here that this change is some evidence that recognition is beginning to be given on the floor to the weakening of the two-party system. As far as estimates days are concerned, although an estimate forms the peg for the debate, the subjects are set down by resolution of the Liaison Committee and so enable select committee reports relating to expenditure to be debated. Usually these days are treated as six half-days, so enabling more topics to be covered.

THE ORGANIZATION OF BUSINESS

An essential feature of the House of Commons is that its business is primarily controlled by the government of the day. Ministers provide the framework within which business takes place and their wishes normally take precedence. Of course there is a measure of co-operation between the two major parties and particularly between the business managers of the government and the official opposition, 'the usual channels'. These mechanisms are usually sufficient to settle such issues as to whether to hold certain debates on certain days, or whether to continue beyond the normal hour for closing. Without a measure of agreement on such matters, life would quickly become intolerable for all concerned. The outcome of these discussions is announced by the leader of the House each Thursday after Question Time when he gives details of business for the following week.

While some items of business are unavoidable, Question Time four days a week, the daily adjournment debate, and so on, there is scope for argument about others. Items such as private members' bills and motions have an established place, with currently twelve Fridays for bills and nine Fridays and parts of four Mondays for motions being set aside. (For further discussion of these areas see the chapters by Gavin Drewry and Helen Irwin respectively.) Precisely which Fridays and which Mondays is subject to some discussion between the parties. Likewise some subjects have a regular place and discussion will be only over the timing, for example the annual consideration of the Defence White Paper or debates on foreign affairs. Opposition days can be used to debate subjects that enable the government to be portrayed in a poor light. Other topics may or may not be accommodated. At times it may seem that the front benches of the two major parties are in league to keep discussion of certain topics off the floor of the House; such allegations were made during the miners' strike of 1984–5, when some Labour back-benchers were critical of the Labour leadership's attitude to the conduct of the dispute by the National Union of Mineworkers.

If the parties disagree about the ordering of business it is likely that the government will have its way, and can usually ensure that debate is confined to the time they make available by means of the closure and, occasionally, the guillotine. In essence the closure represents a check against unlimited debate. It is the Speaker's decision

61

whether or not to accept a closure motion. 'That the Question be now put'. In making that decision, he has to have regard to the interests of majorities and minorities. If the Speaker accepts the motion, there must not only be a majority in its favour for it to be carried but also at least 100 Members voting in support of it. In practice, therefore, the closure is very much a device for governments; private members find it more difficult to secure the necessary numbers on their own legislation.

In cases where a government judges that too much delay is occurring on a bill, it may take steps by way of an 'allocation of time order' (guillotine resolution) to limit debate in the House.[12] Such a motion normally sets out dates by which remaining stages of a bill must be completed or the amount of time available for particular stages. Within that framework the Business Committee may work out more detailed arrangements. The penalty for a government in resorting to the device, aside from political capital made by opponents, is that such resolutions have to be debated on the floor, but for a maximum of three hours. In 1984–5 two bills received this treatment and in 1985–6 three.

This style of arranging matters leaves a modest place for minor parties. We have noted the right to three opposition days, and in recent years it has been usual to allow a vote on an Alliance amendment on the final day of the debate on the address in reply to the Queen's Speech but otherwise there has been little formal recognition of change. As the Liberal chief whip pointed out just before the 1987 general election: 'Labour whips are fully consulted about the scheduling of Parliamentary business while we are usually left out of consultations and merely informed of the result.'[13]

THE PLACE OF THE SPEAKER

Within the framework agreed by the usual channels (or, in the event of their failure to agree, laid down by the government), the control of business is largely in the hands of the Speaker and his deputies. Despite the highly party-oriented environment of the Commons, the office of Speaker has retained its aura of impartiality. The Speaker represents the whole House and has a special responsibility to safeguard the interests of minorities within it. Although many Speakers come with a background of non-partisan committee chairmanship, most recent occupants of the Chair (Speakers Morrison, Hylton Foster, Lloyd, and Thomas) have had very visible ministerial pedigrees.

When the office of Speaker falls vacant, the choice of a successor rests formally with the House as a whole. In practice the government of the day, in consultation with other parties, has had a large voice in the outcome. However, there were suggestions in the most recent case in 1983 that the voice of backbenchers was taken rather more into account.

Once in office, great responsibility falls on the Speaker for the conduct of business on the floor. In his role as presiding officer he is responsible for ensuring that the House's procedures are observed. In some areas he has a large measure of discretion: for example, in dealing with requests for emergency adjournment debates or in the selection or grouping of amendments in debate. His responsibilities for maintaining order range from handling points of order (frequently bogus, as Helen Irwin notes in her chapter) or dealing with irrelevance or tedious repetition to coping with a boisterous collection of larger-than-life characters who may transgress the rules and conventions of the House. His powers here range from calling a Member to order, to taking more serious steps, for example by 'naming' a Member who persistently infringes the rules of the House. This would normally be followed by a motion of the House suspending the 'named' Member. More serious collective disorder may result in the Speaker suspending or adjourning a sitting when he judges that the temperature needs to be lowered.

As far as debate is concerned it is fairly clear that arrangements are a good deal more formalized than is sometimes acknowledged. Phrases such as 'catching the Speaker's eye' exaggerate the extent of spontaneity. For a major debate, or one in which many Members wish to speak, it is usual for the Speaker to be notified in advance by those who wish to participate. There is in effect a batting list from which Speakers may be reluctant to depart. Moreover, in practice, Members have an informal ration of time and their chances of being called depend, in part, on how much of their ration they have used and how long they spoke for when last called. (A 'black list' undoubtedly exists.) Some of these points were well illustrated in a statement by the Speaker at the start of the debate on airports policy in June 1985; drawing attention to the fact that thirty-eight Members had indicated to him their wish to take part he said:

I shall give some priority to those hon. Members who were not called during the questions on the statement made on 5 January [*sic*], as I said I would. In drawing up my list of those hon. Members who may take part today I have taken into account those who spoke on 31 January when we last debated this matter and, incidentally, how long they spoke for.[14]

The Chair calls Members from each side alternately, with (from 1983 to 1987) normally, one Alliance Member in each full day's debate and perhaps another representative of a minor party. One result is that where a party has a large majority (as with the Conservatives after 1983) frustration about speaking opportunities is likely to be greater among its backbenchers. It is part of the duty of Speakers to give a hearing to minorities (including those within major parties). The priority accorded to Privy Councillors to be called in debate is widely unpopular among backbenchers.

One partial solution to the problem of Members being squeezed out of debates is to encourage brevity. Persuasion has some influence when many people want to take part but the House has recently strengthened the Speaker's hand here. In October 1984 it agreed to an experiment (which followed an earlier, more limited one in 1979–80) with a ten-minute limit on speeches within a two-hour period in the middle of popular debates. This experiment evidently proved more popular than its 1979–80 predecessor in that it was extended in February 1986. In November 1986 the Procedure Committee pronounced the experiment a success and recommended that it be incorporated into Standing Orders.[15] However, as of June 1988 this had not been done.

In other areas too the Speaker has a discretion which affects the conduct of business, for example over the style of Question Time. There is a basic choice between hurrying on to cover as many questions as possible, without allowing time for proper ventilation of the issues, or being content with reaching fewer questions but dealing with them more adequately. Recent occupants of the Chair have tended to choose the latter alternative whereas their predecessors preferred the former. Similarly the Speaker exercises control over whether to accept a request for a private notice question or for an emergency debate under SO No. 20 (formerly SO No. 10). In practice, in both areas there are well developed informal conventions. Private notice questions are allowed at the rate of one or two a week.

Requests for emergency adjournment debates are unlikely to succeed as the figures in table 5.2 in Helen Irwin's chapter show.

If the Speaker accepts a request for an emergency adjournment debate, the House's agreement is also needed for it to be held. Unless the matter is judged especially urgent, in which case the debate will be held at 7.00 p.m. the same day, the debate will be held after Question Time on the next sitting day (except for debates granted on Thursdays which are held over until the following Monday). The debate is limited to three hours. In 1984–5 the only successful applicant was the shadow environment spokesman, Dr Cunningham, who raised the issue of restrictions on local-government capital expenditure. In the following session the solitary successful candidate was the Leader of the Opposition on the controversy surrounding the leaking of the Solicitor General's letter during the Westland affair. This provided one of the most dramatic debates of the Parliament, for it was held against a background of speculation that the survival of the Prime Minister and her government depended on a credible performance in the debate. In both these examples the debate was opened and closed by frontbench spokesmen; in the Westland case about half the time available was occupied by the four frontbench speakers. This tends to confirm the view that such debates have become as much a part of the party battle as a weapon of the backbencher.

THE REPORTING OF THE FLOOR

Much of the literature on Parliament assumes that it is an important centre of national life and that within the House of Commons it is the Chamber which is, or should be, the focus of attention. Phrases such as 'the Grand Inquest of the Nation' were once more commonly applied to the House than they are today.[16]

As we noted earlier, the House sits for long hours and for much of each year. What is less clear is how far these deliberations have an impact on what happens outside or how far the world outside Westminster cares about, or even notices, what happens there. In part the answer to this depends on the way in which and the degree to which the House is projected in the main elements of the mass media: newspapers, radio and television.

Without doubt press coverage of the House has diminished in quantity 'There is no longer the same reporting in the press of what each member says. Debates are summarised in such a condensed way that a member is very lucky if a couple of sentences are reported.'[17] No longer do even the serious newspapers offer extended coverage of proceedings on the floor of the House (except for the Budget debate). Readers are perhaps unwilling to plough through long accounts of speeches. In part the change must reflect a perception on the part of editors and others that what happens in the House itself is simply less important than it was. One must be careful here to distinguish between the floor and other aspects of Parliament. In part there may be less reporting of the floor because other aspects of the House have grown in importance, accessibility, and variety. Committee work, party meetings, and informal lobby contact are all part of what constitutes the 'House' but are not part of the House considered purely as the Chamber.

One striking feature of reading the Parliamentary report in, say, *The Times* of twenty or more years ago is how far it was simply a summary of proceedings in the Chambers of the Lords and Commons. It is certainly true that much more attention was paid to the variety of speeches made, even to the extent of simply listing the names of some Members who contributed to the debate when nothing of their words is reported. Today it is not unusual to find the main debate totally ignored on the parliamentary page of a serious newspaper in favour of reporting items arising in Questions, statements, and the like.[18]

One factor relevant here is that despite, or because of, modern technology national newspaper deadlines rule out coverage of a large part of each day's proceedings in most of their editions.[19] In that respect some other aspects of the House's work, for example select committee activity, often have a better sense of timing for newspaper deadlines. It may also be that increasingly they can offer 'news'. It is perhaps no accident that a number of newspapers call the page on which Parliament is reported by a title which indicates a broader coverage: for example 'The day in politics' (the *Guardian*) and 'Parliament and politics' (the *Independent*).

To a degree it is not surprising that newspaper coverage of Parliament should have suffered a decline. That medium has undoubtedly in certain respects been overtaken by radio and, especially, television. As far as radio is concerned, while there has long been reporting of parliamentary proceedings, it is only relatively recently that direct broadcasting has been permitted.[20] As in former times with newspaper reporing, the House's relations with reporting by radio have been marked by great caution. The general oversight of the arrangements for broadcasting proceedings of the House is entrusted to the Select Committee on Sound Broadcasting. It produces reports on a variety of matters: recent areas of its concern have included the arrangements for the permanent storage of Members' speeches via the National Sound Archives[21] and the possibility of a 'Dial-a-Debate' service enabling telephone users to have access to debates.[22]

It is remarkable that the very idea of broadcasting proceedings was not debated in the House until 1959. A closed-circuit experiment was conducted in 1968 but it was not until 1975 that a public experiment was undertaken. This lasted for four weeks, but not until 1978 did permanent broadcasting begin. Initially live broadcasting of Question Time and major debates was undertaken but this has fallen away over the past decade so that there is no longer regular national live broadcasting. Occasions that are judged to be of great interest (for example the Chancellor's budget speech) are covered in this way. Extracts are, however, used in radio and television news bulletins as well as in programmes like 'Today in Parliament' and 'Yesterday in Parliament'. In addition, a good deal of use is made by local radio stations of items relevant to their areas.

Live broadcasting of the House's proceedings has been subject to some criticism: for example, that it magnifies the farmyard impression of the House and exacerbates the adversarial style of politics. Whatever its faults (and perhaps the early focus on Prime Minister's Question Time was not the best possible advertisement for the House) it is now well established as a means of communicating what takes place on the floor of the House. Radio coverage of major debates (for example on the Falklands in April 1982 or on Westland, especially the emergency adjournment debate on 27 January 1986) provides a wider audience with a ring-side seat for occasions of considerable tension and national importance. To that extent sound broadcasting has helped to make the House of Commons a little less remote.

Despite, or because of, its experience with sound broadcasting, the House has been slow to accept the idea of its proceedings being televised. For some years the only exception permitted was the summons to attend the House of Lords for the reading of the Queen's Speech as part of the State Opening of Parliament. Since 1966 the House has periodically addressed the matter of television. In

November 1985, it reaffirmed its opposition, although by a very narrow majority and against the expectations of many observers. However in February 1988 the House voted by a majority of 54 for an experiment in the public broadcasting of its proceedings by television.

To the advocates of televising the House's proceedings, the rejection of the idea until 1988 represented evidence of a reluctance to come to terms with the most powerful medium of communication in contemporary society. This reluctance contrasts with the eagerness with which the House of Lords has embraced television and the obvious alacrity with which individual Members of the Commons agree to appear on television. For most Members, it has been said, 'a minute on regional television is far more important than a speech in the House of Commons'.[23] Those who favour allowing the cameras into the Chamber argue that the House's work has become increasingly remote from much of society and that television may be the only means by which vitality can be restored to proceedings on the floor. To keep the cameras out is regarded as being on a par with the House's efforts to prevent publication of its debates in an earlier age.

Those who oppose the introduction of the cameras argue that they will merely encourage some unfortunate trends in existing behaviour: a tendency to play to the gallery, a further decline in parliamentary behaviour, an even greater concern with constituency matters, and the irresistible desire of some Members to inflate their own egos. There is also a fear that extracts will be used so selectively that only the dramatic will be deemed newsworthy. Moreover, smaller parties are hesitant because they fear losing out in the coverage to the larger parties. Some opposition derives from the feeling that the necessary technology with its heat and light will be an intrusion which would erode further the intimate atmosphere of the Chamber.[24]

Concern about the way the House is perceived outside and the way proceedings in the Chamber are handled in the media are aspects of a wider problem, namely the standing of the Chamber as a focus of national issues and a source of legitimizing influence. We now turn to this wider problem.

'THE DECLINE OF THE FLOOR'

There has probably never been a time when concern was not expressed about the quality of proceedings in Parliament. The 'things-are-not-what-they-were' school has long flourished in relation to the House of Commons. At the beginning of the century Lord Hugh Cecil was concerned about this: 'Why is it that nobody cares, outside these walls, about the rights of private members? Because there is a deep-seated feeling that the House is an institution which has ceased to have much authority or much repute'.[25] It is true also that the House has a long way to go in its standards of behaviour before it reaches the depths described by observers of the early nineteenth-century House.[26]

All that said, however, there is probably greater concern today about the health of the floor and its proceedings than there has been for a very long time. Expressions of that concern are widespread among those who have been Members or observers of the House. Among the newcomers in either category the sense of dismay may be as great. These concerns centre mainly on attendance, behaviour, and the relevance of what takes place on the floor.

Attendance, like the status of the Chamber generally, has worried previous generations too. Writing some thirty-five years ago, for example, Earl Winterton observed that:

> They [the younger members of the Conservative Party] are in the Chamber only when they want to speak or are interested in the particular subject. So, all too often in the 1945 and 1950 Parliaments, the Opposition back benches were sparsely filled by a handful of M.P.s too engrossed in thinking out what they were going to say, if they were fortunate enough to be 'called', to encourage by cheers those of their own side who were actually speaking.[27]

However bad things seemed to Earl Winterton, it is possible that they have since become a deal worse.

It is impossible to be precise about the level of attendance in the Chamber since no official figures exist. What evidence there is comes from such sources as unofficial counts by journalists and others, the impressions of those with long memories and from those occasions when parties have been found short-handed. All are open to the objection that they are fragmentary and likely to dwell on the occasions when attendance has been noticeably poor. In 1984, for example, it was reported by one observer that for the opening speech by the Secretary of State in the defence debate there were just nine

Labour backbenchers present (plus a similar number of front-benchers).[28] Later that year the Labour opposition, anxious to demonstrate that their attendance in the Chamber had improved, issued figures showing that during a two-day debate on the Local Government Bill their attendance had never dropped below twenty-five.[29]

In the 1980s problems of attendance have been associated particularly with Labour Members but no party has a monopoly of virtue here. It is difficult to know whether Labour's difficulties reflect particular factors (the lack of heart for tackling a government with an overwhelming majority, the associated problem of a very low number of MPs after 1983, and the need to work hard in the first half of each Parliament at cultivating their constituency parties in order to ensure their reselection) or whether they reflect longer term, more general factors. Certainly some seasoned observers would echo and extend the views expressed by Earl Winterton above. A former Speaker of the House referring to the late 1970s and early 1980s he said: 'the attendance in the Chamber became deplorable in the evenings because once members had found out whether they were likely to speak or not, those who knew they were not would be away'.[30]

Explanations for the decline in attendance are plentiful. Aside from those mentioned above, they include the growth in demands made on Members by constituents, interest groups, and others. There is little doubt that the general constituency case load of members has grown considerably, while equally, especially in the Labour Party, constituency parties have become much more anxious to monitor their Member's activities. Another explanation offered is that the provision of office facilities for Members has reduced the need for them to spend time in or around the Chamber itself.[31] It is suggested that the changing nature of Members has meant that there are fewer, on either side of the House, who are content simply to make up an audience. Such are the pressures on the time of Members that many would regard attendance at a debate merely to listen (unless it were to the frontbenchers or a speaker of unusual ability, or an occasion of outstanding interest) as an act of self-indulgence.

More dubious as an explanation is the assertion (often made by Members themselves) that the growth in the volume of committee activity is responsible for the decline in interest in proceedings in the

Chamber. There is little evidence for this as the numbers involved in committee work while the House is sitting are very limited;[32] certainly in the first six months after the 1983 election, when the fourteen 'new' select committees had not yet been re-established, there was no evidence that attendance was better.

Attendance may have declined because the quality of speaking is less compelling and there are simply fewer stars to draw in the crowds. Probably there are fewer Members whose very name on the annunciator can draw an audience. However, great orators may be more recognizable in retrospect. What may be true is that there has been a general rise in the average competence but that the competent are not compelling.[33] It may also be that the new style of political conversation, which stresses the ability to communicate via the television screen with the public in their own homes, requires different techniques than those valued on the floor of the House. Certainly some do not succeed in adjusting, Michael Foot being an obvious example of one whose parliamentary reputation was not translatable to television.

Two other factors are perhaps closer to the heart of the matter. The first is that much of what takes place in the House is not seen as being of great importance. According to this argument the decline of Britain as a great power and the sense that decisions in domestic politics are taken elsewhere have meant that many debates are simply less significant. This point was made by John Mackintosh in 1978 when he suggested that there had been a decline in the quality of frontbench performers due in part to the fact that: 'Britain is no longer a world power, the House of Commons spends very little time on crucial world events, and more and more debates are about boring and detailed problems of economic policy'.[34] A similar point was more recently made by Francis Pym when he argued that 'with the reduction in the international influence of Britain, the Commons has "dealt far less often with wider issues of major significance and far more with trivial matters" '.[35] The argument is clear, if debates are about less important things why should busy people spend large lumps of time listening to them.

Secondly, much of what takes place in the Chamber is pre-determined as to its outcome. Either to make speeches or to listen to them is unlikely to have any impact on the result, notwithstanding the decline in the strength of party solidarity in voting in the House over the past two decades. There are fairly rare exceptions, when members are influenced by what is said in debate. The logic of this view might seem to point in the direction either of leaving speeches undelivered or of having them entered into the record without taking up the time of the House if their only audience is the local paper in the Member's constituency. Much debate in the Commons hardly deserves that name but is rather a series of largely unconnected speeches often delivered to a near empty House.

However it is important that when occasion demands the House is available to express the views and emotions of the nation. In that respect no committee rooms or television studio can provide a substitute. On more humdrum occasions however we should perhaps not be surprised if Members find other things to do.

Those who are most pessimistic about the health of the floor would probably argue also that there is a growing streak in British political life which simply does not believe in parliamentary politics. This tendency takes various forms, one of the mildest being those who believe that the only acceptable 'democratic' verdict is that offered by the 'people' themselves via referenda. More worrying perhaps is the tendency of some groups not to participate in parliamentary politics as a protest: the boycott of the Commons by Unionist Movements in 1986–7 reflects this sentiment. Most worrying of all are those who despise much of the style of parliamentary politics and believe, or affect to believe, that issues will ultimately be resolved on the streets.

Concern about attendance is often linked to disquiet about standards of behaviour in the House. Some see growth of a 'yobbish' streak in the House's behaviour. (No doubt one might plead that here the House is merely reflecting changes in society outside.) Anxiety has been expressed about a tendency to unruliness, the development of organized barracking, and a decline in the standards of parliamentary dress.

Again the evidence tends to be anecdotal and, perhaps for obvious reasons, to come disproportionately from those who are leaving the House. For example one Conservative MP announcing his intention to retire from the House put it thus in 1986: 'Historically, the chamber was enriched by genuine wit and debating skills. Today, such niceties are all too often submerged beneath raucous abuse.'[36] But historians and former politicians have borne frequent witness to extensive rowdiness in earlier Parliaments – 1909–11 for example – so perhaps behaviour is not so very different today. However, in November 1984 the Speaker was forced to abandon a sitting after a campaign of organized disorder by a group of Labour Members.[37] Suspensions of sittings occur from time to time, often to the embarrassment of a party's front bench. The protestors would no doubt plead provocation by ministers suspected, for example, of trying to avoid making a statement on some controversial issue.

CONCLUSION

Whatever the shortcomings of proceedings on the floor it is nevertheless important that the Chamber is available for issues to be raised. The ability or, perhaps equally important, the threat to raise a matter on the floor is of value – to government, opposition parties, or backbenchers. Equally it is important that the floor provides an outlet for the individual dissident: the Tam Dalyell or the Dale Campbell-Savours in the present age or the Gerald Nabarro, Dame Irene Ward, or Sydney Silverman a generation earlier. That is not to say that the floor is the only forum available to individuals or groups; letters to ministers, party backbench committees, as well as committees of the House are just some of the other available avenues.

It is important also not to overlook the fact that the floor is the scene of a struggle for political power between parties with different aims and attitudes. Perhaps that struggle is conducted in ways which seem less acceptable than was the case in the past. Adversarial politics have not enjoyed a good press in recent years and are blamed in some quarters for contributing to some of the shortcomings in British economic and political performance. Behind the ritual clashes, however, there is a genuine attempt to convince the electorate; whether that attempt succeeds or is even heard is open to doubt. Yet one of the main functions of the floor is to provide an opportunity for backbenchers and opposition parties to hold the government of the day accountable and likewise to provide that government with a platform on which to explain and defend its policies. For much of the time such activities are conducted in a low-key way: the House may more often be boring than boisterous.

There are a number of criticisms about proceedings in the Chamber. First, they offer a paradox: many Members want to speak in some (though by no means all) debates but few want to listen. Secondly, the House spends time debating topics in which members appear to have little interest and yet cannot find time to debate others.[38] Thirdly, there are clearly problems in projecting proceedings on the floor into the public domain. It remains to be seen whether the Commons will come to terms with television before we reach the last decade of the century.

To some extent what happens on the floor of the House is a reflection of what Members want. However much they may blame governments for dominating their lives, in principle they have it in their own power to change things,[39] whether it be the lateness of sittings, the topics that are discussed, or whatever. In practice change is less easily achieved and governments are accorded considerable latitude in their organization of the House's procedures. That things are done as they are suggests that present arrangements suit many people. Change may occur if there are different party configurations in the House or if enough Members become convinced that present practices are inadequate.

That such a shift in opinion is possible is suggested by the willingness of Members to alter the committee system of the House when enough of them accepted the truth of the proposition that the balance between executive and legislature had been tilted too heavily towards the former. That change gave proceedings *off* the floor of the House a greater degree of prominence than they had hitherto enjoyed. The committee system is unlikely to revert to its pre–1979 form, so the floor must live with the knowledge that it is no longer the best tool for some aspects of executive scrutiny. Nevertheless, much committee work is preparatory to, and enriches and informs, debate on the floor; the two are essentially complementary. Whether more effective ways can be devised of sharing the burdens (or even the time) between floor and committees remains to be seen.

Inevitably when a government has a majority in the region of 100 seats there are likely to be fewer upsets and uncertainties in the proceedings in the House. Nevertheless as the Parliament of 1983–7 shows, these are not to be ruled out entirely. On issues such as Westland the government found itself very much on the defensive; on a number of other matters (such as the proposal to charge fees to the parents of students in higher education) it judged that concessions were the prudent course. Most spectacular of all was the defeat on the floor of the House of a major piece of legislation, the Shops Bill.

In situations where governments have smaller majorities, or perhaps no majority at all, the floor will become more important. A degree of uncertainty about outcomes, as between 1974 and 1979, is undoubtedly an asset in drawing attention to the floor both within Westminster and outside. As a result of the election of 1987 we are again in a period when the floor may seem of limited interest to many (especially opposition) Members. Two successive Parliaments with government majorities in excess of 100 is hardly the ideal prescription for a revival of interest in the Chamber. A degree of difficulty for governments is undoubtedly a tonic for the health of the floor of the House.

Chapter Five

OPPORTUNITIES FOR BACKBENCHERS

HELEN IRWIN

Several quite distinct sets of opportunities exist for private Members (i.e. backbenchers) to raise issues in the House. Some of these can conveniently be described as opportunities in 'prime time' – the period immediately after the House meets at 2.30 from Monday to Thursday during which the House is most likely to be full, and which receives the maximum coverage on radio and television. The other main opportunities for backbenchers occur during 'off-peak' hours, whether late at night, or during days set aside in whole or in part for private members, and in written procedures.

'Prime-time' opportunities include oral parliamentary questions and private notice questions, motions to introduce bills under SO No. 19, applications for emergency debates under SO No. 20 (adjournment on specific and important matter that should have urgent consideration), and points of order. 'Off-peak' time reserved specifically for backbenchers includes the half-hour adjournment debate at the end of business each day, debates on motions for holiday adjournments, debates on a motion to adjourn the House following the Consolidated Fund Bill and private Members' motions, as well as private Members' bills, which are described in chapter 7. In addition to these opportunities on the floor of the House, Members also have at their disposal two opportunities to raise issues in writing: parliamentary questions for written answer, and early day motions.

Standing Orders and successive decisions by the House governing the rules for each backbench opportunity mean that, to take full advantage of all opportunities, a Member has to be fairly persistent and conversant with the rules of the House governing matters such as the admissibility of parliamentary questions, and the content of adjournment debates. For example, debates on any motions for the adjournment of the House should not be used to call for new legislation, but a Member may ask a minister to introduce the legislation he desires in question, table an early day motion demanding the legislation he has in mind, seek to introduce a bill himself (see chapter 7), or raise the whole issue of the desirability of a change in the law in a private member's motion. An energetic Member, campaigning on a particular issue, may use several or all of these opportunities to draw it to the attention of the House, the press, and ministers.

PRIME TIME

Question Time

On the face of it, it is perhaps odd that Standing Orders say remarkably little about parliamentary questions, given their high profile. Standing Order No. 17 (Questions to Members) sets out the time during which oral questions can be taken (from not later than 2.45 p.m. to, normally, 3.30 p.m. on Mondays and Thursdays) and the complex rules governing the period of notice for different types of question. Nothing is said there, however, about the rules governing the content of questions (or answers) nor about which minister will be answering on any particular day. Questions are not orders of the day and are not recorded in the votes and proceedings (minutes) or the journal of the House. They are informal proceedings and their conduct is determined by successive decisions of the House and Speaker's rulings.[1]

Space does not permit an exposition in this chapter on the history of questions, which can be found in successive books and articles by the late Sir Norman Chester,[2] tracing their evolution from a virtually unlimited (but much less used) weapon of the nineteenth-century Member to the heavily regulated Question Time of today. In large measure this trend may be seen as a consequence of the steady accretion to the government of the day of control over the time of the House. Within the time set aside for questions, decisions are determined, through discussions between the 'usual channels' (see p. 61) after which a rota is published setting out the days on which each minister will answer.

Ministers from most departments answer questions once every three or four weeks. The rota also provides for the Attorney General, the Leader of the House (mainly in his capacity as Chairman of the Services Committee) the Chairmen of the House of Commons Commission and of the Public Accounts Committee, and the Member answering for the Church Commissioners, to answer questions for a few minutes every few weeks. Departments who answer on Wednesdays get a whole Question Time – these are at present the Foreign and Commonwealth Office (FCO), the Scottish Office, and the Departments of Trade and Industry and of the Environment. Ministers from departments who answer questions on Tuesday and Thursday answer only until 3.15, and between 3.15 and 3.30 on those days the Prime Minister answers questions. The rota is not sacrosanct. Following complaints about the amount of time available to question particular ministers the time available for some departments has been altered during a session, and, for example, the separate period allocated on FCO questions day to questions on European Community matters since 1973 has now been done away with and questions on EEC matters have since April 1985 formed an integral part of FCO Questions. Although Members *may* table questions for oral answer to other ministers than those answering on a particular day, such questions are now very rarely reached, except occasionally on Mondays.

The evolution of a strict timetable allocating Question Time on particular days to one or a few ministers has obvious advantages for ministers, who therefore can plan their other duties with greater certainty. It is a consequence of the greatly increased *volume* of questions tabled for oral answer (see table 5.1). Another consequence of that growth has been the development of strict rules governing the period of notice required for questions for oral answer. A minimum notice of two sitting days is now required, but because of the volume of demand the maximum period of notice (ten sitting days – usually a calendar fortnight) has in practice become the minimum; and even then the questions may not be reached. Manuscripts of questions tabled for oral answer ten sitting days hence are shuffled (like a pack of cards) by staff of the Table Office and are then numbered in random order before being printed in that order. Out of between 100 and 150 questions tabled for answer by a single minister on any one day, only the first twenty or so questions in the list have a chance of being reached during Question Time and far fewer of the questions tabled to the Prime Minister. Questions tabled after the first opportunity are in practice not going to receive an oral answer, and receive a written answer which is printed in the official report, along with answers to all questions not reached by 3.30. This effective requirement of a fortnight's notice of an oral question, coupled with the rule since 1972[3] that no Member may have more than eight questions awaiting oral answer at any one time, have had significant effects on the content and style of Question Time.

Ostensibly the parliamentary question is a device to enable a Member to obtain information from a minister about a matter for which the minister is responsible. To some extent (see below) written questions represent a means of obtaining information from the government. It is arguable whether oral questions and Question Time now perform that function at all. The other main function of questions, as used by Members since the nineteenth century, is to draw attention to a topical subject and, through a supplementary question, put the Minister on the spot and oblige him to give an answer there and then.

Question Time on the floor of the House can perhaps best be seen as an instance of direct political accountability of ministers to the House. In that process, it is the supplementary questions rather than the original question tabled which are now of most significance. One recent identifiable change has been the reduction in length of most questions tabled for oral answer, most of which now occupy no more than two lines of type compared with anything up to six or even eight lines in the 1950s. Oral questions are either extremely specific or very general – 'if he will make a statement on . . .'. This trend has been accompanied, however, by a significant increase in the length of supplementary questions, and the Speaker now regularly makes pleas for shorter supplementary questions.

Other Parliaments, such as Canada's, have not emulated the United Kingdom's pattern of progressively constraining and regulating Question Time, but have opted for a system of questions without notice, which has the advantage of enabling Members to raise any issue at the earliest opportunity and demand an explanation. Paradoxically, the strict practice at Westminster of requiring a fortnight's notice of oral questions may have had almost the same effect. Members are increasingly giving notice of questions in sufficiently general form to enable them to raise virtually any supplementary on a wide topic. But the requirement of notice does enable ministers to be briefed in the area of interest to the Member. Ministers take great pains with such briefings and can usually field questions without too much difficulty. Sometimes, however, they are caught out.

An interesting trend in Question Time is the extent to which it is now orchestrated in advance, both by opposition Members and by government supporters. Although some Members work alone, others appear to be planning their line of attack together. For example, of the questions tabled to the Chancellor of the Exchequer for oral answer on 29 January 1987, eleven, tabled by government (Conservative) backbenchers asked: 'What representations he has received from political parties for increases in public expenditure'; a further six Conservative Members asked very similar questions about the personal equity plan scheme, and seven opposition (Labour) Members asked: 'if he has any estimate of the cost to the Exchequer of the present level of unemployment in [a particular region of the country]'.

Similarly identical areas of interest can be seen in questions tabled to ministers in other large departments. This trend has recently spread to questions to smaller departments as evidence by the recent rise in the number of questions to the Minister for the Arts.[4] Some of this may perhaps be attributed to greater organization by opposition parties planning in advance issues to concentrate on, while other sets of remarkably similar questions from government supporters suggest that some attempt is being made to use Question Time to back up ministers. It is likely that a considerable number of oral questions tabled emanate from sources other than the Member actually tabling the question, including some outside organizations, some of which use the services of the many firms of parliamentary consultants which have grown up during the last few years.

Because tabling of an oral question is in effect entering a lottery, planned action by a group of like-minded Members clearly increases the likelihood of one, or several, questions on the issue they wish to pursue being reached in the time available, giving not only the Member tabling the original question, but also others interested in the same subject, including the front bench spokesmen, an opportunity to have a go at the minister. To the extent that orchestrating the tabling of oral questions increases the odds against a single Member, acting alone, being able to raise an issue, this development could be interpreted as a potential abuse of Question Time. Certainly some Members see it as such. On the other hand, it can equally be interpreted as an illustration of the infinite resourcefulness of Members as a whole and of the adaptability of the institution. Instead of continually giving all the advantage to ministers, by enabling them and their officials to prepare extensively answers to all possible supplementaries in the generous two weeks' period of notice given of the text of a particular question, the development of more general questions, planned in conjunction with similar questions by a variety of other Members, may still provide the House, and backbenchers on both sides of the House, with a real opportunity to use Question Time to hold ministers to account and, occasionally, elicit from them an unguarded admission of political value. It has also had the effect of transforming Question Time from a fairly rapid question-and-answer period on a wide variety of maters, to something like a series of mini-debates – as witnessed both by regular appeals from the Speaker for shorter supplementary questions and answers[5] and on some occasions by the Speaker deliberately allowing a longer run of supplementaries on matters of current political concern.[6]

One complementary effect of this trend in Question Time is the opportunity it gives to frontbench spokesmen to participate in Question Time. Junior opposition spokesmen frequently table oral questions themselves and shadow ministers also regularly ask supplementaries to backbenchers' questions. For example, on 25 November 1986, during oral questions to the Secretary of State for Social Services, out of eleven questions answered, opposition spokesmen intervened with supplementaries on four.

Questions to the Prime Minister are now mainly (but not exclusively) 'open' questions, usually in the form of 'if she will list her official engagements for [the day on which the Question is due for answer]' which permits a virtually infinite number of potential topical supplementaries on the lines of 'if, in her busy day, the Prime Minister will consider . . .'. (This formula has almost entirely replaced earlier popular open questions such as 'when she last met the TUC or the CBI' or 'if she will pay an official visit to [a town in the Member's constituency]' although this latter form is still used by a few Members.) The open question developed as a consequence of the practice of successive Prime Ministers of transferring all questions on specific subjects to the minister primarily responsible for the area of policy covered by the question.[7]

Not withstanding statements by the Prime Minister that she would no longer transfer questions,[8] the use of open question has grown and grown. Well over 100 oral questions are tabled to the Prime Minister for each Question Time. Substantive questions are now a rarity, about 3 per cent, although they are stoutly defended by those who use them. Although the rules for supplementary questions are in theory the same as for original questions, of which the most important is that questions must relate to matters for which ministers are responsible, in the noisy hurly-burly of Prime Minister's Question Time enforcement of the rules is virtually impossible.[9]

By convention, the Leader of the Opposition never tables a question for oral answer to the Prime Minister,[10] but it has become usual for him to intervene with supplementary questions to the Prime Minister at every opportunity, often as many as three times.[11] Mainly as a consequence of this, Prime Minister's Question Time has become almost an instance of gladiatorial combat between the leaders of the two main parties, often with additional intervention of the leaders of smaller parties in the House. The noise level has risen, with both sides cheering on their leader and booing their opponent, and attempts from both sides of the House to prevent other spokesmen getting a look in at all. At his election on 17 June 1987, Mr Speaker Weatherill told the House he had been 'appalled' to hear the noises broadcast from Question Time on the radio[12] and in the 1983–7 Parliament he regularly appealed for better (and quieter) behaviour at Question Time. During that Parliament there were a number of calls for a new examination of Question Time by the Procedure Committee and these will no doubt be repeated in the new Parliament.

Private notice questions and business questions

Private notice questions (PNQs) are an extension of Question Time. By giving notice before noon (10 a.m. on Fridays) any Member may seek to ask a PNQ on a matter which is urgent and for which ministers have some responsibility or which relates to the business of the House. The Speaker has to decide whether the matter is sufficiently urgent and important to justify a PNQ.

The number of PNQs allowed has varied with different Speakers. In 1975–6, for example, forty-two PNQs were allowed. In 1981–2 (the last full session of Mr Speaker Thomas) their number had shrunk to nine, but in 1985–6 forty-three were permitted. Topics raised in PNQs range from the very local – for example, a railway or industrial disaster – to issues of major national importance. The most usual formulation of a PNQ is 'if he will make a statement

Table 5.1 The number of questions tabled[a] in each session 1979–80 to 1986–7

Session	1 Questions for oral answer	2 Questions for ordinary written answer	3 Questions for priority written answer	4 Questions for written answer (total) [cols 2 and 3]	5 Total no. of questions tabled (cols 1 and 4)	6 Average no. of questions per sitting day[b]
1979–80[c]	12,453	20,119	19,793	39,912	52,365	215
1980–1	8,175	11,634	11,054	22,688	30,863	189
1981–2	8,991	11,450	11,989	23,439	32,430	186
1982–3[d]	6,125	8,752	8,343	17,095	23,220	202
1983–4[c]	13,386	18,521	21,598	40,119	53,505	251
1984–5	14,800	13,395	18,128	31,523	46,323	269
1985–6	18,139	12,548	19,260	31,808	49,947	290
1986–7[d]	12,766	8,202	13,129	21,331	34,097	313

Notes: a Statistics collected by the Journal Office, House of Commons. The figures in this table differ from those produced by POLIS in the House of Commons Library which refer only to questions answered and do not take into account questions subsequently withdrawn or not answered. Questions tabled are used in this chapter as a more accurate representation of the intentions of Members.
  b Figures rounded to nearest whole number. In practice, most questions, especially oral questions are tabled on Mondays to Thursdays.
  c unusually long session.
  d unusually short session.

on. . .'. Although it is open to any Member to ask a PNQ, and backbenchers regularly seek to raise topical matters by this device, a high proportion of those allowed are asked by opposition frontbench spokesmen. PNQs are asked immediately after the end of Question Time, at 3.30 p.m. (or they may interrupt the business on Fridays at 11 a.m.). They represent a halfway house between a parliamentary question and a full ministerial statement, and a limited number of supplementaries are permitted after the initial answer to a PNQ.

Normally the business for the coming week is announced by the Leader of the House in response to a PNQ from the Leader of the Opposition at 3.30 p.m. on the Thursday of each week. After he has asked a supplementary question, the occasion is pre-eminently an opportunity for backbenchers. In the guise of requests for time to be found in the coming week for a debate on a particular matter, Members can and do raise virtually any issue. Unless he is minded to arrange such a debate in the near future, in which case he will suggest that the matter be discussed through the 'usual channels', the Leader of the House frequently replies by undertaking to refer the issues a Member wishes to see debated to the responsible minister. This is particularly the case in response to supplementaries drawing attention to early day motions (EDMs).

Application for emergency debates

Applications for debate on a matter which is 'specific and important and should have urgent consideration' are regulated by SO No. 20 (formerly SO No. 10 and SO No. 9). Table 5.2 sets out the number

Table 5.2 SO No. 20 applications 1979–87

| Session | Number of Applications | | |
	Made	Refused	Accepted by Chair
1979–80	89	87	2
1980–1	48	47	1
1981–2	61	59	2
1982–3	50	48	2
1983–4	84	81	3
1984–5	61	60	1
1985–6	87	86	1
1986–7	48	46	2

Source: Sessional diary of the House of Commons (unprinted).

of such applications and the number which were successful between 1979 and 1987. Most of those granted were requested by the opposition front bench.[13]

In 1983 the Standing Order was amended to provide that a Member seeking to obtain an emergency debate should speak for no more than three minutes in support of his application. The Speaker does not give his reasons for refusing an application although he occasionally qualifies his refusal by acknowledging the seriousness of the issue which has been raised. Applications are heard at the commencement of public business, immediately after Question Time and any PNQs or ministerial statements. It might be thought surprising that so many backbench Members seek to move the adjournment under SO No. 20 when they can be virtually certain that their applications will be refused. But the opportunity to propose that there should be an emergency debate enables any Member to speak for three minutes at prime time when the House is fullest and when ministers are likely to be present. Issues raised range from impending redundancies in a particular industry in a Member's constituency to issues of national security. Whatever the subject, the Member raising it can be virtually certain of media coverage. SO No. 20 applications, therefore, represent probably the most significant means by which a backbencher, virtually without notice, can draw the attention of the House and the media to a particular topic.

Points of order

In principle, points of order raised with the Speaker relate to matters of procedure on which he can rule. They can, by definition, be raised at any time. Besides genuine points of order, it is frequently the case that Members seek to raise other issues, usually at prime time, by means of points of order in order to obtain publicity for, for example, a minister's refusal to act in particular circumstances or the Member's inability to find a formal means of raising the issue on the floor of the House because it relates to a matter for which the government is not directly responsible.

In his letter to the Procedure committee of 21 November 1986[14] the Speaker stated his view that if new restrictive rules about EDMs were to be introduced (see below), there might be many more 'bogus' points of order in the Chamber. Table 4.1 in Borthwick's chapter (p. 57) demonstrates the increasing amount of time being taken by points of order in the early afternoon. Points of order are, by their very nature, unregulated, and not susceptible to rules. In 1987, faced with a daily barrage of points of order, the Speaker developed a practice of postponing them until after other business, such as SO No. 20 applications, ministerial statements, or PNQs, in an attempt to curb the prolongation of Question Time by successive points of order arising out of answers to questions.[15] This new practice, although welcomed by some Members, remains controversial and there are some who would prefer to be able to raise points of order at the moment when they seek to do so, even during Question Time.[16]

Private Members' bills – the ten-minute rule

Consideration by the House of Private members' bills is discussed more fully in chapter 7. A significant and regularly used backbench opportunity, however, is the ten-minute rule, whereby at the commencement of public business on most Tuesdays and Wednesdays in a session a Member may seek leave to introduce a bill and may in so doing make a brief explanatory statement, followed by a similar statement by a Member opposing the motion (see SO No. 19). This procedure provides a free-standing opportunity at prime time for a backbencher to make a speech and enable the House to vote on a proposal he has initiated. Some ten-minute-rule applications are agreed without a vote, either because they are extremely uncontroversial or, one suspects, because their subject matter is so extraordinary, and their chances of becoming law so slender, that Members do not bother to oppose them.

OPPORTUNITIES ON THE FLOOR OF THE HOUSE AT OTHER TIMES

Daily adjournment debate

Each week Members may let the Speaker have notice of a topic which they wish to raise on the daily motion for the adjournment of the House. A ballot is held in the Speaker's office every Thursday for the topics to be raised on Monday, Tuesday, Wednesday, and Friday in the coming week. The adjournment debate on Thursdays is, by tradition, in the Speaker's gift – he often uses it to permit a

Member who has been putting the same topic unsuccessfully into the ballot for a number of weeks an opportunity to state his case, probably on a constituency matter. The debate itself takes place at the end of each day's business and usually lasts no more than 30 minutes (see SO No. 9(7)). Virtually any matter which engages a minister's responsibility may be raised on the adjournment, although direct calls for new legislation are not allowed (see SO No. 29).

The following list of subjects proposed to be raised on the motion for the adjournment of the House between 30 March and Monday 6 April 1987 illustrates the range of topics so raised:

Monday 30 March	Mr Tom Pendry	Tameside urban aid
Tuesday 31 March	Mr Patrick McLoughlin	Proposals of the Derbyshire County Council to reorganize sixth-form education
Wednesday 1 April	Mr Ted Garrett	The Northumbria ambulance service
Thursday 2 April	Mr Michael Marshall	Opportunities for British investment in Japan
Friday 3 April	Mr George Howarth	Control of toxic emissions from incinerators
Monday 6 April	Mr Michael Colvin	The future of Play Board

The normal pattern of the daily debate is for the Member raising the issue to speak for about half the time available and for a responsible minister to reply. Occasionally, with the agreement of the Member raising the topic, another Member may also intervene – perhaps from a neighbouring constituency affected by the same issue. On the occasions when the main business of the day finishes unexpectedly early, other Members may seek to raise other matters on the adjournment by giving notice by 8.00 p.m. to the Speaker. To be allowed to do this, the Member needs to secure the agreement of a minister to reply. The chances of getting a considered reply to a debate on a topic thus raised at the last minute are not very good. To prevent such unexpected extra debates being used to cause serious political embarrassment, government whips often seek to engineer a friendly extra debate if they anticipate that business will collapse, by suggesting that the opportunity is seized by a government supporter. Hence to take full advantage of opportunities available to them, Members need to be constantly alert to the opportunities likely to crop up.[17]

Private Members' motions

About eleven days each session are designated as private Members' motion days and offer rare opportunities for a backbencher to determine the business of the House. Most private Members' motions days are Fridays, but two are usually taken in the form of four 'half' days until 7 p.m. on Mondays.[18] (The exact number and dates of such days is decided each session on a motion to vary the provisions of SO No. 13 which provides for ten days.) Ballots are held some days in advance (see SO No. 13(9)) and the three Members who are successful in the ballot may table motions for debate. In practice it is only the Member coming first in the ballot who is guaranteed a debate on his or her motion, although sometimes the debate finishes early enough for the second Member at least to make a speech in support of his motion.

Subjects raised on private Members' motions days range from the very wide to the particular. On one occasion (31 January 1958) a motion was debated and agreed to appoint a Select Committee on Procedure. Usually, however, the days are used for debate on fairly broad themes. Opposition spokesmen and ministers speak in the debate. Although almost always fairly low-key in nature, and although they are unlikely to be widely reported in the press, the fact that every ballot for such motions is always well subscribed suggests that the opportunity is valued by Members. Since the debate does not take place on a frontbench motion, it is less likely to be dominated by long set-piece speeches from frontbenchers and Privy Councillors and affords greater opportunity for a number of backbenchers to claim the attention of the House than is open to them in debates on government or opposition motions.

Other motions for the adjournment of the House

On about seven other days in an average session, on motions for the adjournment of the House, backbench Members can initiate short debates. These arise either during the all-night debate (governed by SO No. 54) on a motion for the adjournment which follows proceedings (now entirely formal) on a consolidated fund or an appropriation bill, or on the last day the House sits before a recess, when, by custom, the day is available for a series of 'adjournment' debates on a government motion 'That this House do now adjourn'.

In both cases the Speaker arranges for a ballot of Members wishing to participate in the debates, and the subjects they wish to raise are listed on the order paper. The rules regarding the subject matter of such debates are the same as for the daily adjournment debate, and a minister replies to each debate. On these days, however, each debate may last for longer than the daily half-hour. During the adjournment debates after the passage of a Consolidated Fund Bill, most debates last for 1 hour 30 minutes, and a few, on subjects which a number of Members wished to raise, may at the Speaker's discretion last for up to 3 hours, thus enabling a number of Members to take part. Notwithstanding the fact that they take place in the middle of the night, there are invariably more subjects listed for debate than can be reached before the debate concludes at 9 a.m. the next day (8 a.m. if it takes place on a Thursday night). On days before recesses each debate usually lasts for about three-quarters of an hour.

A rather different opportunity to raise matters on the floor of the House is afforded by the motions tabled by the government determining the dates of a forthcoming recess. On such motions there can be a 3-hour debate during which Members may raise issues which, ostensibly at least, they feel should be debated before the House adjourns for a holiday. On these occasions there is a general 'winding-up' reply by the Leader of the House, who usually undertakes to refer issues raised to the relevant responsible minister in very much the same way as he does in response to issues raised at business questions.

OPPORTUNITIES ON PAPER

Written questions

Questions tabled for written answer far outnumber questions for oral answer (see table 5.1). Not all Members of Parliament make use of this device and the Members asking the largest numbers of written questions are almost all opposition Members. The object of all questions is defined as 'to obtain information or press for action'.[19] Backbench Members of the government party probably make less use than opposition members of written questions because they make greater use of letters to ministers, which are not bound by any of the rules relating to parliamentary questions, nor subject to any deadlines.[20]

Of questions tabled for written answer, roughly half (see table 5.1) are known as 'priority written' questions and distinguished on the order paper by the letter 'W' beside the number of the question. This means that the Member tabling the question has indicated the date on which he requires the answer. Roughly speaking, a minimum of two sitting days' notice is required for such questions (for detailed rules on the period of notice see SO No. 17). Originally designed as a means to enable Members to obtain quick answers to urgent written questions, at a time when limits were being imposed on the number of oral questions a Member could table, the priority written question is now used indiscriminately by many Members. As a consequence, perhaps, a high proportion of such priority questions now receive holding answers, thus negating the objective of this procedure.[21]

A few question are tabled for ordinary written answer the day after they are tabled. More often than not, such questions, distinguished in the order paper by a 'blind p' (¶) are inspired or 'planted' questions, tabled by Members at ministers' request to enable an announcement to be made by written answer to the House. Although frequently criticized by Members, as the Speaker said on 2 April 1987, 'the parliamentary undergrowth is strewn with planted Questions and has been so over the decades'.[22] The obviously inspired question is an accepted method of making announcements. Occasionally major statements are also made as written answers 'pursuant' to earlier answers to questions. For example, on 9 February 1987 a written statement on policies for the use of agricultural land appeared 'pursuant' to an earlier answer. Although not infringing any of the rules relating to questions and answers, announcements made in this way frequently lead to protests from the floor of the House, as happened on that occasion.[23]

Why do Members ask written questions? The first reason, and the most obvious, is to obtain the answers. A written question probably represents the quickest and easiest way (from the Member's point of view) of finding something out about an area of government responsibility. In theory it is not in order to seek 'readily available information' by means of questions, but in practice even when the answer could be found, for example by detailed examination of published documents available in the House of Commons Library, Members prefer to seek it by question which, of course, apportions to them some credit for having extracted the answer from the executive as well as providing an authoritative answer fairly quickly. In 1985, after detailed information broken down by electoral ward, postcode areas, and other categories on rates of unemployment in each constituency had been made available to the House of Commons Library, ministers in the Department of Employment sought to stop answering questions seeking such information, whether written or oral. In the face of considerable opposition, however, ministers began again to provide the information in answer to questions.[24] Once published in Hansard, as a written answer by a minister, information appears to acquire a status, as a formal statement by government of the position, which is politically more significant than information obtained or deduced from published sources. For this reason alone, although it has often been mooted as a way of saving money, Members are likely to resist any attempt to restrict the number of written questions any Member may ask.

Another reason for asking questions, probably equally important to Members, is obtaining publicity for an issue; for example a Member campaigning on a particular issue can announce in a media interview that he or she has tabled, say, twenty questions to the Minister concerned for urgent (i.e. priority written) answer. Linked to this reason, a written question, whose answer has to be personally approved by the minister concerned, can serve to bring an issue, hitherto dealt with in a relatively quiet backwater of a department, on to the minister's desk, perhaps at least stimulating the minister to take an interest in it and, at its most successful, leading to a change of policy. Sometimes a Member will table very many, even hundreds, of written questions in the course of a campaign. Of these, the most prolific recent examples have probably been the campaign in 1983–4 by Mr Tam Dalyell to bring the issues surrounding the sinking of the *General Belgrano* during the Falklands conflict to the forefront of political debate, and the series of questions tabled during the same period by Mr Tony Banks on arrangements planned for local government in London following the abolition of the Greater London Council which must have concentrated the minds of many civil servants in the Department of the Environment over a long period.

Reading the pages of the official report containing answers to written questions reveals many little-known aspects of ministers' responsibility – ranging (random examples culled from a single day) from hedgehog ladders, to deaf and dumb children in St Helena, to a conference centre in Harrogate, to the number of chiropodists in

Cornwall and the Isles of Scilly, to redundancies at Pinewood film studios.[25] Questions for written answer may at most be a seen as a powerful device in the hands of a persistent backbencher or, at least, as a source of fascinating material on the involvement of government in aspects of daily life.

Early day motions

Each day the bundle of daily papers of the House of Commons includes a quantity of blue pages. Generally speaking, these record notices of questions, amendments to bills, and motions set down for future days. Most of these motions are ostensibly motions tabled for debte on 'an early day'. In practice it is virtually certain that most early day motions (EDMs) will never be debated at all. The main exceptions are EDMs in the form of a 'prayers' against a statutory instrument (chapter 10).

Any Member may table an EDM. Other Members may append their names to an EDM at any time during the session and every time a Member adds his name to the motion it is reprinted, along with the names of the first six 'sponsors' of the motion. Members may also table amendments to EDMs which are printed each time the motion is reprinted and which also attract additional names of supporting Members. The number of EDMs tabled has increased dramatically in recent sessions (see table 5.3).

Besides 'prayers' the subject matter of motions varies widely. The rules of the House governing the form and content of motions are few: so long as the motion is no more than 250 words long and is couched in temperate and parliamentary language, and provided criticism of the personal conduct of certain categories of people (Members of either House of Parliament, judges, or the royal family) is drafted in the form of a substantive motion and not an amendment, virtually anything can be said.

Despite their ostensible role as motions which Members wish the House to debate, the prime function of EDMs is probably to gain publicity. Many concern very local issues and may perhaps congratulate a local football team on a recent victory, or highlight an important achievement by an individual constituent, or continue on the order paper of the House of Commons a local battle, such as disagreements between different parties on Liverpool City Council. Such 'local' EDMs are probably tabled with a view to obtaining

Table 5.3 Number of Early Day Motions Presented since 1939

1939–40	21	1955–56	116	1972–73	448
1940–41	30	1956–57	96	1973–74[a]	174
1941–42	41	1957–58	105	1974[a]	245
1942–43	77	1958–59	99	1974–75	759
1943–44	88	1959–60	111	1975–76	701
1944–45	64	1960–61	169	1976–77	475
1945–46	71	1961–62	154	1977–78	611
1946–47	37	1962–63	176	1978–79[a]	368
1947–48	79	1963–64	180	1979–80[b]	907
1948[c]	3	1964–65	356	1980–81	631
1948–49	77	1965–66[a]	164	1981–82	716
1949–50	55	1966–67[b]	640	1982–83[a]	502
1950–51	97	1967–68	446	1983–84[b]	1058
1951–52	106	1968–69	443	1984–85	979
1952–53	135	1969–70[a]	300	1985–86	1262
1953–54	102	1970–71[b]	717	1986–87[a]	1000
1954–55	52	1971–72	474		

a Short session.
b Long session.
c Very short session.
Source: Library Fact Sheet No. 30, May 1985, updated.

publicity in local newspapers. Other motions are tabled at the instigation of pressure groups, which regard (whether justifiably or not) the accumulation of large numbers of Members in support of an EDM as a major part of their campaigns.[26] Sometimes Members of a select committee may table an EDM to seek to gauge support in the House for their proposals or to seek a debate on them. In 1981, following the rejection by the government of most of the recommendations in a report on the role of the Comptroller and Auditor General,[27] Members of the Committee of Public Accounts tabled an EDM commending their proposals which was supported by nearly 300 Members.[28] Thereafter Mr Norman St John Stevas successfully introduced a private Members' bill which enacted many of the committee's original proposals.[29]

Many other EDMs consist of attacks on the policies of the government or on other Members of the House. Occasionally there are motions critical of the Chair which, if not subsequently withdrawn (as often happens), are usually given time for a debate. Motions critical of government policies are occasionally taken over by an opposition party and debated on opposition days. Most, however, simply remain on the notice paper and are never debated, except in the sense that a 'debate' takes place on paper as other related motions or amendments are tabled. It is possible to regard EDMs as little more than a parliamentary graffiti board.

Another category contributing to the recent huge increase in EDMs is motions drawing attention to matters which Members have been unable to raise by any other legitimate parliamentary device. Private Members' motions days provide a similarly unrestricted opportunity to table a motion on virtually any subject, but the chance of winning a place in the ballot for such days is slender and there are only a few such opportunities in a year. EDMs enable a Member to draw immediate attention to matters which may not be raised by the more conventional devices of questions or adjournment debates. A novel example of this was the series of forty EDMs tabled in 1986–7 by Mr Dale Campbell-Savours calling on the government to answer specific questions related to the government's attempt to stop publication of a book about MI5. Mr Campbell-Savours has described such motions as 'early day questions' which he was tabling to draw attention to what he believed to be a deficiency in the procedure relating to questions which enabled ministers to refuse to answer further questions on a topic.[30] Of course he equally received no answer to his motions. Other motions may be tabled to express criticism of various people either inside or outside Parliament in a way which could not readily be done either in questions or debate, or (without fear of prosecution) in the press (see chapter 11 on parliamentary privilege).

The large increase in the number of EDMs in the 1983–7 Parliament, and the increase in the number of such motions which, under the protection of parliamentary privilege, attacked individuals, led to many calls for 'reform' or regulation of EDMs, including EDMs on the subject.[31] Following a short investigation in 1987 the Procedure Committee published a report which explored the recent development of EDMs.[32] It concluded that apart from certain small changes designed mainly to reduce printing costs no change in the present practice should be made. In this decision they were supported by a letter from the Speaker which, while acknowledging that 'we do get some pretty poor notices on the paper from time to time', concluded that 'this is something I am prepared to live with in the interests of freedom of expression'.[33]

CONCLUSION

Given that, in any Parliament, if the government has a sufficient majority, backbenchers either together or individually are unlikely to be able to defeat the government or force it to change its mind by voting, the two remaining weapons of backbenchers are delay, and publicity. Backbenchers demonstrated the extent to which the procedures of the House can be adapted to delay business on 7 June 1985 when debate on a private Member's motion intended to provide extra time for debate on a private Member's bill was delayed for several hours by the ingenious use of two little-used procedures, the moving by a backbencher of a new writ for a by-election and the lengthy presentation of a large number of public petitions.[34] In that instance both the supporters of Mr Andrew Bowden's initial private Member's motion (itself an unusual use of a private Members' motions day) and those who succeeded in preventing it being thoroughly debated, seized opportunities open to them but rarely used; and the latter succeeded thereby in killing an exceptionally contentious bill. However the rules regulating procedures are amended, imaginative backbenchers will continue to seize and make full use of all conceivable opportunities.

More conventionally, by making full use of the range of opportunities available, a Member can bring an issue to the forefront of political debate. Nevertheless, the biggest drawback, from the point of view of backbenchers, of most of the formal opportunities provided for by the rules of the House is that most of them are either written opportunities (such as EDMs and written questions) or can only be used to the full if the Member is successful in a ballot (such as with oral PQs, private Members' bills and motions). With 650 Members in the House, the chances of one Member being successful in a ballot on any given occasion are not good. In 1987, a new Member, Mr Graham Allen, described such procedures as 'parliamentary bingo'.[35] Hence the increase in the use of unregulated 'prime-time' opportunities to gain publicity and demand a government response. However much the rules for questions and motions are re-examined, it is unlikely that Members will be willing to resist the temptation to raise matters in prime-time, if necessary as bogus points of order. Nonetheless, many Members have stated that it is their inability to raise matters through the conventional backbench devices that leads them to make successive applications under SO No. 20, or table large numbers of EDMs, or raise lengthy points of order.

The particular rules which seem to cause problems are first, in relation to questions, the rule which prevents further questions once a minister has 'blocked' a subject by refusing to answer any further questions on it, and secondly, in relation both to questions and to motions for the adjournment, the rule confining such questions and motions to matters for which ministers are responsible. This latter rule can appear to operate wholly in the interests of protecting the minister since, by convention, ministerial responsibility can be extended if ministers begin to take an interest in a subject. For example, questions are now permitted on the internal affairs of many foreign countries because successive foreign secretaries have expressed views on such matters.[36] In such circumstances it is perhaps unsurprising if backbenchers wishing to raise topical matters with ministers feel frustrated when ministers refuse to answer questions on them. Sustained pressure by means of SO No. 20 applications, points of order (however bogus), and EDMs, may succeed in provoking ministers into making a response or an intervention on an issue and thus bring the issue within the bounds of ministerial responsibility on which Members are then entitled to seek information through more conventional parliamentary channels. To that extent, the recent increase in prime-time activity can be seen to be in part an attempt to push back the frontiers of the rules governing questions and motions.

Whether ministers would be prepared to countenance a relaxation of the rules governing the subject matter of questions is open to doubt, not least on grounds of cost, since it can be assumed that such a relaxation would inevitably increase the total number of questions. The most recent figures for the average cost of officials' time of replying to questions were estimated at £75 for an oral question or £45 for a written question to which needs to be added the cost of printing them on the order paper and motion paper (£842,000 in 1985–6) and printing replies in the official report (£430,000 in 1985–6 for written answers alone).[37] Excluding the cost of printing oral answers and the time of the staff of the House of Commons, the total cost to officials and printing costs of all written and oral questions in 1985–6 (the last full session) was over £4 million.

Although the government has control over the majority of the time of the floor of the House, the opportunities discussed in this chapter, in different ways, enable backbench Members to dictate the issues discussed by the House. In addition, there are also occasional opportunities for backbench Members to initiate debates in standing committees, especially on 'prayers' against statutory instruments and on European documents. Table 5.4 sets out approximately the amount of time on the floor taken by business initiated by back-benchers in 1985–6 (the last full session of Parliament). In that Parliament the House sat for approximately 1,535 hours. Hard and fast distinctions between front- and backbench time are not easy, and these calculations exclude time taken by SO No. 10 (now 20) applications (5 hours), PNQs (58 hours) and points of order (14 hours) which are initiated by backbenchers as well as opposition frontbenchers. As a rough estimate, backbenchers' time as listed in table 5.4 amounted in 1985–6 to approximately 400 hours or more than 25 per cent of the time of the House although, as stated above, some of this time (notably Question Time) is increasingly being hijacked by opposition spokesmen.

Table 5.4   Time spent on business mainly initiated by backbenchers, 1985–6

Parliamentary questions	127 hours
(approximately 55 minutes per day, Monday–Thursday. Some questions are tabled by opposition spokesmen)	
Daily adjournment debates	81 hours
(30 minutes per day, plus longer debates on certain days when the designated business finished earlier)	
Other adjournment debates	55 hours
(of which 'Consolidated Fund' debates amounted to 37 hours; debate on days before recesses to 18 hours)	
Motion for the dates of recesses	12 hours
Motions to introduce private Members' Bills (ten-minute rule)	11 hours
Private Members' motions	57 hours
Private Members' bills (see chapter 7)	57 hours

Note: All figures are rounded to the nearest hour.
Source: Sessional diary of the House of Commons (unprinted).

The Procedure Committee concluded in May 1987 that

> experience at Westminster continues to suggest that there is a great deal of demand for Members to be able briefly to draw attention to topical or constituency matters. This demand is shown in the great number of unsuccessful applications for emergency adjournment debates (under Standing Order No. 20)

the growth in the number of Early Day Motions, the large number of bogus points of order and the increasing prevalence of 'open' oral Questions.[38]

Although used most vociferously by opposition Members, SO No. 20 applications and points of order are utilized by Members from all sides of the House. Together they amounted to just under 1.3 per cent of the total time the House sat in each of the three sessions for 1984–5 to 1986–7.[39] However much their growth may be deprecated in some quarters, not least by the Speaker, on whom they exercise severe pressure, and notwithstanding the fact that the time they take eats into the time available for debate on the formal business of the day, it may be that these 'unregulated' opportunities for back-benchers fit the mood of the House of Commons in the 1980s more appropriately than many of the formal opportunities provided by backbench Members of Parliament.

Chapter Six

OPPOSITION TO GOVERNMENT

PHILIP NORTON

Opposition in the House of Commons is often characterized as Opposition with a capital O. Two monolithic parties – comprising Government and Opposition – sit facing one another in the House, the relationship between the two characterized as an adversary one. The Government governs, the Opposition opposes, and backbenchers on both sides loyally support their leaders in the division lobbies.

Such a perception is a popular one. However, it is both simplistic and misleading, increasingly so. To see the House solely in terms of government and opposition is to ignore the complex composition of the Commons. There is, on both sides of the House, a well-developed party infrastructure. Emphasis on the adversary relationship between the two sides is to neglect the consensual nature of the House. The efficient despatch of business is dependent upon agreement between the parties. The opposition more often supports (or at least does not oppose) than it opposes government bills. Furthermore, stress on the opposition *qua* opposition and the adversary relationship detracts from what may be termed opposition with a small 'o' – that is, opposition within rather than between parties. Opportunities to express opposition to government policies are not confined to the official opposition, and increasingly – certainly since 1970 – those opportunities have been utilized.

The complex political composition of the House of Commons is illustrated in the diagram of the layout of the chamber on p. 2. The government, represented by ministers on the Treasury bench, with backbench members of their party sitting behind them, sits facing an opposition front bench, backbench members of the opposition, and other opposition parties (comprising for more than the past decade five or more parties). The House, stripped of its partisan configurations, may also be seen as a far from cohesive body of 650 Members, each with a different perception of constituency, and moral, responsibilities. But a description of the Chamber cannot illustrate the channels for opposition. It does not encompass the party infrastructures, primarily the party backbench committees, nor – overlapping but not coterminous with this omission – does it point to all the opportunities available to express opposition, several of which are available off the floor of the House.

Focusing upon the different sources from which opposition to government may emanate allows the different means of opposition to be identified. For ministers, the most sustained opposition comes from the benches opposite; the most worrying comes from the benches behind them.

THE OPPOSITION BENCHES

The three principal sources of opposition on the benches to the Speaker's left are the official opposition (as a collective party), other opposition parties, and backbenchers acting on their own initiative when the opposition front bench is silent. The means available to each to express disagreement with government differ both in form and extent.

The opposition

The existence of an 'opposition' in the House is not a recent development. Party groupings – though not a party system – can be identified before the Glorious Revolution of 1688. At some stage in the eighteenth century, Members opposed to one another began to sit on different sides of the House. The term 'His Majesty's Opposition' was coined by John Hobhouse (later Lord Broughton) in a speech in 1826 and the term has been employed ever since. Gradually, the opposition began to acquire a recognizable structure: an opposition front bench (comprising the leading members of the party),[1] a leader,[2] and a more developed whipping system: though whips have their origins in the eighteenth century, the modern role ascribed to them as managers and communicators developed concomitantly with the growth of organized party in the nineteenth.[3] To this has been added, in the twentieth, internal party organization: weekly party meetings of the parliamentary party, elected officers, and a series of party committees shadowing the main responsibilities of government. The Parliamentary Labour Party (the PLP) was formed in 1906; the Conservative 1922 Committee first met in April 1923.[4]

The growth of a party infrastructure is indicative of the complex nature of opposition. The opposition comprises a party which has contested an election on a manifesto which is different to that of the party returned to government. It may thus be expected to be critical of government and to express opposition to much of what it brings before the House. This essentially negative role necessitates some measure of organization, both for the expression of disagreement in debate and for its expression in the division lobbies. The opposition, though, also constitutes the alternative government (that is, by definition it is the largest minority party prepared, in the event of the resignation of the government, to assume office).[5] This imposes a different perspective. Indeed, it imposes two different (not always compatible) perspectives. *If* the opposition is to be returned to government, it has to be able not only to oppose the policies advanced by the existing administration but also to advance alternative policies of its own. This constitutes a more positive role than that of sheer resistance, hence the value of specialization by party committees; nonetheless, it still motivates a critical stance. Contemplating *when* it is returned to power motivates the opposition – and the opposition front bench in particular – to adopt a more conciliatory role, not wishing to generate problems which it will then have to contend with when in government. Members of the opposition front bench may thus adopt a consensual as opposed to an adversary approach in responding to government proposals.

Indeed, in quantitative terms (that is, the number of bills opposed on second reading), a consensual model fits the House of Commons better than an adversary model. In the thirty-nine sessions between 1945 and 1983, 79 per cent of government bills were not divided against on second reading. The opposition forced divisions against only 18 per cent of bills, the remaining 3 per cent being forced by backbenchers of other opposition parties.[6] This degree of consensus is explicable in terms of the governmental perspective of opposition front benchers, the number of measures of a technical or administrative nature,[7] and a degree of bipartisanship in certain sectors (most notably in defence and foreign affairs).[8] In qualitative terms, the picture is somewhat different. On matters of what may be termed high policy, introducing significant changes to existing policies, the adversary model assumes greater relevance. The House disposes of non-contentious matters in order to concentrate on issues that divide the two sides of the House. Given the decline of the Keynesian consensus of the 1950s and early 1960s, when both parties shared similar views on managing the economy, it is perhaps not surprising that there is a greater number of such issues, the extent of consensus declining since 1970. 'Whereas 85 per cent of new Government Acts went through unopposed between 1945 and 1970, the proportion since has dropped to 69 per cent.'[9]

The opposition thus needs a complex infrastructure in order to generate effective criticism of – and alternatives to – government policies, in order to determine which measures should be opposed or supported, and in order to marshall its forces effectively to speak and vote against government when it deems such a course necessary.

When it does determine to oppose a particular bill or policy, what means are available to it? And how effective are they? The three primary means available are those of debate, vote, and obstruction. The first two are often seen as ineffectual, indulged in for form's sake, with the third – obstruction – constituting the only effective if not always legitimate weapon at the opposition's disposal. This perception, though widely held within the Palace of Westminster (and hence affecting MPs' behaviour), is misleading.

Debate constitutes the most-time consuming activity of the House (see Borthwick, chapter 4). Except where private legislation and private members' legislation are involved, the opposition has a clearly understood place in the proceedings. The opening and winding-up speeches are provided by the two front benches. In between, opposition backbenchers alternate with government backbenchers in being called (except for one or two speeches from Members of the other opposition parties). At the end of the debate, the House divides, the number of opposition members entering the division lobby depending in large part upon the strength of the whip issued: a three-line whip maximizes attendance, a one-line whip allows many, usually most, Members to be absent.

Is it not possible to dismiss debates as largely ritualistic and the outcome of divisions as predictable, as they have been for more than a century? In part, the answer is yes, but the statement fails to convey the significance for the opposition – and parliamentary government – of both debates and divisions. The point was well put by Ivor Jennings:

Because the Government is criticised it has to meet criticism. Because it must in course of time defend itself in the constituencies it must persuade public opinion to move with it. The Opposition is at once the alternative to the Government and a focus for the discontent of the people. Its function is almost as important as that of the Government.[10]

Debates, in short, serve several important purposes. They provide the opposition with an authoritative public forum in which to challenge government. They provide a platform for the expression of alternative views. They serve an important tension-release function, allowing the opposition to give voice on behalf of groups excluded from the policy-making process. The significance of debates for parliamentary democracy can best be grasped by contemplating what would be the position if Parliament did not exist. The significance of debates for the opposition can best be grasped by comparing the high public visibility achieved by the Labour opposition in the 1983–7 Parliament with the restricted public visibility achieved by the smaller opposition parties.

Divisions at the conclusion of debates are also not lacking in significance. If parties are united the outcome may be predictable, but forcing a vote provides the opportunity to demonstrate one's opposition. The use of one-, two-, or three-line whips allows the opposition to make clear the strength of its feelings; indeed, by issuing a three-line whip it may help raise the political significance of an issue beyond that accorded it by government. And by calling a division the opposition requires government to give more attention – managerially as much as intellectually – to the issue in question. Finally, but most importantly, the opposition entering the lobby against the government is a necessary but not sufficient condition for dissent by government backbenchers (or, in the event of a minority government, other opposition parties) to result in defeat for the government – a point of more than academic significance, especially since 1970 when defeats have become more frequent. The debates which attract the least interest, and to which government usually accords least priority, are those which are to end without a division.

One final, but often overlooked, point is that debates may actually influence government. This is least likely to happen in set-piece debates on major principles of public policy, but in other debates – including detailed discussion in standing committee – it is not un-

PHILIP NORTON

known for ministers to be influenced by what is said from the benches opposite. This influence may take different forms: direct influence, resulting in the minister conceding the point; less direct and unobservable influence, the force of the argument being recognized but not publicly acknowledged (possibly resulting in later modification); and influence derived from embarrassment (the minister recognizing that the opposition has got the better of the argument and resolving not to let that happen again). Influence may even derive from the threat of debate: a particular motion or amendment can worry both ministers and officials. One such instance – an opposition amendment to a National Insurance bill – was recorded by Social Services Secretary Barbara Castle in 1974: 'As someone very recently a backbencher', she confided to her diary, 'it fascinates me how much consternation an Opposition can cause in a department by its activities'.[11] The extent of such influence cannot be quantified. Relative to the bulk of public business, items affected are likely to be small in number but arguably sufficient to justify the exercise.

What, then, of obstruction? This is often seen as the opposition's most tangible weapon, the threat of non-co-operation or of filibustering causing the government to make concessions. The Select Committee on Procedure in 1977–8 advanced this supposition as the basis for opposing automatic timetabling of legislation.

> The Opposition may at present legimately use their power of delay to cause the Government to consider making concessions in their bills. If timetabling were general such a power would be lost. This would amount to a significant constitutional development, to the detriment of all non-ministerial Members.[12]

However, reviewing this 'time-hallowed argument', the Procedure Committee of 1984–5 came to a different conclusion. It was unable to find many occasions when delay had induced the government to make concessions.[13] Rather, as the evidence it received made clear, delaying tactics serve primarily to irritate government and to make it less responsive to opposition arguments. A long-drawn out campaign results in the government introducing a guillotine motion. The opposition may derive some marginal political capital from the government's action but it has no tangible impact on the legislation. The methods of delay do little to enhance the reputation of the House and, in the opinion of the Procedure Committee in 1985, were not sufficient to justify the existing deficiencies of legislative scrutiny by standing committee. It therefore recommended the timetabling of controversial bills.[14] The House, however, still adhered to the folklore of the power of delay and voted against the committee's recommendation.[15] Interestingly, the debate was one in which roles were reversed, the government adopting the position of the alternative opposition, wishing to have the presumed power of delay should it occupy the benches opposite. The irrelevance of the argument of delay was lost on both frontbench speakers as well as many backbenchers.

The role of the opposition, then, is more subtle – certainly more intricate – than is popularly portrayed by the adversary model. It is part-adversary, part-consensual, and more besides. And not only is opposing the government not its sole activity, it is an activity not confined to Her Majesty's Opposition.

Other opposition parties

The House proceeds largely on the basis of the existence of government and opposition. Other parties are generally viewed, politically as well as procedurally, as marginal. They are, nonetheless, an established feature of the parliamentary landscape. No Parliament this century has comprised solely the two parties of government and official opposition. The 1983 and 1987 general elections each witnessed the return of forty-four MPs representing other parties.

Throughout the 1950s and 1960s the third party in the House was the Liberal Party (no other party witnessed the return of more than one Member). In the 1970s it was joined by Scottish National, Plaid Cymru, Ulster Unionist, Democratic Unionist, SDLP and – in 1981 – Social Democratic parties. Once a party has two or more Members, the practice has been to create some form of organization, however rudimentary. Even where there are only two Members, one has been designated as whip. The larger the party, the greater the organization: an elected leader (sometimes with a deputy or deputies), regular meetings, and a written whip. Portfolios are shared between Members. In the 1983 Parliament, the size of the Liberal Party was sufficient to allow some Members to be official spokesmen on designated subjects and for some, by choice, to be the equivalent of backbenchers (that is, with no portfolio). Some of the parties, in-

105

cluding the SDP and Scottish National Party, have variously introduced standing orders.

In the House, these parties constitute in many respects mini-oppositions. Usually they sit on the opposition side of the House, on the benches just below the gangway. They respond to government policies, adopting a critical stance; like the main opposition party, they have sought election on distinct manifestos. They have some input into the 'usual channels', albeit – unlike the official opposition – input that is *ad hoc* and occasional. (It is this input that justifies the designation of a whip in a two-man party.) When the opposition does not divide the House, they may do so. In debates, they have spokesmen that can expect recognition by the Chair. And now, since 1985, the third largest party in the House (up till 1987 the Liberal Party) can play an agenda-setting role in debate: the topic for debate on three opposition days is selected by the party leader, the topic on the remaining seventeen days being chosen by the leader of the opposition.

In terms of having some influence on government, there are two situations in which third parties cease to be marginal. First, where they have sufficient numbers to be a potentially disruptive force in the House. Such occasions are rare, at least in recent history, though recently the Liberals – now the Social and Liberal Democrats – appear to have had a little more input into 'the usual channels' as a result of their increased numbers. Second, and more important, when there is a minority government. In such a situation, one or more third parties holds the balance of power. In return for not voting against the government on a vote of confidence, they may negotiate or expect concessions from government. This was the position that pertained in the three years from 1976 to 1979 when the Labour Government of James Callaghan was in a minority in the House. The relationship between the government and the Liberal Parliamentary Party took the form of a pact from 1977 to 1978 under which several Liberal measures were introduced in return for support in the lobbies.[16] Less formal, but arguably much more effective, was the relationship between the government and the Ulster Unionist and Plaid Cymru parties. The Ulster Unionists achieved one of their main goals (an increase in the number of parliamentary seats in Northern Ireland) and in the 1978 Queen's Speech the Plaid Cymru Members got five of the six things they asked for.

However, assuming a government with an overall majority and

third parties with limited numbers, the impact of such parties in the House is slight. This is especially apparent when compared with the position of the official opposition. The problem is partly a managerial one. With a small number of MPs, it is difficult to maintain a permanent presence in the House (though, given their limited numbers, the Liberals tended to have a better showing than their critics in the two main parties suggest).[17] It is also political and procedural. The lion's share of the participation in debate from the opposition side of the House is taken by the official opposition. In a full-day debate in the 1983/87 Parliament, one Liberal spokesman would normally be called and sometimes, but by no means always, an SDP spokesman. (For a number of weeks at the end of the Parliament, the two Alliance parties appointed joint spokesmen; the SDP opted out of the arrangement in the new Parliament.) Ulster Unionist Members concentrate on debates affecting the Province. Plaid Cymru and Scottish National Members normally consult with one another to decide whether a Nationalist should seek to take part in debate; they recognize that they could not expect speakers from both parties to be called in second-reading debate. In short, speakers from third parties are dwarfed by those called from the two main parties. Which way they vote at the end of a debate is unlikely to influence the Treasury (front) bench. (Indeed, since 1979 the voting of opposition parties has been largely predictable and the government's business managers consequently take little interest in them.) The Liberal and SDP parties in particular further suffered from the fact that both main parties in the House prefer the maintenance of the two-party dominance, and hence tend to adopt a relatively dismissive attitude toward what they consider to be interlopers.[18]

Compared with the official opposition, the marginal role of third parties is apparent. However, compared with parties not represented in the House, the benefits of having some parliamentary representation also emerge. Being represented in Parliament gives a party a particular legitimacy, not least in the perception of the mass media. Seats rather than votes are what matter. In the 1979 general election, for example, the National Front achieved a greater aggregate vote than Plaid Cymru, but Plaid Cymru achieved two seats and the National Front none. Concomitantly, representation in the House provides an authoritative public platform. Third parties can raise issues – though the formal opportunities are limited – when the two main parties are silent. They can force a division when the opposition front bench remains seated. As such, they may be able to carve out a distinctive stance. The reasons why the stance is distinctive is in the short term self-defeating: it is distinctive because it has the support of no other party. However, over time it is possible that it may have some impact inside or outside the House. The point was well summarized by former Liberal leader, Jo (now Lord) Grimond:

> Many Members and groups, I would include the Liberal Party, appear to have been weaving sand for decades yet their toe-hold on the political process has given them influence. Had there been no Liberal Party, in the wings at least, and spasmodically making some impact from the stage, the Tory and Labour Parties would, I believe, have been different.[19]

The value of the floor of the House as a platform for third-party opposition to government measures was well shown in the 1983–7 Parliament in the experience of Ulster Unionist Members. In order to express their rejection of the Anglo-Irish Agreement signed in 1985, they all – with the exception of Enoch Powell – boycotted proceedings in the House. The effect was to deny them an important and authoritative means of conveying their views to the government front bench. Immediately following the 1987 general election they abandoned their boycott, returned to the House and promptly proceeded to divide the House on a variety of motions affecting the Province.

Third parties in the House thus play a limited oppositional role. They have, largely by virtue of increased numbers, had greater visibility over the past ten to fifteen years. Their impact is maximized at times of minority government. At other times, they are largely marginalized by the two main parties.

Opposition backbenchers

A third source of opposition is that of opposition backbenchers. On a number of issues, the official opposition may decide not to oppose the government; as we have seen, most bills receive a second reading without the opposition dividing against them. Indeed, on occasion the opposition will support, by vote if necessary, certain measures. The same applies in the case of third parties. Such a stance does not always find favour with opposition backbenchers. As a result, the government may find the principal opposition to a particular measure emanating, by voice and vote, from the opposition backbenches. It may come from an individual Member, from an *ad hoc* body of Members, or from an organized group. Such occasions may not be frequent but they are often newsworthy.

Opposition to government from an individual opposition Member (on other than constituency grounds or personal moral conscience) is rare and is usually ignored. Indeed, it is difficult for one Member to have much impact; without the support of a second, for example, it is impossible to force a division. However, persistence pays. Tabling a large number of questions (especially for written answers, upon which no limit is set), springing to one's feet in the chamber whenever the occasion permits, and writing and speaking in public can attract public attention. The most notable example in the 1983–7 Parliament was the Labour Member for Linlithgow, Tam Dalyell. His pursuit of government ministers on a number of issues, but most especially the sinking of the Argentinian battleship *General Belgrano* during the Falklands conflict, demonstrated the way in which an opposition Member can use parliamentary procedure to upset the occupants of the Treasury Bench, including the Prime Minister.

Dissent expressed by a group of opposition backbenchers is more common. On occasion, a number of Members may oppose the Government in order to act as a ginger group, prompting the opposition front bench to be more vigorous in its opposition. At the beginning of the Heath Government in 1970–1, for example, several Labour MPs led by James Wellbeloved formed such a ginger group and forced several divisions on government motions.[20] A number of Conservative Members performed a similar role in the short Parliament of 1974.[21] On other occasions, divisions are forced because of opposition to the policy or bill in question. There have been various examples in most recent Parliaments. In 1968, for example, forty-five Conservatives voted against the third reading of the Race Relations Bill; twenty-seven voted against the Rhodesian sanctions order the following year. In 1971 sixty-eight Labour MPs voted against the policy of internment in Northern Ireland; the following year thirty-two voted against the Northern Ireland Detention of Terrorists Order. In the 1974–9 Parliament, Conservative backbenchers regularly voted against the continuation of the Rhodesian sanctions order: in 1978 no less than 116 voted against. Since, 1979, Labour backbenchers have variously forced divisions when the opposition front bench has been content to abstain, a practice carried over into the 1987 Parliament. Within three weeks of the Parliament having met, twenty-three Labour Members voted against the Summer adjournment motion.

On occasion, divisions may be forced by an organized group of backbench Members, for example the Tribune Group of Labour MPs. It is rare, though, for this to happen when the Labour Party is in opposition. Today, the Tribune Group has been succeeded by the Campaign Group of Labour MPs as the keeper of the Socialist conscience, but the latter appears to play little role in organizing opposition in the House independent of the opposition as a whole. On the Conservative side, there are no equivalent attitude groups of Members; some Members belong to groups such as the Monday Club, though such bodies are not exclusively parliamentary, and some belong to private dining groups (more prominent since 1979), but none of these bodies has provided the basis for a planned campaign of opposition in the House, at least not during periods when the party has been in opposition.

Occasions when opposition backbenchers oppose the Government in voice or vote can embarrass the opposition front bench as much as the government. Such opposition, though, can serve various beneficial purposes. The potential for opposition helps keep the government on its toes; its business managers know that gaining the support of the opposition front bench may not be sufficient to ensure the speedy and unopposed passage of a measure. Allowing backbenchers to express views that opposition spokesmen may be reluctant to voice can serve an important expressive function, allowing various disaffected groups to find an outlet for their opinions in an authoritative forum. Hence, and ironically, such opposition can serve an important role of regime support.

Clearly, then, the picture of a government facing a monolithic and persistent opposition is a misleading one. The opposition they face may emanate from different parts of the benches facing them, it may be and usually is intermittent rather than persistent, and it can and usually does take different forms. The picture of government versus opposition also masks the various functions fulfilled by the different elements on the opposition benches. Opposition can have some impact, though achieving a clear reversal of government policy is extremely rare. The likelihood of that happening is greatest when opposition is not confined to one side of the House. The time for ministers to begin sweating is when the voices of dissent come from behind them.

THE GOVERNMENT BACK BENCHES

Each parliamentary party comprises like-minded Members who by virtue of political philosophy and political socialization want to support their party and its leaders in the division lobbies. No party philosophy, though, is so hegemonic as to preclude scope for disagreement. There are different philosophical strains within most parties. Members may disagree over the best means to achieve agreed goals. It is thus quite possible for backbenchers to disagree with their leaders.

Prior to 1960, backbench disagreement with party leaders was not always made public. Members usually either kept their doubts to themselves or else expressed them privately to the whips or frontbenchers or gave voice to them in private party meetings. There was often a reluctance to make disagreement public. There was an even greater unwillingness to take it as far as voting against one's own side in the division lobbies. This was especially so on the government side of the House, given that voting with the opposition could result in the government losing the vote. In the view of many government backbenchers, a government defeat could bring the government down. There was no constitutional basis for such a belief but it was one that the whips, for reasons of self-interest, did nothing to discourage.

Not surprisingly, dissent by government backbenchers in the division lobbies was notable for its rarity. There were actually two sessions in the 1950s when not one Conservative Member cast a vote against the government. Government backbenchers were more independent in Parliaments in which the government had a large overall majority and hence in which they could cross-vote without threatening the government's majority. The Conservative government of 1959–64 faced dissent from a disparate range of backbenchers on a range of issues. The Labour government of 1966–70 faced particularly persistent dissent from the left wing of the PLP, primarily the Tribune Group, but like its Conservative predecessor never lost a vote. Indeed, the chances of it doing so were even smaller given the source from which the dissent was expressed: when Tribune Group MPs voted against the government it was normally on issues on which the Conservative opposition either abstained or supported the Government.

All this was to change in the period from 1970 onwards. Government backbenchers in the 1970–4 Parliament proved willing to vote against their own side on more occasions, in greater numbers, and with greater effect than ever before. On six occasions, cross-voting by Conservative backbenchers resulted in government defeats. Three of these defeats took place on three-line whips, the most important taking place on the immigration rules in 1972.[22] This change is in part explicable in terms of new issues coming on to the political agenda, cutting across normal party lines (though many of these issues pre-dated the Parliament); more significantly, it is explicable in terms of the leadership style of the Prime Minister, Edward Heath. His autocratic approach had the effect of shutting off the usual private outlets for the expressions of dissent.[23] The only way backbenchers could register their opposition effectively was to go public and use their ultimate weapon: entering the 'No' lobby against the government.

The government defeats in the 1970–4 Parliament helped provide precedents for subsequent Parliaments. They helped dispel myths as to what would happen if the Government lost a vote. (There was never any consideration of resignation following the Heath defeats.) They were also reinforced by seventeen defeats suffered by the minority Labour government in the short 1974 Parliament, the consequence of opposition parties combining against the government. The 1974–9 Parliament saw forty-two defeats of the government in the lobbies. The majority of these (twenty-three) were the result of Labour backbenchers entering, sometimes in large numbers, the opposition lobby. The most persistent dissent witnessed by the Wilson and Callaghan governments was from Tribune Group Members, but the most effective was that expressed by Members drawn from different parts of the party: they were more likely to enter a whipped opposition lobby.

This greater degree of independence by government backbenchers has been maintained since 1979.[24] It has, though, been somewhat less publicly visible and commented upon. In part this is because the size of the government's overall majority has been sufficient to absorb most dissent. More importantly it is because much of the dissent has not taken public form. The threat of government backbenchers voting against their own side has been sufficient, especially when it looked as if the government might not win the vote, to force a change in government policy. During the 1979–83 Parliament various measures were modified under threat of defeat and two bills were withdrawn. Remarkably, in the 1983–7 Parliament, despite an overall majority of almost 140, the government retreated under threat of defeat on at least two issues: student grants and the sale of parts of British Leyland to Americans. On other occasions, when government concessions were not forthcoming, backbenchers entered the opposition lobby. In 1982 this produced a defeat for the government on the immigration rules and in 1986 it resulted in the loss of the second reading of the Shops Bill, only the third time this century that a government has lost a second-reading vote (and the first time that a government with an overall majority has lost such a vote). The government was also variously defeated on a number of House of Commons matters, including procedure and Members' allowances, as well as suffering the loss of a number of votes in standing committee. The 1986 Financial Services Bill, for example, was variously amended as a result of cross-voting by Conservative Members.

Within weeks of the 1987 general election, the Thatcher government was facing threatened cross-voting by backbenchers on its plans to introduce a community charge to replace domestic rates. Despite an overall majority of 101, the Cabinet began to discuss plans to soften the impact of introducing the new charge.[25] The Government also refrained from opposing the proposed increase in Members' pay (by more than 20 per cent) in July 1987.[26] A similar reluctance to face backbench opposition had led the Cabinet in 1979 not to object to the creation of the new investigative select committees.[27]

There has been a significant change in parliamentary behaviour, introducing a new dimension to the nature of opposition in the House of Commons. Before 1970 a government could proceed on the basis that, if it pushed ahead regardless, it would have a majority in the lobbies. Since 1970, it has not been able to make such a presumption. It may assume that it will normally have a majority – but it cannot take it for granted. Consequently, anticipation of parliamentary reaction has become a significant factor in the deliberations of Cabinet and the government business managers. Parliamentary opposition now means much more than implied by the adversary model of politics.

The willingness of government backbenchers to enter the opposition lobby has supplemented rather than supplanted the private party channels available to express disagreement with government policy. Cross-voting is, after all, an admission of failure that earlier attempts to persuade government to alter its stance have failed.

The whips constitute the most regular and established channels for the transmission of disquiet from backbenchers to ministers. The Government Whips Office is a well-manned and organized institution at the heart of parliamentary life. Fourteen government whips are now normally appointed. They maintain a permanent presence during proceedings on the floor of the House and in standing committee. There is a whip responsible for each regional grouping of government supporters, and a whip attends each meeting of a party backbench committee. Any disquiet among backbenchers is quickly noted and passed on to the chief whip and to the appropriate minister. Significant backbench dissent will be reported to Cabinet: the chief whip attends though is not usually a member. Ministers and whips will seek to meet backbench criticism in order to ensure that it is not made public and, if it is, to ensure that it does not result in cross-voting. If dissenters are numerous and remain unpersuaded it is the chief whip's task to tell the Prime Minister. During the period of the Heath government, the chief whip had on occasion to tell the Prime Minister that he could not guarantee a majority in the House for a particular proposal. The Prime Minister's reaction was to insist that the measure be proceeded with, the consequence being the embarrassment of defeat. Other Prime Ministers have been more responsive, hence the effectiveness of the threat of defeat.

Party committees also provide an important conduit for backbench dissension. This is especially so on the Conservative side of the House where committees are better attended and have greater political clout than Labour subject groups. (This is attributable in part to the proximity of Conservative committees to the fount of policy-making in the party – the party leader; PLP groups are more divorced from Labour's policy-making organs.) Harold Macmillan once claimed that the committees had been set up 'by the whips after the 1931 election to keep the majority out of mischief'.[28] Given that he got the date and the identity of the creators wrong (they grew largely in the 1920s on backbench initiative), it is perhaps not surprising that he should have misstated the purpose. The committees fulfil important functions, allowing backbenchers to specialize in a particular subject area (the only structured and regular means available prior to the creation of the departmentally-related select committees in 1979) and to keep themselves abreast of current developments; meetings are addressed by appropriate experts and public figures. Some committees go on fact-finding excursions. All will normally discuss any forthcoming legislation, usually some time before its second reading. If one or two backbenchers express dissenting opinions, then the committees may serve to absorb their dissent. The Members will have had the opportunity to give voice privately to their views and the whip present will be able to report back whether or not those views have found a receptive audience; if they have not the Members may decide not to pursue their objections and the whips are not likely to be unduly concerned. However, if dissent is more widespread the committees serve as important agents for the expression of dissent. Conservative committees are open to all Conservative backbenchers. Attendance may serve to indicate when backbench disquiet on a particular issue is significant. A normal committee meeting may attract no more than a handful of Members; it is far from unknown for less than ten to be present. When backbenchers are worried the number may swell to nearer a hundred. Thus, for example, in July 1987 between eighty and a hundred Conservative backbenchers packed a meeting of the party environment committee to discuss the Government's plan to abolish domestic rates. At various times, particular committees have served as the principal vehicles of dissent. In 1973, for example, opponents of the government's plans to build a third London airport at Maplin used the aviation committee to channel their opposition, consulting expert opinion that was on a par with that consulted by Government. The election of committee officers at the beginning of each session may also serve to indicate backbench disquiet, critics of government policy being elected to serve. Increasingly, committee elections have been fought between different sections of the party, with particular groups nominating slates of candidates. During Edward Heath's premiership, the finance committee was a battleground for the dispute between supporters and opponents of the government's economic policy. Today, most committees are contested on a left versus right (or 'wet' versus 'dry') basis. At the beginning of the 1987–8 session, government supporters got the lion's share of the officerships; critics, nonetheless, made some important gains.[29]

Critics of government policy may also employ other party and parliamentary means of voicing their disquiet. They may use the full meeting of the parliamentary party, they may table critical parliamentary questions, or they may table early day motions (though now so over-used for other purposes that critical motions do not stand out in the way they used to); they may, of course, go public – not only on the floor of the House (if the opportunity presents itself) but also outside the House. These channels are usually supplementary to the main private channels available and will be used selectively only if dissent expressed via the whips or party committees is ignored.

The government side of the House is thus a more complex political entity than the term itself may imply. The government front bench cannot necessarily assume that, on a particular issue, opponents will be confined to the benches opposite. Indeed, on occasion it may find the opposition more supportive than some of its own backbenchers. The time for a minister to panic is when dissenting voices are raised in all parts of the House. For a minister to face a baying House is not only bad publicity for the government it is personally unnerving. It is an experience that ministers prefer to avoid. A failure to handle dissent effectively can mar, possibly destroy, a ministerial career.

THE CONSTITUENCY MEMBER

There are occasions when Members operate outside the context of party. These include debates on private Members' legislation, for which government has no collective responsibility, as well as divisions in which a free vote is conceded. At a different level, involving ministerial responsibility, are those instances when Members pursue constituency casework: in other words, pursue a particular complaint against a department on behalf of a constituent or group within the constituency. If dissatisfied with the minister's response the Member may pursue the case to the extent that he or she may raise the issue on the floor of the House.

In many instances, constituents contact their MP with complaints which are not the responsibility of central government; about half concern local-authority responsibilities. Of those that fall within the remit of a central department, constituents are often satisfied with an authoritative reply. The main means of conveying constituents' particular concerns to ministers is by correspondence. About 10,000 letters a month are received from MPs by ministers (in some cases the letter writers themselves are ministers); a similar number of letters go from ministers to the Members. Most concern constituency cases rather than matters of policy. The Department of Health and Social Security is the ministry receiving the largest mailbag.[30]

In most cases, a full ministerial letter – and some are long and detailed – is sufficient to deal with the constituent's problem. However, if the constituent's Member is dissatisfied with the response then a more oppositional stance may be adopted. This may involve 'going public' – issuing press releases, tabling questions (oral or written) and seeking a half-hour adjournment debate. Some Members will also refer cases to the Ombudsman.

More significant at a political level, government policy may affect not just an individual constituent but the interests of the constituency as a whole. This may lead the Member, regardless of party, to oppose the government and, if necessary, to vote against it in the division lobbies. Reorganization of local government boundaries and the closure (or transfer) of public establishments such as military bases are among the issues most likely to generate opposition from constituency MPs. Among recent examples are the support of GCHQ workers by Cheltenham Member Charles Irving, the local Conservative MP for the communications base, when the government required workers to resign membership of trade unions, and the opposition to the siting of low-level nuclear waste dumps in their constituencies by four Conservative MPs: three were government ministers and they used other Members to speak for them; the fourth, Michael Brown, threatened to resign his seat. Coupled with local and well-reported protests, the opposition appears to have had some effect: it was decided not to pursue exploration of the sites.

Opposition to government measures on constituency grounds may also overlap with opposition expressed by the same or other Members on grounds of political principle or personal conscience. This combination may generate a significant number of opponents. One notable example was during the 1974–9 Parliament when the Labour government introduced its Scotland and Wales Bill to devolve power to elected assemblies in Scotland and Wales. A number of Labour Members were opposed to the proposal on principle, fearing the break-up of the United Kingdom. Labour Members in the North of England were worried that it would work against the interests of the North and hence their constituencies. The opposition was sufficiently broad and deep to result in the guillotine motion for the bill being defeated. The retreat of the Thatcher government in 1984 on the issue of student grants was largely the result of pressure from constituents on Conservative MPs; a number of Conservative Members were also influenced to vote against the Shops Bill in 1986 as a result of constituency pressure.

Members who pursue a constituency matter in opposition to government or departmental policy usually gain the respect of other Members for so doing. If the government objects to a Member's activity, there is little it can do. However, where the issue concerns only one Member, the government may be able to proceed regardless. The greater the number of constituencies affected, the greater the likelihood of effective opposition; similarly when the issue attracts opposition on other grounds as well.

CONCLUSION

Opposition to government is not as persistent or as predictable as the adversary model of politics would suggest. When government measures are opposed – and only a minority are – that opposition is most likely to be expressed by the official opposition. Such opposition, though, constitutes but the largest element of a much larger configuration of opposition. That opposition can be characterized not in terms of a static government-versus-opposition relationship but rather as analogous to a chemical reaction, the nature of the opposition shifting from issue to issue.

For the government, and especially the whips and business managers, parliamentary life has become more complex – and demanding – over the past fifteen years. Opposition to government may emanate from the opposition as such, from minority parties, from groups of opposition backbenchers, from government backbenchers and, most seriously, from a combination of these, the nature of that opposition taking different forms: private communications, vocal dissent in party committees (or meetings of the parliamentary party), the tabling of critical questions or EDMs, speeches on the floor of the House, or, most dangerous of all, voting against the government in the division lobbies. In most – but no longer all – cases, voting is predictable and the government assured of a majority. What ensures that high level of predictability is the ground work done beforehand by the whips.

The effects of opposition to government are various. It can, but (expressed as a proportion of the total number of times opposition is expressed) rarely does, effect a change in government policy, though given the importance of anticipated parliamentary reaction by the government the extent of this effect cannot be quantified. Opposition helps fulfil an important symbolic and political function, fulfilling to some extent Bagehot's expressive function. It allows the views of outside groups or worried constituents to find expression. It forces the government to justify itself and to do so in a public forum presided over by a neutral figure. It may even result in government being persuaded to change tack. And the more that opposition is seen as extending beyond the predictable adversary relationship of one side versus the other, then the greater the likelihood of public support for the institution of Parliament.

Chapter Seven

LEGISLATION

GAVIN DREWRY

Laws, mainly in the form of legisla*tion*, made by a legisla*ture*, are the major vehicles through which public policies are delivered. In the United Kingdom, each session of Parliament opens with a Queen's Speech (written nowadays, of course, by Her Majesty's ministers and not by Her Majesty) heralding around twenty particularly important government bills that will dominate the parliamentary agenda in the months to come. We nowadays take it more or less for granted that it is the job of government (through Parliament, in which, via party discipline, it normally controls a majority of the seats) to legislate, and to do so on a heroic scale; post-1979 Conservative administrations, dedicated to cutting back the scope of state activity via programmes of 'privatization' and 'deregulation', have been every bit as productive as their predecessors in passing new laws. However, we should bear in mind that the working out of such large, detailed, and carefully planned legislative programmes is quite a recent development in our constitutional history.[1] The creeping development, over the last century and more, of massive economic and social intervention by government can in fact be traced through the growth (in number and in bulk) of Acts of Parliament and of various other kinds of legislation.[2] Laws, it has been pointed out, are a major resource of government activity, along with public money and bureaucratic manpower.[3]

But 'law' itself is, as successive generations of legal theorists have pointed out, a slippery concept, and 'legislation' wears many different disguises. A lot of law-making happens without much help or hindrance from Parliament, and parliamentary legislation itself takes many forms. Apart from the familiar public general Acts of Parliament, of which there are various sub-species, a quick glance along the shelves of any law library, through the *Sessional Information Digests* produced by the House of Commons Library, or through the index of Erskine May's *Parliamentary Practice* discloses the existence of private Acts, provisional order confirmation Acts, and Church of England Measures. Moving gradually away from Westminster itself, we find delegated legislation, including statutory instruments (made by or in the name of ministers and subject, more in theory than in practice, to parliamentary approval: see below), by-laws (made by local authorities and other public bodies, and subject to no parliamentary scrutiny at all), and rules of court procedure (made by judges). Each of these can be further sub-categorized according to various criteria, such as the procedures to be followed for promulgation and scrutiny. European legislation, again divisible into several distinct types, has, since the United Kingdom joined the European Community in 1973, impinged increasingly on the work of the Westminster Parliament and on the lives of citizens represented in it. The picture is further complicated by the proliferation (in parallel with the growth in modern times of a vast array of 'quasi-government' bodies, commonly if misleadingly called quangos) of 'quasi-legislation', in various forms – including administrative circulars, codes of practice, and extra-statutory tax concessions (putting a gloss on the formal legislative provisions of the Annual Finance Act).[4] Parliament's capacity to influence directly the 'Acts' promulgated in its name (but originating for the most part in government initiatives) is in practice quite limited; its capacity to superintend the making of delegated legislation is little more than nominal; its influence on many areas of quasi-legislative activity is virtually non-existent.

To make matters still more complicated, as the authors of a major textbook on the subject have pointed out, the term 'legislation' is commonly used in at least two senses.[5] It is often used as a generic term for a body of rules (in numerous forms, as indicated in the preceding paragraph); but we have also to remember that those rules are merely the printed products of various legislative *processes*. In talking about 'legislation' in its second sense, as a process, we quickly encounter reminders of the well-known doctrine of separation of powers, which seeks to draw a sharp distinction between the constitutional functions of 'legislatures' (which make laws), 'executives' (which execute laws), and members of the 'judiciary' (who interpret laws in the context of litigation). In practice the demarcation lines between these functions can never be sharply drawn in any real-life political system, but it is still not uncommon to hear expressions like 'legislation by [administrative] circular' or 'judicial legislation', used not only to indicate the indisputable fact that administrators and judges have important roles to play in the legislative process but also, sometimes, that the user of such expressions implicitly disapproves of officials and judges trespassing on the territory of the legislature (i.e. Parliament). However, some would question whether in reality the Westminster Parliament, dominated as it is by a powerful executive, able in most circumstances to mobilize majority support in the division lobbies, can properly be called a 'legislature' at all.

At the turn of this century a distinguished parliamentary draftsman, Sir Courtenay Ilbert, wrote an illuminating treatise under the title, *Legislative Methods and Forms*.[6] The present chapter is concerned to some degree with 'forms' (of which, as already noted, there is a bewildering variety), to a greater extent with 'methods' (though not with techniques of legislative drafting, in which Ilbert had a particular professional interest) and, above all, with the legislative *process* and Parliament's place – a small, but important one, as we shall see – in that highly complex area of activity.

PARLIAMENT AND THE LEGISLATIVE PROCESS

The House of Commons spends at least half its time talking about legislation, and a lot of time in addition talking about matters which may give rise to legislation and matters arising, directly or indirectly, from past legislation.[7] Yet – and this brings us back to the doubt, mentioned earlier, as to whether or not Parliament is a 'legislature' in the full sense of the word – it is nowadays widely recognized that Parliament's role as a law-making body belongs more in the realms of rarified constitutional theory than in the domain of hard political reality. As S. A. Walkland once put it:

> The legislative process is now complex: it comprises deliberative, Parliamentary and administrative stages, over all of which executive influence is predominant. Legislation is now an almost exclusively executive function, modified, sometimes heavily, by practices of group and Parliamentary consultations.[8]

And:

> In so far as there is a 'deliberative' stage in the legislative process,
> this is now found much earlier than the Parliamentary stages, in
> the interplay between political parties, pressure groups,
> Departments and the Cabinet, which together form a complex
> decision making structure, involving a variety of social and
> political forces.[9]

Conventional wisdom, unmodified in the twenty years since
Walkland wrote these words, is that the parliamentary stages of the
legislative process are, for the purposes of getting policy intentions
converted into laws, the least creative ones; that Parliament has
relinquished any significant capacity for legislative initiative that it
may once have possessed to the executive that sits in its midst and
dominates its proceedings; that Parliament 'legitimates' and (perhaps)
'ventilates' but does not 'legislate'; so far as subordinate legislation,
and *a fortiori* quasi-legislation is concerned it barely does either of
those things.

Accepting that Parliament is not, whatever constitutional theory
might suggest to the contrary, at the centre of the universe so far as
the legislative process is concerned, where does it stand in relation to
other institutions involved in that process? Indeed, does this particular
universe have a centre at all? Figure 7.1 seeks to provide an answer,
in diagrammatic form. It assumes that the legislative process can be
broken down into four sets of interlocking and overlapping functions:
1, 'Inspiration'; 2, 'Deliberation and formulation'; 3, 'Legitimation';
4, 'Application' – plus a capacity for 'Feedback', or learning by
experience.

According to this model, Parliament (assuming for the moment
that the latter is distinguishable from the executive that sits in it)
impinges hardly at all on functions 1 and 4. It has rather more of a
part to play in 2, both overtly in so far as limited facilities exist for
debates on white papers, etc., and less formally in the day-to-day
intercourse between MPs and ministers, for example in party committees and in corridors, tea rooms, and bars. It has been suggested
that the Finance Bill (giving legislative effect to the tax changes
announced in the annual Budget statement) can be an important
exception that proves the general rule.[10] The most sensitive and
important parts of Finance Bills, unlike most other government
measures, are formulated in strict secrecy, with non-government

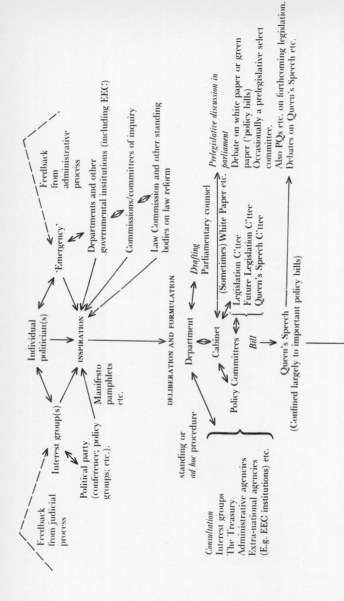

Figure 7.1 GOVERNMENT LEGISLATION

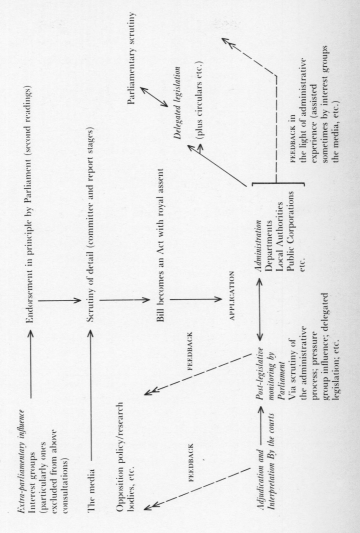

'outsiders' strictly excluded; this gives peculiar importance to its parliamentary stages, during which substantial changes are sometimes made following pressure-group lobbying of a kind which, in the case of most other bills, will usually have happened much earlier. Most bills are the products of hard bargaining in Whitehall, with Parliament being presented, in effect, with a *fait accompli*, too late to exert any real influence; sometimes (for example with Finance Bills and with exceptionally urgent measures, put together in a great hurry, without much time for prior negotiation) parliamentary scrutiny becomes more meaningful.

But Parliament's main legislative function, as already indicated, lies largely in legitimation, i.e. in helping to secure public acceptance of and obedience to the legislative actions of the state. Even if we do not like a particular law, most of us accept it, once it has duly passed through a (partly) elected Parliament, as being 'the law of the land', and so binding upon us. Moreover, parliamentary sovereignty, together with the absence of a codified British constitution (note the sharp contrast here between Britain and many other countries, notably the United States), means that we cannot challenge the legality (or the constitutionality) of an Act of Parliament in the courts, though there may in some circumstances be scope for doing so in the case of delegated and quasi-legislation. Thus Parliament's legitimating role is based on deep-rooted cultural attachments to traditions of representative government, reinforced by constitutional doctrine, rather than on any illusions about its actual impact upon legislation, which most of us recognize as being slight.

In this context, private Members' bills (see below) can be treated as a peculiar species of government legislation. The minority that reach the statute book do so only with government approval (and are often completely redrafted as a condition of retaining that approval); I have described elsewhere one striking, but by no means untypical, instance of this phenomenon, in the 1985–6 session – the Children and Young Persons (Amendment) Bill, dealing with the subject of child abuse.[11] Backbench bills that fail (see discussion of table 7.1, below) are often propaganda exercises rather than law-making ones.

Lest these remarks seem unduly dismissive of Parliament's importance in the legislative process, let us remember that legitimation is an essential function in any ordered society (even though some people, particularly supporters of the Alliance parties, have argued that the arithmetically skewed results yielded by the present electoral system cast serious doubt upon the legitimating capacity of the House of Commons). It is also arguable that the facility Parliament provides for public ventilation of policy issues cannot be brushed aside as worthless merely because it falls short – even a long way short – of a Utopian view of what representation and democracy in a complex pluralist society should really be about. Let us remember, too, that 'influence' goes a good deal deeper than being able to thwart the legislative ambitions of ministers by defeating a government bill at second reading (though a rare instance of this is cited below) or by forcing important backbench amendments through committee and report stage. As Bachrach and Baratz once pointed out,[12] power is something with two faces; it is necessary to look not only at decisions, but also at non-decisions, at why some issues never get into the political agenda at all. The number of concessions forced from ministers in the shape of bills abandoned or hostile amendments carried may not amount to much, but what we do not know is how often an idea fails to get even beyond the 'inspiration' stage or through its 'formative and deliberative' stages simply because a minister shrinks from having to justify an unpopular policy in public. Herein lies much of Parliament's real influence, though because of its invisibility we can never measure its magnitude.

PUBLIC BILLS: SOME PROCEDURAL ASPECTS

The minutiae of procedural arrangements in Parliament for the scrutiny of legislation lie outside the scope of this chapter, but something does need to be said, briefly, about the arrangements for passing public bills – a subject that has given rise to a lot of parliamentary discussion and academic theorizing over the years. Let the following outline suffice by way of factual background.

Bills can begin in either House (all important financial measures and nearly all politically contentious ones begin in the Commons rather than the Lords). Bills are debated in principle at second reading, then in detail, clause by clause, at committee stage (normally taken 'upstairs', in a small standing committee, in the Commons, but on the floor of the House in the Lords). The bill, with any amendments agreed in committee, is reported back to the House, providing further opportunity for changes to be made (including concessions promised in committee by ministers). The bill is then debated again in principle, as amended, at third reading (though this stage is often taken formally). Having passed these stages in one House (the detailed procedural arrangements of the two Houses differ significantly, though the principles followed are broadly the same in both), the bill goes through a similar process in the other House. Amendments made in that House are then considered by the first House. There are arrangements for resolving disagreements between Lords and Commons, and, in circumstances of total deadlock, the Parliament Acts 1911 and 1949 provide a mechanism whereby the will of the Commons can be made to prevail over that of a stubborn House of Lords – though this has not happened for some forty years despite the fact that governments of both main parties have sometimes, in the 1980s as well as in the 1970s, found it difficult to get contentious bills through the Lords unamended.[13]

Members of Parliament have, in recent years, done a lot of tinkering with their legislative procedures. The Commons Select Committee on Procedure looked at public bill procedure no fewer than five times between the late 1950s and the mid-1980s.[14] These committee assessments have not, on the whole, come up with proposals for any major restructuring: parliamentarians tend to be conservative and introspective about their own institution and to see reform in terms of balanced 'packages' that trade off the respective procedural interests of government, opposition, and backbenchers. This is perhaps a sensible approach, given that proposals have to be 'sold' to suspicious parliamentary colleagues with divergent interests, fearful that the procedural balance may be tilted to their disadvantage. These exercises have resulted in various minor innovations, such as a facility, since 1965, for uncontroversial bills to have their second reading in a standing committee and, more radically, the tentative introduction, in 1980, of 'special standing committees', which precede the traditional clause-by-clause committee stage of a bill by up to four evidence-taking sessions (see below).

Standing comittees have long been seen as the Achilles heel of legislative procedure, and a lot of the attention of reformers has been focused on them. They take up a lot of man-hours: in 1984–5, twenty-nine government bills took 201 committee sittings, at which between twelve and forty-six members attended; sixteen private Members' bills accounted for a further twenty-three sittings.[15] There are also standing committees on statutory instruments (seventy-one sittings in 1984–5) and on European Community Documents (seven sittings). There is a feeling among many parliamentarians that much of this expenditure of effort is a waste of time. Richard Crossman wrote as follows of his experience as a member of the Labour government's ministerial team steering the National Superannuation Bill through committee in 1970:

> It is utterly futile to have this method of taking a Bill to pieces in order to improve it and moreover it's utterly debilitating. The Government backbenchers waste their time in Standing Committee, where they are hardly allowed to speak because that would prolong the business and anything they say may provoke another Tory speech. The Opposition arguments are amateur and bogus, because half the time they don't really understand the details of the clauses they are discussing.[16]

A major analysis by J. A. G. Griffith of standing-committee proceedings in the three sessions, 1967–71,[17] showed that the great majority of successful amendments are moved by ministers; he found that on only sixteen occasions was the government forced to modify a principle of a bill as a result of proceedings in committee. Miers and Page point out that this was less true in the mid/late 1970s, when Labour was in office with a small or non-existent majority. Mrs Thatcher's government has not laboured under this handicap. Since 1979 the House of Commons on its own has done little to impede the government's legislative ambitions, and it has often been left to the House of Lords (sometimes working in tacit co-operation with MPs) to force ministers onto the defensive and to undertake detailed scrutiny: a recent study by Donald Shell highlights several instances (such as the field of local government reform) where the House of Lords has made a major impact on government legislation.[18]

One can, of course, argue that governments are elected to legislate and that the absence of parliamentary obstruction should be welcomed. But this is, at best, a half-truth: governments must govern, but need all the time to be forced to think hard about what they are doing; there needs to be an adequate procedure for the informed parliamentary scrutiny of complex laws that affect so any people's lives. It is arguable that traditional standing-committee procedure fails adequately to meet either of these needs.

One suggestion (with a number of variations) that has found favour over the years with parliamentary reformers is to allow standing committees to inform themselves and then perhaps bring informed influence to bear on ministers, by borrowing the well-tried interrogative procedures of select committees. The first report of the Select Committee on Procedure in the 1977–8 session proposed a new kind of 'public bill committee', empowered to take up to four sessions (one in private, three in public) of evidence before reverting to the traditional adversarial format of a standing committee.[19] The government accepted the recommendation, on an experimental basis, the new-style committees being titled 'special standing committees'; but in the event, the government (originally, only ministers were allowed to move that bills be committed to such committees after second reading) has sanctioned use of the procedure only on five occasions – three times in 1980–1 and once in each of the sessions 1981–2 and 1983–4.[20] Backbenchers like the procedure, and ministers have also seen virtues in it,[21] and the Select Committee on Procedure, in a later report in the 1984–5 session,[22] recommended that permanent provision for the new-style committees be enshrined in Standing Orders. The government agreed to this, but has shown little sign of any willingness to extend its use of the procedure. Against ministerial wishes, the House voted in favour of a recommendation that non-ministerial MPs be allowed to move for committal of bills to special standing committees. The trouble with achieving worthwhile procedural reform is that almost anything designed to make legislative scrutiny more effective also makes ministers' lives harder.

The 1984–5 Procedure Committee report also addressed itself to the vexed issue of timetabling bills in committee. The real problem here is with a small number of really big and contentious bills – even in an era of high inter-party polarization and of Thatcherite 'conviction politics' a surprisingly large percentage of government bills is in fact uncontentious in principle as between the parties, any dispute being mainly over more or less important matters of detail. The opposition's only weapon against what it regards as a wholly obnoxious measure is to play for time; it slows down committee proceedings so that only perhaps a dozen clauses out of a hundred are debated in thirty sittings; the government is then provoked into moving an allocation-of-time ('guillotine') motion which stipulates time limits for the completion of the remaining stages; thus all too often an important bill eventually passes through the Commons having undergone very little in the way of constructive scrutiny, and it is left to the House of Lords to justify its existence by picking up the pieces. this happened, for instance, in 1984–5 to the high controversial Local

Government Bill (98 clauses) and to the Transport Bill (114 clauses).

The Procedure Committee recommended the establishment of a new Legislative Business Committee to lay down timetables in advance for the committee stages of Bills likely to require more than twenty-five hours in standing committee. It argued that:

> we are convinced that whatever view is taken of the purposes of committee stage, whether it is seen as an opportunity to scrutinise Government's proposals and genuinely to improve a Bill, or primarily as an opportunity to draw attention to weaknesses in it, or just to harass Ministers, the House as a whole expects its committees to give their attention to all parts of Bills. The related imposition of timetables means that this is most unlikely to happen on Bills arousing great political controversy.[23]

In the result the proposal proved unacceptable to many MPs including the Leader of the House and the opposition frontbench. One objection to it was that it would deprive the opposition of its residual (though not particularly efficacious) powers of delay; it was also pointed out that the number of bills affected by the new machinery would in practice be very small indeed. The proposal having been rejected, after a wide-ranging Commons debate on 27 February 1986, the Procedure Committee subsequently produced another, much amended, variant of the idea in another report,[24] but this made no further headway in the 1983–7 Parliament. A good deal of the work of standing committees remains as futile as it was in Crossman's day; but the real problem of legislative scrutiny (if there really is a 'problem') is not procedural at all, it is constitutional. Parliament's role *vis-à-vis* the executive is reactive and supportive; many parliamentarians, invoking constitutional dogma and democratic theory, feel that it should have a more active and meaningful role. But no amount of procedural tinkering can ever achieve that.

PUBLIC BILLS: SOME FACTS AND FIGURES

Any quantitative (or qualitative) analysis of legislation requires us to draw a very sharp distinction between public and private bills. The former (to which most of this chapter relates) are measures affecting the general public interest, though their actual scope may be quite narrow; private bills single out particular interests for discriminatory treatment (e.g. by giving statutory powers to one, named, local authority, but not to local authorities in general), and are subject to a special, quasi-judicial procedure, with the 'promoters' of the Bill (for example, a local authority seeking new powers) and any objectors being given an opportunity, usually through counsel, to argue their respective cases. Unlike public bills, private bills that fail to complete their passage through Parliament in one session can be carried over to the next. Eighteen such bills received the royal assent in the 1985–6 session. Private bills are of considerable historical interest and, up to at least the early part of the last century, private legislation outweighed public legislation both in volume and in importance. But although academics and parliamentarians still show intermittent interest in the subject (e.g. in the wake of the Local Government Bill 1972),[25] our main concern here must be with public legislation.

Table 7.1 shows the progress of the 650 public bills introduced in the 1983–7 Parliament (government bills in columns 1–4 and backbench bills in columns 5–8). Columns 1–4 distinguish between 'ordinary' government bills (further distinguishing between those first introduced into the House of Commons and those that began life in the Lords), and two other, special categories that need to be considered quite separately. It should perhaps be remarked in passing that lumping together government bills under the heading 'ordinary' in the first two columns conceals important differences: 'ordinary' measures vary enormously in size (see below); some are controversial, many are not; some ('policy bills', as a colleague and I have called them elsewhere)[26] effect major policy changes, other ('administration bills') merely tidy up and/or update earlier legislation.

As for the two special categories,[27] Consolidated Fund bills are 'legislation' only in name, but are included in the table for the sake of completeness: they give formal legislative approval to the government's estimates, go through both Houses without debate, and are used as pegs upon which to hang general debates (on adjournment motions) on subjects chosen by backbenchers. Consolidation bills serve the function of tidying up the Statute Book. Over a period of time, many Acts are passed on the same subject – housing, company law, road traffic, etc. – and each new Act refers back to and amends, or repeals, parts of its predecessors. After a while, it becomes very difficult to discover how the law on a given subject actually stands without ploughing back through a mass of old statutes. Consolidation bills bring together in a single measure all the existing statute law on

Table 7.1 Progress of public bills, 1983–7 Parliament

| | Ordinary government bills | | Special government bills | | Backbench bills | | | | |
	1 Introduced in House of Commons	2 Introduced in House of Lords	3 Consolidation bills	4 Consolidated Fund bills	5 Ballot	6 10-minute rule	7 SO 58a	8 Backbench peers	9 Total
Not printed					3	78	11	—	92
One reading only	1		1		13	111	77	9	212
Second reading lost/ adjourned etc.					18	3	4	8	33
Two readings or more					4	1	1	9	15
Passed first House only	1	1			1	—	—	17	20
Withdrawn	4	1	—	—	1	—	1	3	10
Royal Assent	101	56	29	14	39	2	13	14	268
Total[b]	107	58	30	14	79	195[c]	107	60	650

Notes: a formerly SO No. 39.
b all government bills: 209, of which 95.7% enacted; all backbench bills: 441, of which 15.4% enacted.
c total excludes 23 refusals of leave to introduce.

a given subject. Since 1965 the Law Commissions have had a special responsibility for preparing Consolidation bills. They are always introduced into the House of Lords and are looked at by a joint committee of the two Houses, whose main task is to make sure that the law is not actually being altered, either accidentally or by design (except for specifically permitted minor amendments in some cases). Consolidation bills are quite numerous and are often very bulky (see below); they are normally completely uncontroversial (something will have gone badly wrong if they are not) and serve a special legislative purpose. They therefore need to be considered quite separately from ordinary bills.

Columns 5–8 of table 7.1 deal with bills introduced by back-benchers. Government business dominates the parliamentary time-table, but a small amount of time is made available to enable backbenchers to pursue their own legislative ambitions. In recent sessions this has amounted to twelve Fridays (a day when many Members want to rush off as early as possible to go to their constitu-encies and/or their loved ones); the first six allotted Fridays are set aside for second readings; the next six for the later stages of bills that have managed to make progress beyond second reading. Members ballot for priority on these Fridays, and the first twenty (sometimes someone subsequently drops out, which is why the total in column 5 is 79 rather than 80) choose 'slots' on the available days, in order of their success: getting a place in the first six means that a Member can choose the first slot on one of the precious second-reading days.

Ballot bills are usually serious legislative exercises; many un-balloted bills (columns 6 and 7 of table 7.1) are not. They serve a propagandist purpose; most make no progress beyond formal first reading and many are not even printed. On Tuesdays and Wednes-days, just after Question Time, a Member who has given notice in advance can ask the House for leave to introduce a bill, making a speech of up to ten minutes (hence the 'ten-minute rule') in support of his motion. Anyone who wishes can then oppose the motion with a short speech; there may then be a division; sometimes (twenty-three times in the 1983–7 Parliament) leave is refused, which means that the 'bill' is strangled at birth and does not count in the main body of legislative statistics. Any Member can introduce a Bill (under SO No. 58) at any time by simply presenting it to the House: this does not, of course, give the Member concerned any opportunity to make a speech (as with the ten-minute rule procedure) or any special claim upon the small quota of private Members' time, but some of these bills do make progress, often without any formal debate in the House, but with government blessing (the key to success with *all* categories of backbench bill). Finally, we should mention the opportunity for backbench peers to introduce bills (column 88), many of which pass the House of Lords but fail to make any progress in the House of Commons for want both of time and of ministerial support.

Quite a lot of backbench bills (sixty-eight in 1983–7) reach the Statute Book; the success rate of balloted bills is, as one would expect, particularly high (nearly half in 1983–7). But it has to be remembered that the government decides which bills will live and which will die; some backbench bills are in fact government-inspired; backbench bills that make progress are often extensively redrafted at ministerial insistence. It would be little exaggeration to say that most backbench Acts of Parliament are really a special sub-species of government legislation. The government, after all, has to take responsibility for them, administer them, and underwrite any financial consequences, once they become law.

The most striking thing about government bills (though it should come as no surprise, given earlier remarks about Parliament's essentially supportive role in the legislative process) is that nearly all of them become law. Of 165 'ordinary' government bills in the 1983–7 Parliament, just eight failed to reach the Statute Book. Four of these instances were purely technical 'failures', being hybrid bills (that is, measures, such as the Channel Tunnel Bill, which combine the characteristics of public and private bills) which failed to complete their progress through a special-committee procedure (at which objectors can be heard) in one session, and were carried over to the next. The other four were:

1 *Civil Aviation Bill* (1984–5), withdrawn in Commons standing committee, 9 May 1985. The bill, intended to restrict aircraft movements at Heathrow, provoked a rebellion by Conservative backbench opponents of the proposed third London Airport at Stansted. The minister agreed to postpone the bill until decisions had been taken on the Stansted proposal following an inquiry inspector's report.
2 *Education (Corporal Punishment) Bill* (1984–5), dropped at report stage in the Lords in 1985 after passing through the Commons.

The bill, the government's reluctant response to an adverse ruling by the European court of Human Rights in 1982, gave parents of children at state schools the right to exempt them from corporal punishment. The Lords inserted an amendment banning corporal punishment in schools altogether. Rather than seeking to reverse this defeat in the Commons, where a lot of Conservative backbenchers had earlier shown considerable hostility towards the bill, the government decided to abandon it altogether. In the following session the Lords again defeated the government on the issue, this time in the context of a quite different Education Bill; on this occasion the government allowed a free (i.e. unwhipped) vote in the Commons, and abolition was carried by the margin of a single vote.

3 *Land Registration and the Law of Property Bill* (1984–5). The Lord Chancellor withdrew this rather technical law reform bill after its Lords second reading, in the face of a hostile amendment put down for the committee stage which, if carried, would, he thought, completely defeat its purpose. He echoed the words of his famous predecessor, Lord Campbell, that law reform must be 'by consent or not at all'.

4 *Shops Bill* (1985–6), the most remarkable of the four government 'failures'. Despite the opposition of religious groups and many of its own backbenchers, the government decided to legislate to repeal the archaic legislative restrictions on Sunday trading. It introduced the bill in the Lords (a controversial decision in itself, given the strong feelings aroused by the bill), where it met oppoosition from some of its own erstwhile supporters (including the former Conservative Prime Minister, the Earl of Stockton), from the bishops, and from the formidable ex-Master of the Rolls, Lord Denning. Having been defeated on an important amendment in the Lords, the government faced a major rebellion from its backbenchers in the Commons. While imposing a three-line whip at second reading, it promised to send the bill to a 'special standing committee' (see above), to allow free votes on amendments at later stages, and to refrain from imposing a guillotine to force the Bill through. Notwithstanding these concessions, sixty-eight Conservatives defied the whips, they were joined by all fourteen Ulster Unionsts (protesting against the Anglo-Irish Agreement), and the bill was, almost unprecedently, defeated on the motion for its second reading, by 296 votes to 282.

It will be noted that three of these instances were ones where the government (with a nominal majority of more than 140 in the 1983–7 Parliament) faced rebellions in its own ranks. It is only rarely that Conservative and Labour Members find themselves in the same division lobbies, and when it does happen their motives for being there are often very different. These episodes only go to demonstrate the old truth about 'strong government': even if the executive has a working majority in the House of Commons it has to be able to *mobilize* that majority if it is to remain effective. This recalls our earlier remarks about the importance of the 'invisible' face of power.

It seems on the face of it remarkable that the early dissolution of Parliament, in June 1987, did not force the outright abandonment of any of the government's major bills. A June dissolution in 1970 forced the abandonment of nearly 40 per cent of the legislative programme.[28] Part of the explanation probably lies simply in good management by those in charge of government business, and in avoiding the introduction of too many controversial items in what was always likely to be the last session of the Parliament. However, the story is not quite as simple as the bare statistics in Table 7.1 might suggest. The Thatcher government, like its predecessors, had to do some hard bargaining with the opposition parties to salvage all that it could of its legislative programme; the Finance Bill and the Criminal Justice Bill were among those salvaged, but at a cost. What the raw figures do not show is that these, and other controversial bills, went onto the Statute Book shorn of all but their least contentious clauses. The remainder had to be retrieved by further legislation in the 1987-8 session.

This brings us to one further point about the statistics relating to public bills, that they vary enormously in size. This is shown in Table 7.2, over.

Government bills introduced into the Lords tend to be bigger than those introduced into the Commons, many of them being intricate and technical law reform measures (the figures for 1985 are distorted by the presence of the massive Insolvency Act 1985, with 236 sections and 10 schedules). Consolidation bills are often enormous (the Companies Act 1985 has 747 sections and 25 schedules), for reasons already indicated. But the most striking contrast is that between government and non-government Acts. 'Ordinary' government Acts passed in 1985 outnumbered backbench ones by a ratio of 41:20, or about two to one; if we break down Acts into their component

Table 7.2   Size of public acts, 1985[a]

Type	Number	Average number		Range	
		Sections	Schedules	Sections	Schedules
Government (Commons)	29	22	3	2–140	0–8
Government (Lords)[b]	12	44	4	2–236	0–10
Consolidation (Lords)	11	158	8	6–747	4–25
Balloted backbench (Commons)	11	3	0.5	2–6	0–3
Unballoted backbench (Commons and Lords)	9	4	0.5	2–7	0–3
Total	72				
Average		41	3		

Notes: *a* Excluding Consolidated Fund and Appropriation Acts.
   b Excluding consolidation bills

sections, the ratio becomes 1,162:73, or about sixteen to one. Most successful backbench measures are not only, as has been noted, government bills in disguise, they are also very emphatically, as someone once said, 'little laws for little occasions'.

SUBORDINATE LEGISLATION

The massive growth of government activity in the last decades of the nineteenth century could not be accommodated entirely through the constricted and rigid medium of public Acts of Parliament. A growing bureaucracy needed to be able to fill in the details of legislation to meet changing administrative exerience and unforseen contingencies. It became increasingly the practice to include in Acts of Parliament a facility for ministers and their armies of civil servants to make detailed regulations to meet changing needs and circumstances, thus freeing Parliament (or so it was claimed) to debate the really important issues of public policy without getting bogged down in unnecessary detail. An Act that confers such delegated (or subordinate) legislative powers is called the 'parent Act', with reference to instruments made under the exercise of such powers. Statutory Rules and Orders (as they were then called – in 1946 they were rechristened Statutory Instruments) were first collected together in annual volumes in 1890.

By and large, the delegation of legislative powers was recognized as inevitable and necessary, but there were critics, some of whom disapproved in principle of growing state intervention, and saw delegated legislation as a nasty symptom of an even nastier disease. The defence of the Realm Act, enacted at the beginning of the First World War, produced an explosion of government rules and regulations (twenty-five years later, the Emergency Powers (Defence) Act 1939 produced a similar explosion in the Second World War). The 1920s saw only a partial dismantling of the wartime regulatory state. In 1929, Lord Chief Justice Hewart published a widely read polemic, *The New Despotism*,[29] attacking the growth of delegated legislation as symptomatic of unchecked bureaucratic power. The Donoughmore Committee on Ministers' Powers[30] (set up in response to Hewart's complaints) cautiously endorsed the principles underlying the use of delegated legislation, though it did recommend various safeguards, and since then the constitutionality of the practice has never seriously been questioned. However, the perennial problem of determining where 'detail' ends and 'principle' begins remains unresolved, and probably unresoluble.

Public concern has shifted to the manifest shortcomings of the procedures for parliamentary scrutiny of statutory instruments – about 2,000 of them a year, many of them of extremely wide-ranging effect. In this context it is important to remember that most SIs fall into one of three broad categories, depending on the form of parliamentary scrutiny to which they are subject. 'Negative' instruments come automatically into effect after being laid before Parliament, unless a motion for annulment (technically called a 'prayer') is carried within forty sitting days by either House. 'Affirmative' SIs (in theory, though not always in practice, the most important and far-reaching ones) must positively be affirmed by resolution, usually of both Houses, before coming into effect. Thus the government is obliged to find time for approval of affirmative instruments, but has every incentive to *avoid* finding time for prayers against negative ones. Few prayers are debated, and the government has no difficulty in fending off the feeble threat posed by those that are.[31] Since the mid-1970s, debates on many affirmative instruments (and a few prayers) have been hived off to standing committees, to avoid cluttering up the floor of the House. A further species of instrument has only to be submitted to Parliament for information, and is not subject to any special procedure for approval or annulment.

Statutory Instrument procedures leave a lot to be desired (there is further discussion of them in chapter 10); but, as with discussion of the shortcomings of parliamentary scrutiny of public bills, the real issues – and the ultimate obstacles to meaningful reform – are constitutional rather than procedural. And if there are worries about how to monitor the deluge of subordinate legislation, what about quasi-legislation[32] – administrative circulars, internal rules for the guidance of administrators, codes of practice (some statutory, some not), extra-statutory tax concessions, etc. – much of which is promulgated without even token reference to Parliament? Its extent is vast: it is to be found lurking in numerous corners of the welfare system, the tax system, immigration procedures, police powers. Its legal status is often ambiguous. It is here that anyone wishing to make a reformist impact upon the legislative process might most usefully begin.

Chapter Eight

THE HOUSE OF COMMONS AND PUBLIC MONEY

ANN ROBINSON

In theory the House of Commons has control over all public expenditure and all taxes. Parliament is sovereign and its sovereignty is expressed nowhere so clearly as in respect of public money. But the theory of parliamentary sovereignty over finance is hardly borne out by the practice of modern government. Government is now so vast that no single body of men and women could scrutinize all its parts. And, furthermore, much of public money is actually spent either by individual recipients of social security or by bodies only loosely connected with central government departments, some of which have sources of income in addition to the funds voted by Parliament. In such circumstances, Parliament cannot completely control either the total amounts spent or the manner in which the funds it does vote are spent.

Parliament has recognized the realities of modern government by deliberately casting aside some of its powers to exert detailed control over finance. At one end of the spectrum it has given over to the European Community a share of the national wealth in the form of the Community's 'own resources' – up to 1.4 per cent of a notionally harmonized VAT base and all external levies and customs duties. At the other extreme, Parliament has given to local authorities the right to raise taxes through the system of local rates and certain rights to determine priorities in spending. Of course what Parliament has given, it may, being sovereign, take back unto itself. What has been given over to the European Community could, in theory, be regained were we to leave the partnership. But the Treaty of Rome provides no method of secession and for the time being at least it is reasonable to assume that about 1 per cent of the national wealth may be appropriated by the Community as of right. In December 1987

ANN ROBINSON

a bill was introduced to replace the local rates with a community charge, although it is not clear at the time of writing whether that bill will succeed and in what precise form. The constitutional position of local authorities is, however, that in the last resort they are subordinate to Parliament, being creatures of Parliament and having no constitutional autonomy of their own. These examples seem to leave the theory of parliamentary sovereignty over finance intact: when the British Parliament determines so to do, it stands supreme in control of the public purse strings, able to fill and empty the purse at its own will.

The analogy with a purse, however, creates a false impression of the nature of parliamentary sovereignty over finance. Certainly, the House of Commons has considerable powers over taxation but so far as expenditure is concerned its powers are limited in two ways. It cannot alone determine the total amount of money expended by public bodies, for some have revenue-raising capacities of their own. And it cannot determine the details of how much of public money is spent, and on what objects. In periods of limited government or in periods such as the 1930s when expanded government functions were performed increasingly by central government departments, Parliament might expect to determine both the total amount and the direction of public expenditure. And it might expect, too, to be able to check up to ensure that public funds were actually expended as it had wished. That was the expectation, at least, of the reforms introduced by Gladstone when, setting up the Public Accounts Committee in the House of Commons, he hoped to 'close the circle of control'.[1] Today, however, the vastly expanded sphere of public activities and the loosely articulated structure of modern government together are bound to limit Parliament's capacity. Public expenditure represents a sizable proportion of the national wealth and much of it is expended by bodies and individuals remote from the House of Commons. The effect is that much of public spending is 'relatively uncontrollable' in any detailed manner by the House (see table 8.1).

The House has thus to work within the constraints imposed by the size, complexity, and structure of modern government. In order to appreciate how far Members of the House of Commons try, within these constraints, to control both the incoming and outgoing of revenue and expenditure it is convenient to consider their role as they themselves see it – that is, on an annual basis. The financial year does not correspond either to the calendar year or to the

Table 8.1 The limits of parliamentary control of public expenditure

Function	% Total public expenditure	Spender	Method of altering total spent^a	Audit machinery	Public Accounts Committee scrutiny
Social Security	31	Individual beneficiaries	No cash limits. Changes to rate structure and eligibility rules requires legislation.	NAO^b (on the administration only)	—
Health and Personal Social Services	13	Health authorities	Total is cash limited	NAO (on general management issues)	—
		Local authorities	Partially cash limited via rate support grant	Audit Commission	
Education and Science	11	Local authorities	Rate support grant	Audit Commission	—
		Universities and research councils	Cash limits	NAO	Yes
European Community,	12	European Community	Legislation	Court of Auditors	—
Northern Ireland, Scotland, Wales		Northern Ireland, Scotland, Wales	Cash limits (but see education, personal social services, etc.)	NAO	Yes
Defence	13	(1) Ministry of Defence	Cash limits	NAO (except firms)	Yes
		(2) Defence contractors			
Employment	3	Department and Manpower Services Commission	Cash limits	NAO	Yes
Home Office	4	Department and prisons, etc.	Cash limits	NAO	Yes
Department of Environment	5	(1) Department	Cash limits	NAO	Yes
		(2) Local authorities	—	Audit Commission	—
Foreign and Commonwealth Office	1	Department	Cash limits	NAO	Yes
Other	7	Various	—	—	—
Total	100				

Note: a Cash limits are set each year via estimates process.
  b National Audit Office.
Source: Figures derived from Public Expenditure White Paper, 1986.

parliamentary year and we could thus commence our examination of the cycle at any point, but we should begin, as Members of Parliament begin, at the start of the parliamentary year in the autumn (see table 8.2).

The first event of the annual parliamentary cycle comes shortly after Members return to Westminster from their long summer recess when they are confronted by the Chancellor's Autumn Statement. The Chancellor makes a verbal statement to the House introducing the document and, as a rule, the main debate on the statement takes place some weeks later when the Treasury and Civil Service Committee has produced its report. It is, of course, up to the opposition to decide to debate the statement earlier by making it the subject of one of their days, as they did in 1986. But any such early debate cannot be informed by the reasoned arguments of a select committee report.

The Autumn Statement is a relatively new procedure first formally used in 1982 when Sir Geoffrey Howe made it the forum for presentation of the economic forecast required by the Industry Act 1975. The Autumn Statement consists of three elements: the forecast of the economy; an outline of the government's expenditure plans for the coming year as agreed in Cabinet at the conclusion of the annual expenditure round; and details of changes to National Insurance rates and charges. These last will also generally have been the subject of a statement by the Secretary of State for Social Security.[2] The forecast for the economy taken together with the coming year's public expenditure total gives some indication of the likely room for tax changes in the Spring Budget. The public expenditure total for the coming year forms the basis on which the forthcoming supply estimates, now published at the time of the Budget, will be set. Since the House of Commons will not be able to consider the estimates until the Spring, after the new financial year has already begun, it must pass a 'vote on account' (comprising about 49 per cent of the total of current estimates) in December which will permit departments to continue spending until August, by which time the estimates will have been finally approved. The public expenditure total also sets the level for the rate support grant to local authorities and other items for which parliamentary approval is required during the coming year. The Autumn Statement, and the select committee report which analyses its contents, thus sets the scene for all the forthcoming detailed proposals on both spending and taxation.

Following publication of the statement, the Treasury and Civil Service Committee begins its inquiry so that it can publish its report prior to the debate on the statement which takes place in December. The timetable is tight but the committee tries to get its report published before the House debates the statement. In its 1984 report the committee commented:

> It is right and proper that the House should have the fullest opportunity to examine and discuss important pronouncements from the Government with the prior benefit of an informed Select Committee investigation. We therefore hope that the arrangements made this year can now be regarded as firmly established.[3]

The government, for its part, recognizes the role of the select committee.[4]

The committee generally hears evidence from the Chancellor of the Exchequer and Treasury civil servants. It also commissions alternative forecasts of the economy from teams of economists. In this way the Committee's report provides Members of the House with a basis for critical evaluation of the Treasury's figures. As well as considering the substantive material in the forecast the committee also comments from time to time on the mechanism for establishing the public expenditure totals in the statement. And the committee has also commented on the form of the Autumn Statement itself:

> In our view, the development of the Autumn Statement has been one of the most useful of the reforms which have been introduced in recent years. The document itself is widely acknowledged to be superior in form to its more elderly counterparts.[5]

The debate on the Autumn Statement tends, as do other financial debates, to be dominated by members or ex-members of the Treasury and Civil Service Committee. In their speeches they refer to the contents of the Committee's report, drawing attention to alternative interpretations of economic developments. But other speakers do not necessarily make much use of the committee's work. For example, as the 1987 general election approached the opposition parties concentrated their attack on the government's economic policy using whatever opportunities they could for debate. In the 1986 debate on the Autumn Statement it was noticeable that while the speeches of committee members made generous reference to the committee's

Table 8.2 Finance and the parliamentary timetable

		Committee	Floor of House	Legislation
November/December	*Autumn Statement* 1 Forecast of economy (required by Industry Act) 2 Survey of public expenditure for forthcoming year (result of annual PESC round) 3 Announcement of uprating of social security benefit and contribution rates to take effect the following April	TCSC	Debate (one day)	
December	*Vote on account* This permits Departments to spend between end of the current financial year on 31 March and August, by which time the Estimates will have been approved.	—	Vote (without debate)	Consolidated Fund Bill
December	*Winter supplementary estimates*	—	Vote (without debate)	Consolidated Fund Bill
February/March	*Public Expenditure White Paper* Surveys *all* public expenditure i.e. that covered by Supply Estimates and that, e.g. some local authority expenditure, which lies outside the Estimates. Shows expected figures for three years ahead.	TCSC	Debate (one day)	
March	*Spring supplementary estimates*	Various departmental committees	Vote (without debate or after short debates)	Consolidated Fund (No. 2) Bill

		PAC / TCSC	Vote / Debate	Consolidated Fund
March	Excess votes for previous financial year	PAC	Vote (without debate)	Consolidated Fund (No. 2) Bill
April	*Budget Statement* Survey of public revenue and expenditure and of the economy. Statement of tax changes to be introduced in forthcoming Finance Bill	TCSC	Debate (three to four days)	
April May–July	*Supply Estimates* (published with the Budget) *Legislation* 1 Annual supply estimates	Various departmental select committees. Usually on supplementary estimates only	Some debates (Three or four short debates)	Consolidated Fund (Appropriation Bill)
	2 Summer supplementaries and revised estimates			
	3 Finance Bill	Some parts go to standing committees for their committee stage[a]	Several days. Normal legislation procedure is followed	Finance Bill

a From time to time Select Committees have been established to consider proposals (at Green Paper Stage) for new tax legislation e.g. Select Committee on Corporation Tax (1971); Select Committee on Tax Credits (1972); Select Committee on Wealth Tax (1975). In recent years when Green Papers on taxation have been issued (e.g. Taxation of Husband and Wife, Reform of Domestic Rates) no Select Committee has been set up to study them.

report those of the main opposition speakers paid little attention to it, preferring instead their own 'political' focus. At about the same time as the Autumn Statement and the vote on account, the government presents Winter supplementary estimates to cover additional expenditure to be incurred in the current financial year. These are usually voted in blocks, without detailed scrutiny or debate.

The next major event in the annual expenditure process is the publication of the Public Expenditure White Paper, usually in January or February. While the Autumn Statement shows concisely the overall level of public expenditure for the coming year – in relation to the other economic indicators – the Public Expenditure White Paper is a bulky document in two volumes which shows in some detail the spending plans of the government for three years ahead. The White Paper shows all public expenditure including both that which will later appear in the form of departmental estimates and that which is the responsibility of local authorities. Following pressure from the House of Commons and its committees it now also includes statements of government aims and objectives and a considerable number of 'performance indicators'. Like the Autumn Statement, the Public Expenditure White Paper is always the subject of an inquiry by the Treasury and Civil Service Committee whose report is published prior to the debate on the floor of the House. Evidence is usually provided by the Chief Secretary to the Treasury, who is the minister responsible for co-ordinating the annual expenditure round and for the presentation of the White Paper, by Treasury civil servants, and by the Committee's team of outside specialist advisers.

Because the Treasury and Civil Service Committee and its predecessor, the General Sub-Committee of the Expenditure Committee, have now undertaken numerous successive inquiries into Public Expenditure White Papers they have developed a dialogue with the government. Through repeated recommendations and active pursuit of positive government responses they have had a substantial impact on the contents and presentation of the White Paper. The impact of the committee on the government was recognized by the Chief Secretary to the Treasury speaking in the White Paper debate on 18 February 1986, when he said: 'Treasury Ministers and officials have always appreciated in particular the recommendations on technical and presentational matters.'[6] These recommendations have ensured that the Public Expenditure White Paper now contains information on aims and objectives, on amounts to be spent, and on performance indicators, and also that it is clearly linked to the annual estimates which are published some weeks afterwards, at the same time as the Budget. In some senses the Public Expenditure White Paper can be regarded as one volume of the annual 'Budget' of the United Kingdom. But although parliamentary committees have kept up a steady stream of pressure on the government to present a 'unified Budget' each year,[7] the House still gets the Public Expenditure White Paper first and the Budget (containing taxation proposals) afterwards. The Treasury and Civil Service Committee has commented:

> The Survey [of MPs undertaken by Likierman and Vass] recommends that the Public Expenditure White Paper should no longer be produced as at present in early February or thereabouts, and that in effect the relevant material in Volume I should be included in the proposed new 'UK Budget' document and that most of the material in Volume II should be included in a comprehensive set of Departmental Reports. The first of these documents would appear on Budget Day and the second series shortly thereafter.[8]

So far, however, none of these recommendations have been adopted. The Treasury and Civil Service Committee has also pointed out that the period immediately preceding the Budget is perhaps not the best time for holding a debate on public expenditure in the House of Commons. Interest in the debate is limited: 'The debate is over-shadowed by the immediately impending Budget and is rarely a distinguished occasion in the parliamentary calendar.'[9] As in the case of the Autumn Statement, attendance is largely confined to the specialists. Peter Rees, commenting on the attendance at the 1986 White Paper debate said:

> It is disappointing to those of us who are in the Chamber this evening and who are concerned about, if not dedicated to public expenditure, that so few hon. Members attend these debates. That may be due to what they see as the aridity of the subject. They are wrong.[10]

The Treasury and Civil Service Committee would prefer that a separate public expenditure debate concentrating on future years and based on reports from select committees could be held in June. This recommendation has not yet found favour. It is difficult to see the departmental select committees willingly co-operating to produce comparable reports on their expenditure in time for a regular debate in June, although in the 1983–7 Parliament more of them undertook studies of expenditure on relevant programmes. The experience of several years work by the departmental select committees (other than the Treasury and Civil Service Committee which has always played its part) indicates that their work on the Public Expenditure White Paper is likely to remain subsidiary to their main 'policy' inquiries.[11]

Select committees have equally shown only intermittent interest in playing a part in the next stage in the parliamentary calendar on the expenditure side, scrutiny of the supply estimates. Following a long period during which the House of Commons took no detailed notice of the estimates and passed them simply 'on the nod', a new procedure was introduced in 1984 to enable some estimates to be debated on the floor of the House following detailed study of them by the relevant select committee. On the whole select committees seem to have preferred to examine supplementary estimates rather than parts of the main estimates because supplementary estimates are related to changes in policy or to mistakes which give the committees something 'political' to get their teeth into. The Treasury and Civil Service Committee has, for example, undertaken a number of inquiries into supplementary estimates for the Budget of the European Community. Its 1985 report on the subject provides a good example of the 'political' nature of many supplementaries.[12] Additional money was required so that the UK could make a contribution towards balancing the 1984 Budget of the Community (any money over and above the 'own resources' – see page 141 – has to be approved by Parliament). The government hoped to get the additional funds required through Parliament by laying an order under section 1(3) of the European Communities Act 1972 which would have the effect of declaring the intergovernmental agreement on the additional funds a Community Treaty, ancillary to the Treaty of Rome, thus in turn creating an obligation to make the appropriate payment. The sum needed would have been charged on the Consolidated Fund. However, because some uncertainty arose about the use of this procedure, an application for judicial review was made in the High Court. Although the government thought that its chosen procedure was appropriate for seeking Parliament's authority for the payment, they eventually decided to abandon the court case and instead use the road of supplementary estimate and Consolidated Fund bill. The long and interesting political history of this supplementary had obvious appeal for a select committee, many of whose members were not particularly keen on the European Community. It provides a good example of why supplementaries, rather than sections of the main estimates, appeal to select committees as subjects for inquiry and subsequent debate in the House.[13] It is notable, however, that floor debates on the estimates follow the familiar pattern of domination by the members of the relevant select committee whose report forms the subject of the debate.

The House of Commons has been successful in persuading the government to alter the form of the supply estimates. Following a number of select committee recommendations the form of the supply estimates and the form of the Public Expenditure White Paper have, from 1987, been more closely allied, so that MPs can now, if they wish, cross-refer between the two documents. The Public Expenditure White Paper is now presented on a departmental (rather than 'functional') basis enabling it to be linked to the departmental estimates. And the estimates give targets for the running costs of departments to provide a sort of second-tier cash-limits bringing together the estimates of pay and other general administrative costs.[14] The Treasury, introducing these changes, said: 'An important aim of better links is to enable select committees and others to view a department's estimates in the context of its chapter in the PEWP, which describes the aims and outputs of expenditure and sets out the medium term plans'.[15] The estimates therefore now come before Parliament in a format that focuses on the total cash provision sought for running costs in each vote. The new format means that MPs can now actually find out how much it costs to run schools, or higher and further education, or the agricultural advisory service.[16] Members of Parliament are no longer faced with a list of 'inputs' – salaries, lighting, accommodation – unrelated to the global figures for spending on functions set out in the White Paper. It is too early yet to say what use Members will make of these new facilities.

While the estimates are before the House, it will be very occupied considering the Finance Bill which authorizes tax changes announced by the Chancellor in March or April. The Chancellor's Budget Statement generally includes a conspectus of the economic situation; a brief summary of the public expenditure plans; and details of proposed taxation changes. The Treasury and Civil Service Committee undertakes a study of the Budget, completing the trilogy of annual reports on regular financial documents. But its Budget report does not concentrate on what might be thought to be the most characteristic items of the Budget, namely the taxation changes which are to occupy so much of the House's legislative time in the early Summer. The Treasury and Civil Service committee has always been hesitant about inquiring into tax policy, preferring its role as shadow of the Treasury as an economics ministry. So when the taxation proposals are brought before the House for detailed consideration, the House does not have at its disposal any detailed 'alternative' analysis from a select committee as it does for the main expenditure documents. On a few occasions in the 1970s, proposals for major tax reforms were given to select committees to examine but this pre-legislative stage has not been employed since 1975.[17]

The Budget Statement is debated by the House usually for four days. Budget debates are broad and wide-ranging. Often the speeches are on subjects hardly related at all to the details of the Chancellor's budget. Many Members take part in this debate for it is a 'political' occasion rather than a narrow 'technical' debate.

Shortly after the Budget debate the Finance Bill begins its long process through the House. It will generally include both changes to existing taxes and any new taxes that are proposed. Some very specialized taxes such as Petroleum Revenue Levy may be the subject of individual legislation.[18] The first major stage of the Finance Bill, its second reading, is often a continuation of the broad budget debate. Detailed examination of the proposed legislation takes place in committee, either of the whole House or in standing committee. Since 1967 the Finance Bill has been divided, with major policy clauses being taken in committee of the whole House and the detailed clauses taken upstairs in standing committee. The House was reluctant to make this change, in part because it was argued that taxation affects everyone and so all members should have an opportunity to take part in committee stage of Finance Bills. But the pressures of time made the move towards standing committee examination inevitable. Furthermore, while all Members may be interested in taxation as taxpayers in general, the number of them who really understand the complexities of the British tax system and are able to make a substantial contribution to the legislative process is very small.

Taxation is a good example of an area of policy which attracts a small, dedicated band of specialists and which repels the great majority of Members.

The annual cycle of expenditure and taxation procedures described above provides Members of the House of Commons with opportunities to scrutinize plans for future public expenditure; to participate in ensuring parliamentary authorization for the coming year's expenditure; to discuss the overall level of required revenue and the balance of different forms of taxation; and to grant legal authority for tax structures and rates. Parliament has also established procedures for *post hoc* scrutiny and control of money actually expended. This is the system designed by Gladstone in the 1860s to 'close the circle' of financial control. Parliament authorizes expenditures, departments (and today also many agencies or 'associated bodies') spend, and Parliament receives the accounts of departments so as to ensure the money has been spent as Parliament intended. In order to carry out this task Gladstone created the Exchequer and Audit Department under the Comptroller and Auditor General reporting to the Public Accounts Committee of the House of Commons. The lynchpin of the system is the accounting officer of each government department who is ultimately answerable to Parliament for money expended by the department or by its 'associated bodies' should they not have their own designated accounting officer.

During the 1970s Parliament turned its attention to the tasks performed by the Comptroller and Auditor General and to the relationship between him and his department on the one hand and parliament on the other, and found that relationship wanting. Through a series of select committee reports Parliament pointed out that the Comptroller and Auditor General was not really a servant of the House of Commons but more a creature of the Treasury; that several areas of public spending apparently escaped the full rigour of state audit – particularly nationalized industries; that the office of the Exchequer and Audit Department was understaffed and underqualified; and that it had begun to undertake efficiency and effectiveness audits but had no clear statutory authority so to do.[19] Gradually the dissatisfaction built up a head of steam until in 1983 Mr Norman St John Stevas, winning the ballot for private Members' bills, introduced the Parliamentary Control of Expenditure (Reform) Bill which became the National Audit Act 1983.

From 1983, therefore, there have been some changes. (1) The Comptroller and Auditor General is an officer of the House of Commons appointed by the House and responsible to it. (2) The Exchequer and Audit Department comprising civil servants has been replaced by the National Audit Office with its own staff (who are not civil servants), and the Budget of the National Audit Office is controlled by a House of Commons Commission. (3) The National Audit Office reports direct to Parliament. The House of Commons was not, however, successful in widening the scope of the new National Audit Office so that it could follow public money wherever it was spent. The National Audit Office is not able to examine the books of either the local authorities or the nationalized industries.

The advent of a National Audit Office has had little impact on the way in which the House scrutinizes expenditure. The Public Accounts Committee acts much as it has always done. It still consists of fifteen members and has no sub-committees. Thus its capacity for work is limited. Although it has, unlike other select committees, the advantage of the support of the National Audit Office staff, it cannot itself look at much of that office's output in any great depth. Furthermore, its questioning of witnesses is not always as rigorous as it might be. Members have neither the skills nor the inclination to probe deeply into the management of the public services except when there are obvious horror stories of incompetence and mismanagement. Nevertheless, in spite of its limitations of scope and capacity the value of the Public Accounts Committee is enormous, for it throws the light of publicity on the actions of those who have the responsibility for spending public money. Permanent secretaries, as departmental accounting officers, know that in the last resort Parliament can call them to account, through the Public Accounts Committee, for anything within the scope of their department's estimates. The threat exercised by the Public Accounts Committee remains even if its capacity to turn on the spotlight is limited and the spotlight is sometimes rather weak. The work of this committee is further considered in chapter 10.

Parliament has certainly altered many of its procedures and sharpened up its capacity to oversee and examine public expenditure and taxation over the past ten years. Yet the results remain disappointing. The generality of MPs remain uninterested in the planning and management of public expenditure and bemused by the complexities of tax legislation. These subjects are too technical and not overtly political enough to encourage most MPs to take a closer look. On the expenditure side the annual debates on the White Paper still attract little attention and cause few hearts to beat faster. Departmental select committees, apart from the Treasury and Civil Service Committee and the Public Accounts Committee, regard their financial scrutiny duties as a chore ancillary to their main political purposes.[20] On the taxation side the House still lacks adequate procedures for considering the details of proposed legislation at an early stage and the debates on the Finance Bill are dominated by a handful of experts.

The general lack of interest evinced by Members of Parliament in detailed financial scrutiny should not be too surprising. It is but an example of how Members of Parliament practice division of labour and specialization in their activities. Although financial matters may seem on the surface to have an appeal to every single member, they are regarded, as are other policy areas, as proper matters for specialization. The House of Commons is not a homogeneous body with all members performing exactly the same roles. It is better understood as a society composed of many sub-groups of which the members of the Treasury and Civil Service Committee, the members of the Public Accounts Committee, and a few well-known 'opinion leaders' or experts on taxation are the three most significant when it comes to the question of public money. For the majority of MPs public expenditure is only interesting when it concerns projects dear to their hearts and to the pockets of their constituents. They feel much the same way about taxation, disliking it in general, and willing to display interest mainly when pressing the claims of interest groups for exemptions and reductions. The great majority of members leave the stage of the House of Commons when financial matters are the subject of debate. The show has been kept going over the past twenty years by a small number of principal actors. There seems little likelihood of change in this pattern of behaviour. What it means, however, for the capacity of the House to control public expenditure, is that a third strain is added to those imposed by the size of the public sector and the poor articulation of the delivery service. The House of Commons could only make better use of its procedures for control of expenditure and taxation if more of its members decided that they would like to play a part. But most would concur with the view expressed by Tim Eggar who, speaking of Parliament's role in ensuring better management in government, said:

> It is important that Parliament itself should be involved in monitoring efficiency and effectiveness. There should be an obligation on each Department to submit an annual standardised report to its relevant Select Committee. That would stress both to Ministers and Civil Servants the importance that Parliament places on good managers. . . . If we can keep up the pressure for a few more years, there will be no need for Ministerial involvement and very little need for Parliamentary involvement.[21]

Regular, permanent, and detailed control over public money is not, as far as most MPs are concerned, the centrepiece of their job. They embody the doctrine of John Stuart Mill that the proper duty of a numerous assembly is not to administer but to take means to ensure that administration is well done by those public servants whose job it is. And most of them are generally happy to leave this task to a small body of 'experts'.

Chapter Nine

DEPARTMENTAL SELECT COMMITTEES

NEVIL JOHNSON

The House's reliance on a select committee system is of long standing, but the addition to it of the departmentally-related select committees in 1979 can now be seen as a major, successful, Parliamentary reform. (*First Report from the Liaison Committee, 1984–85*, 'The Select Committee System, para. 1)

THE REFORMS OF 1979: A TURNING POINT

It is in the judicious but confident terms quoted above that the Liaison Committee, the parliamentary body now responsible for the general oversight of the select committees of the Commons, opened its 1985 report surveying in detail the work of select committees.[1] The Liaison Committee felt able to look back with satisfaction on the activities of the new range of select committees set up in 1979 and to report that the systematization of departmental scrutiny then agreed on had begun to work out well. Much of this chapter is concerned with evaluation of this claim. So it is worth saying right at the beginning that its conclusions will generally endorse the Liaison Committee's assessment of the reforms. Whilst they have turned out to be neither radical in operation nor revolutionary in their effects, they have demonstrated once again the capacity of the House of Commons to adapt its procedures and organization to changing circumstances and demands. Equally they have shown that in an institution deeply conscious of its history change can be successfully reconciled with continuity.

The geography of select committees underwent a radical change in 1979. Before then there was variety and experiment, resulting in a somewhat randomly constructed collection of select committees exercising a range of investigative functions. All this (on which a few further remarks will be made in the next section) could hardly be called a 'system'. The reforms introduced in 1979 changed the map and appear to have given to the select committees of the House of Commons contours likely to endure for a long time to come. There is now a well established system of departmentally related select committtees, fourteen when up to full complement,[2] and covering all important departments of state with the single exception of the Lord Chancellor's Department.[3] Since 1983 the committees have had eleven members each, except in one case (Scottish Affairs) which had until 1987 thirteen, all have the same remit, and all enjoy basically the same powers.[4] They are charged with examination of 'the expenditure, administration and policy of the principal government departments . . . and associated bodies',[5] but each is free to determine how best to interpret that remit and to report to the House. The departmental select committees, in contrast with most of their predecessors, are anchored in Standing Orders and their members enjoy security of tenure for the duration of a Parliament. Similarly, in contrast with most earlier select committees, appointment of members to the departmental select committees has been removed from the untrammelled discretion of the party whips and entrusted to the Committee of Selection. Though the views of the party whips are unlikely to be entirely disregarded in the Committee of Selection, this arrangement means that the new select committees as well as some longer established committees have been given a qualified independence from the influence of party and government. This factor, taken in combination with the procedural freedom possessed by all select committees, enables them to operate with considerable autonomy, for example in deciding what subjects to investigate, how to set about such work, and how to present the results to the House. Naturally, this autonomy is in practice qualified by many constraints, some of which will be considered later. Nevertheless, when introducing the subject of the new departmental committees, it is appropriate to stress their individuality and independence: they are microcosms of the backbenches of the Commons and entitled, within the conventions governing select committees, to proceed as they see fit.

Such in outline is the system of select committees for scrutiny that now exists. Alongside the new pattern of investigative committees there remains, however, a range of other select committees. Some deal with domestic affairs of the House and with procedural question, and we shall not be concerned with them. Occasionally a select committee is used for hearings on bills, and again this is a use of the method of select committee inquiry which will not be examined here.[6] But in addition there are a few select committees which investigate and scrutinize executive activity and proposals, notably the Committee of Public Accounts, the Select Committee on the Parliamentary Commissioner for Administration, and the European Legislation Committee.[7] These three are survivors from the years before 1979, and indeed the Public Accounts Committee founded in 1861) is the most venerable of all investigative select committees.

These scrutiny committees are distinguished from the departmental select committees by the more specific tasks of scrutiny entrusted to them and by the fact that all enjoy more substantial staff support than other select committees. These older committees are considered by St. John Bates in chapter 10. Table 9.1 provides some basic information about the full range of investigative select committees in operation at the end of the 1983–7 Parliament.

The Liaison Committee should also be described in this introductory outline of the present system of select committees. It is essentially a supervisory committee of chairmen, charged with oversight of the select committee system and with advising as requested the House of Commons Commission, a body set up in 1979 to oversee the overall staffing of the House and to control the budget. The Liaison Committee has carried out its tasks unobtrusively, but effectively. It has been responsible for the allocation of funds to the committees for travel (an invidious task which it accepted reluctantly), it has raised general issues affecting the work and proceedings of all the investigative select committees, and has twice presented reports surveying the progress of the new system and offering recommendations for its improvement. These have given committee chairmen the chance to report on their committees' work and have provided well-organized and informative surveys of the achievements of the system seen from the viewpoint of the participants.

Table 9.1 Select committees of scrutiny: factual summary for the 1985–6 session

Name of committee	Number of members	Number of meetings	% attendance of members	Number of UK visits	Number of overseas visits	Number of reports and special reports	Expenses incurred[c] £	Printing Costs[d] £
Agriculture	11	25	68	2	2	1+1	25,461	77,023
Defence	11	63	84.6	5	4	4+3	70,484	102,094
Education, Science and Arts	11	43	64	3	1	3	29,254	81,922
Employment	11	28	72	6	1	3	19,301	69,040
Energy	11	33	65	7	2	6	34,322	99,480
Environment	11	36	67	5	—	5+2	58,298	132,637
European Legislation	16	30	65	—	—	31[a]	62,586	84,615
Foreign Affairs	11	57	66.6	—	1	6	17,713	133,737
Home Affairs	11	16	73	6	2	3+1	29,687	31,236
– Race Relations Sub-Committee	5	15	81	2	—	2[b]	14,069	51,267
Parliamentary Commissioner for Administration	9	15	50	1	—	4	10,654	36,033

Public Accounts	15	46	57	—	—	52	26,217	24,943
Scottish Affairs	13	16	61.5	3	—	—	11,339	48,513
Social Services	11	32	63.9	10	1	2+4	20,600	86,433
Trade and Industry	11	46	68.8	?	?	2	43,363	99,232
Transport	11	33	70	11	1	4+3	22,383	170,227
Treasury and Civil Service	11	36	68.4	3	1	7+2	47,912	84,486
– Civil Service Sub-Committee	5	12	81.6	—	—	1 (b)	8,235	80,749
Welsh Affairs	11	18	56	3	1	1	19,157	54,175

Notes: (i) This list excludes the Statutory Instruments Committee and the Joint Committee on Statutory Instruments which both have the same House of Commons membership of 7, though operating separately. The former met 24 and the latter 34 times in 1985–6.

(ii) In the past a Special Report nearly always contained the Government's reply to a select committee report. This is still often the case, but by no means invariably: for example, the 2 Special Reports from the Environment Committee are follow-up reports by the committee.

(iii) The financial information in the two final columns is indicative only: it takes no account, for example, of House of Commons staff costs, of the cost to the Civil Service etc.

a In addition one volume of Minutes of Evidence on the 1987 Community Budget.

b Also included in figures for the main committee.

c Expenses incurred comprise costs of all visits, fees and expenses for specialist advisers and expenses of preparation for publication of evidence.

d In the case of the printing costs for two sub-commitees these are additional to those recorded for the main committees.

Source: All figures have been taken from the Return for Session 1985–6, HC 172, February 1987.

THE YEARS OF EXPERIMENT: THE BACKGROUND TO THE NEW SELECT COMMITTEES

The focus here is on select committees as they are now. Accordingly, it is not proposed to offer extensive comments on the select committee world as it was before 1979.[8] But a few comments have to be made on the years of experiment, since it was the experience of that period which did much to shape the system of select committees now in place.

It was in the mid-1960s that the idea of parliamentary reform through the extension of select committee scrutiny began to be widely and actively propagated. The years between 1966 and 1979 were then marked by successive attempts to extend and develop the use of investigative select committees of the House. The experiments which took place were certainly in some degree a response to this call for reform, often and vigorously expressed by some members of the Select Committee on Procedure. But what was done did not in the event closely reflect abstract ideas or any fixed plan for select committee development. To a far greater extent it expressed the opportunistic response of governments (and notably that of Mr Wilson from 1966 to 1970) to the mood in favour of reform. Governments became willing to see experiments with select committees, but they had their own political priorities and pursued other aims too, for example to secure a more effective method of dealing with the Finance Bill (in 1967–8) or to accelerate the handling of public bills (in 1976–8). This mixture of motives explains the rather haphazard approach to select committees: a few departmental committees and a few subject committees were set up between 1966 and 1969, most of which did not survive long. Then came other committees for specific purposes such as that for the Parliamentary Commissioner for Administration (1967) and for European Secondary Legislation (1974).

Following a Procedure Committee report in 1969[9] the Conservative government formed by Mr Heath in 1970 did attempt a change which pointed to something more systematic. It accepted the recommendation for an Expenditure Committee, modelled to some extent on the post-1945 Estimates Committee, but having rather wider terms of reference. The outcome was an experiment involving a degree of internal specialization through half a dozen sub-committees loosely related to departments. This model was to influence the Procedure

Committee's recommendations in 1978 for a more extensive and systematic range of departmentally related committees of general scrutiny. But if the Expenditure Committee represented a certain kind of rationalization and a step towards the system now in operation,[10] it co-existed throughout the 1970s with several other committees organized and maintained on different principles. There were one or two subject committees, there was a Nationalised Industries Committee which worked 'across the board', and there were committees with specific tasks related to on-going administrative scrutiny by public officials like the Comptroller and Auditor General. It was this rather luxuriant growth of select committee work that the Procedure Committee subjected to thorough review in 1976–8.

The Procedure Committee of those years was charged with examining the practice and procedure of the House in relation to public business, and representatives of the government, notably in the person of Mr E. Short, then leader of the House, made it clear that what they were after were improvements in the despatch of government business. However, the committee chose instead to give most prominence to proposals for what it commended as 'a rational and effective committee system', making it clear that it did not see its task as

> making the job of Government more comfortable, or the life of the back bencher more bearable, but [with the aim] of enabling the House as a whole to exercise effective control and stewardship over Ministers and the expanding bureaucracy of the modern state for which they are answerable.[11]

The committee was probably inclined to take this line because several of its members were firm supporters of select committee development, and even strong sceptics like Mr Enoch Powell were by this time ready to moderate their root-and-branch opposition.[12] It is also evident, however, that in the party political conditions of the later 1970s, with no single party majority in the House, the committee saw little point in coming out with schemes for strengthening government control of business and accelerating the passage of legislation. Such proposals would have sounded unrealistic and run into strong and diverse opposition. In contrast, the vigorous plea for a rationalization of the select committee experience of the preceding dozen years or so appeared likely to win widespread support.

The committee's efforts in this matter were quickly blessed with success. A Labour government guided on procedural matters by Mr Michael Foot hesitated to act and then tottered to defeat in Parliament and at the polls in the spring of 1979. With remarkable speed the new Conservative government decided to accept the main features of the Procedure Committee's scheme and commended the proposed establishment of a full range of departmental committees to the House in June 1979. As a result by January 1980 fourteen select committees[13] had been appointed and were ready to start work. These changes brought with them the disappearance of several committees, notably those on nationalized industries and on science and technology, although the work of two other committess – on race relations and immigration and on overseas development – was to be continued by sub-committees of the Home and Foreign Affairs committees respectively. In addition, of course, the Expenditure Committee vanished. In this way the system with which observers of Parliament are now familiar was put in place.

When considering the circumstances in which it became possible to conclude a period of experiment and on its foundations establish a coherent and reasonably comprehensive pattern of select committee scrutiny, it is necessary to take account of the political conditions then prevailing. What we might call 'the reform epoch' in relation to the methods and structures of the House of Commons was marked by a steady weakening of governments and growing restiveness on the part of Members of the House. Despite a substantial majority gained in 1966 by Mr Wilson and an adequate majority enjoyed by Mr Heath after 1970, the governments of both prime ministers showed serious weaknesses. Certainly if we compare their record with that of earlier post-1945 governments, there can be little doubt that their ability to maintain support both in the country and in the Commons was less, and one consequence of this was a reduced capacity to sustain their policies in the face of opposition from strategically placed groups or bodies of opinion. Then, after the first election of 1974, it appeared that the familiar two-party alignment might be breaking down. Though the attempt was made by two Labour governments between 1974 and 1979 to play the part of a majority administration, in reality they had no effective capacity to put their policies through Parliament.

It is not surprising that these circumstances were conducive to support for parliamentary reform through select committees. After all, governments were weaker, and it appeared probable that such conditions might persist. Whilst there was no general disposition amongst politicians to follow the American Congress into the illusion that the legislative branch might substitute for the executive in the government of the country, the conditions were propitious for effecting changes which at least would symbolize a renewal of parliamentary authority, give shape and system to developments already in train, and appear to offer to an increasingly professionalized political class more and better career opportunities.

Yet with hindsight it can be seen that there is an irony in the consummation of the campaign for reform achieved in 1979–80. Party political conditions were about to return to something much more like those of the early post-war years than of the 1970s. It is true that the enforcement of strict party discipline has become more difficult in all parties, and that as a result even Mrs Thatcher's governments have had to listen to backbench opinion in the Conservative Party, to tolerate inconvenient and sometimes carping criticism from dissenters, and on occasion to make substantial concessions on matters of policy. Nevertheless, despite all this, the governments headed by Mrs Thatcher since 1979 cannot be regarded as anything other than 'strong' in the traditional sense. They have been headed by a determined and even imperious party leader with a firmly conservative view of the British parliamentary constitution. Her concern has been to pursue a wide range of substantive policy objectives, many of them involving radical economic and social change. To this end she has used the traditional institutions in the traditional way, governing effectively and sometimes dramatically through Parliament. This traditional version of parliamentary government assumes that the executive will shoulder its responsibilities before the Commons, providing leadership whilst still remaining responsive to Parliament's critical reactions. It is not a version of parliamentary government which allows that Parliament should share in policy-making or advance claims to be an equal partner in the business of government. It is a view of the constitution which can accommodate strengthened select committees as critical organs of the House, but it has no place for committees with pretensions to the status of parallel governments.

As we shall see below, the successful consolidation of the new select committees owes much to their members' realistic appreciation of these overarching conditions. They have recognized the shift in party relations and in the style of executive leadership which began to take shape after 1979. They have acknowledged that they should seek success by respecting the limits inherent in a more traditional view of the constitution than that which was becoming fashionable in the 1970s and which for a few more years still was to charm those with visions of 'breaking the mould' of British political life.

THE NEW SYSTEM IN OPERATION

The experience of the departmental select committees now covers two Parliaments, those of 1979–83 and 1983–7. Fortunately, a comprehensive and detailed analysis of the operations of the select committees in the three and half years following their establishment already exists, in *The New Select Committees: a Study of the 1979 Reforms*,[14] and this provides much of the evidence for the general judgements offered here. Within the limits of a short essay it is clearly not practicable to carry forward the kind of detailed description of the work of individual committees which is to be found in this work. However, study of the Liaison Committee's reports of 1982 and 1985[15] as well as consideration of the reports and published evidence of the committees, suggest that in the 1983–7 Parliament no substantial changes took place in the pattern and methods of the departmental select committees. Some gained more self-confidence and probed more aggressively into government affairs, whilst one or two ran into problems and appeared to have little impact. But overall the system was certainly consolidated and by 1987 it had become virtually inconceivable that either the government or any substantial body of opinion in the House would seriously consider major interference with the select committee structure, still less its abolition. Instead, the system received something like a benediction from the government when the Lord Privy Seal and Leader of the House wrote early in 1986 to the chairman of the Liaison Committee saying 'I am sure that there is widespread support for the view expressed in the report that the new Departmentally-related select committees set up in 1979 have now established themselves as a major, successful Parliamentary reform.'[16]

In this evaluation of the system in operation we must start by considering what generalizations can be made about a pattern of select committees in which there is internally great diversity. First, there can be no doubt that the range of scrutiny has been significantly widened. Reporting in April 1985 the Liaison Committee referred to

275 reports produced by the new committees since 1979. More vivid is a scrutiny of the sessional returns for select committees. For example, the return for the 1985–6 session shows that the Foreign Affairs Committee published six reports, several of them very substantial in scale, the Treasury and Civil Service Committee seven reports, the Environment Committee five, and the Energy Committee six. At the other end of the scale the Agriculture Committee published only one report (plus one special report containing a government reply to an earlier report), whilst Scottish Affairs managed two[17]. It is, however, not just a question of more investigations and reports. More important is the fact that the committees are permanent, are necessarily accepted by the departments as regular interlocutors, and can to some extent build on their accumulated experience of the sector of government entrusted to them. All this helps to ensure that the House of Commons, ministers, and the departments all see the committees as regular elements in the processes of discussion, debate, and exchange of information through which public decisions are implemented. As a result organs of the House are latched on to the work of the executive in a more secure fashion than previously.

Secondly, the system has operated to strengthen the sense of accountability to Parliament on the part of the executive, and indeed has added a new dimension to the traditional procedures on the floor of the House for asserting the accountability of government. It is, however, necessary to express this claim in cautious and qualified terms. It is not a matter of government departments going in fear and trembling of parliamentary committees since 1979. It is rather that the government now accepts that for each major sector of public activity there is a select committee that can, if so minded, carry out on a continuing basis a systematic, though selective, examination of what is being done. Such scrutiny is certain to embrace policy and may, of course, extend to financial aspects and to administrative methods if the committee so wishes. Government departments know that they must co-operate to a reasonable degree in such efforts to scrutinize their affairs, and this means that they have to make a serious attempt both to inform and to explain. In addition, however, the government knows that select committees are not confined to such medium or longer-term aspects of public policy. They can also choose to react quickly to issues of current interest and controversy and by so doing subject ministers and their officials to an immediate need to justify what has been done or is proposed. In this way inquisition in committee will supplement interrogation on the floor of the House.

The movement between these two types of inquiry – the policy and administration inquiry and the attempt to assert ministerial accountability for specific decisions – is illustrated by the work programmes of many committees. In 1983–4, for example, the Defence Committee reported on the statement on the defence estimates 1984 (HC 436, 1983–4), on the physical security of military installations in the United Kingdom (HC 397–I and II), and on Ministry of Defence reorganization (HC 584, 1983–4). In 1985–6, however, apart from the regular consideration of defence estimates, it spent most of its time on the fate of Westland plc, reporting on the defence implications of the future of Westland (two volumes, HC 518 and HC 169, 1985–6), and then more controversially still on *Westland plc: The Government's Decision-making* (HC 519, 1985–6). There is no doubt that in these instances the committee was trying to pin the government down in relation to decisions and events which had attracted much comment and criticism, and indeed for a short time had put a question mark over the government's capacity to survive. Moreover, in this case the pressures of accountability were applied both to ministers and to the most senior officials concerned. Nor was the Defence Committee alone in getting in on the Westland affair: the Trade and Industry Committee also did so, examining in 1986 the sponsoring role of the Department of Trade and Industry in relation to Westland plc. A report finally appeared early in 1987 with lengthy evidence.

Thirdly, the committees have for the most part recognized that partisan politics have as a rule got to be held in check if they are to achieve anything. This is apparent at virtually every stage of their work: in the choice of topics for inquiry, in the conduct of inquiries by chairmen, in the efforts normally made to allow all members a fair share of questioning (provided they want it), in the deliberative sessions when draft reports are discussed and finally voted on, and more generally in the style and tone which committee members seek to maintain before the public. All this is not to say that party commitments are laid on one side, that party feelings never find expression, or that there is no disagreement about the conclusions to be drawn from particular inquiries. Naturally such arguments and differences of opinion do occur, and are then usually resolved by a vote as the minutes of proceedings of select committees often show.

But disputes within committees are restrained by the presence of government majorities and by the realization that the very effort of inquiry itself is likely to be unproductive and perhaps nugatory if members focus chiefly on their disagreements rather than on those matters on which they can agree and, therefore, report to the House.[18] In the readiness to moderate partisan commitments the departmental committees conform fully to long-established traditions of select committee behaviour. And in so doing they both impose limits on the extent and quality of the changes which they can effect in the working of the House of Commons and in the relations between the Chamber and the Government, and at the same time lay the basis of their own consolidation and powers of persuasion. It is all a far cry from changes once heralded by Mr St John Stevas, the leader of the House who had a decisive influence on the establishment of the new system, as 'revolutionary'.

Fourthly, the new committees have as a rule gained a satisfactory degree of co-operation from the government, and this embraces both ministers and officials. The quantity of evidence offered to committees, oral and written, remains impressive, and there is no doubt that departments – and this means officials at very senior levels – go to considerable trouble when preparing themselves for appearances before the committees. Ministers too have normally been very willing to appear before committees, though one or two senior ministers have found it an irksome and time-consuming task. Occasionally things have gone wrong in the relations between committees and departments, and the government has refused requests they have made. The Defence Committee's desire in 1986 to interview the officials who acted directly on behalf of ministers in the Westland affair ran into an insistence on confining the committee to officials who were the hierarchical superiors of those the committee wanted to see. This meant that Sir Robert Armstrong, the Cabinet Secretary, had to put on two of his virtuoso performances,[19] though whether he convinced the committee is uncertain. Disagreement on the availability of witnesses and on what information can be given to a committee arises usually when the subject of inquiry is a matter of current controversy and dispute – the Westland affair just quoted, for example, or the banning of trade unions at GCHQ, the government intelligence agency, in 1984. Such difficulties are far less likely to occur when a broader and longer-term aspect of public policy and administration is under review, though in the earlier years of the departmental select committees there was sometimes reluctance to provide documents prepared for planning purposes.

Fifthly, and this will be the last general comment before we turn to a number of more specific features of the operation of the committee system, the committees can plausibly be regarded as making a contribution to the desire felt by many backbenchers to specialize in particular areas of government activity and to demonstrate their own professionalism. Evidence for this view is to be found in the relatively low rate of turnover on most committees and in the frequency of levels of attendance at meetings in excess of 65 per cent. It is also known that the Selection Committee has in each Parliament so far had more candidates for membership of committees than there are places to fill. There are also signs that select committee membership is particularly attractive to new and younger members of the House, especially in the Conservative Party. Moreover, it must be remembered that in 1985–6 307 Members served on select committees, 195 of them on departmental committees. These figures[20] alone illustrate the extent to which Members are now drawn into select committee work: the best part of two-fifths of the 'available' backbenchers are so engaged. This is not to suggest that select committee service has become the dominant preoccupation of many members, and indeed it is quite clear that this is not so. But it does now constitute for a significant part of the House an element in a complex and varied pattern of political activity to which most MPs are committed full-time. Select committee service has for the young and ambitious become a useful staging post in 'career development', though so far there is little evidence that it regularly leads to ministerial decks.[21] And at the other end of the seniority scale there are still those middle-aged and experienced members, some of whom have held middle-rank ministerial office and whose judgement carries weight in the House and in their parties. Such people still secure many of the committee chairmanships and do much to keep the committees on an even keel. 'Professionalism' in the House of Commons necessarily includes an instinctive grasp of the habits and reactions of those who make the institution work.

STAFFING: THE ROLE OF CLERKS AND SPECIAL ADVISERS

In the years when parliamentary reform was a cause dear to many hearts a familiar call was for more and better qualified staff for select committees. If such committees were to be the House's principal instrument for the investigation and scrutiny of executive action, then clearly, so it was argued, they must have effective support in carrying out their work. Moreover, the committees have an informative function: they collect large amounts of evidence (much of which is published) and need skilled assistance in evaluating it. Such arguments pointed towards an increase in staffing and perhaps towards the introduction of people from outside the Department of the Clerk to bring specialized knowledge and experience to the task of assisting committees in their inquiries.

Only to a very limited extent have such ideas proved practicable or even attractive to members. Undoubtedly the workload of the new select committees has been heavy since they are, after all, small bodies trying to produce annually several more or less substantial reports. But the burden of work has been dealt with principally by reliance on the well-tried servicing of select committees by clerks of the House and their assistants. There has been a modest increase in the establishment of the Committee Office, so that by 1986 the majority of departmental committees were serviced by a senior committee clerk, assisted by three or four other staff. But in some instances the establishment was a shade larger (Treasury and Civil Service had in addition to the clerk a staff of five), whilst in others it was smaller (a clerk and two others for Agriculture and for Welsh Affairs, for example). A handful of committees have also engaged temporary committee assistants who work full-time and bring an element of specialization to the staffing arrangements. Differences in the scale of staffing reflect in some degree conclusions about the breadth of a committee's remit and the amount of investigation it is likely to undertake.

Alongside the full-time staff, nearly all of whom mirror in their qualifications, mode of recruitment, and pay and conditions the generalist grades of the Civil Service, there are specialist advisers, a form of support introduced at Westminster well before 1979. The numbers per committee vary enormously. For example, Agriculture listed three in 1985–6, Energy eight, Foreign Affairs six, Social Services thirteen, Treasury and Civil Service ten. However, these figures have to be treated with caution, since to be listed as a specialist adviser is not necessarily proof that the person concerned actually did work for a committee in the year to which the return refers. In many cases committees engage a specialist adviser and then keep him or her on the list even though the adviser may not be called upon for assistance. Committees vary in the significance they attach to the support of specialist advisers. Those, like the Energy Committee, with difficult technical problems to handle tend to draw substantially on the work of their specialist advisers, others, like Home Affairs or Social Services, dealing with subjects on which every layman tends to think that he knows the answers, expect less from such advisers. And there is too the rather exceptional case of the Treasury and Civil Service Committee which has shown a predilection for pitting (albeit indirectly) its economists against those of the Treasury in its annual reviews of economic policy, public expenditure, and budgetary proposals. On the whole, however, specialist advisers now generally perform only an ancillary role, offering technical advice to their committees when this is required, assessing evidence as it is submitted, and providing often substantial assistance when the stage of preparing the guidelines of a report has been reached. The small amounts spent on the remuneration of specialist advisers, usually no more than a few thousand pounds by each committee per year, testifes to their limited role. The main burden of managing a committee's affairs, providing policy advice, and above all giving shape to a report which by reflecting the spread of opinions in the committee is also likely to gain its approval does, therefore, rest on the clerk and his or her assistants. Indeed, in some cases there can be little doubt that the clerks make sure that 'experts are on tap, but not on top', carefully maintaining their own position as the channel of communication with the chairman and the focal point for members seeking guidance and briefing. And, of course, it is the clerks who possess the drafting skills.

The staffing of select committees has, therefore, settled down into familiar patterns. No longer do we hear of aspirations to imitate, if only in a very qualified way, the staffing enjoyed by Congressional committees. Nor do we hear much of the need for committees to develop their own bureaucratic resources to enable them to challenge the departments of state on terms nearer to equality. Instead, we find that the administrative backing for committees closely follows principles long established in the Civil Service, and that the relationship between a committee and its permanent staff is very like that between a minister and his officials, or perhaps we should say between a minister and his private office.

All this means that the committee staff must be sensitive to the style and methods of work of committee chairmen. These are important variables affecting the operation of committees. Some chairmen are active and keen to take initiatives, some prefer to develop a style of chairmanship emphasizing fairness and even detachment, and there are others whose main interest is in the appearance of thorough and well-supported reports. Again, some chairmen prefer rather formal relations with the staff, with witnesses and departments, and with specialist advisers, whilst others have an easier and more friendly approach. These as well as other differences in personal characteristics make for many variations in the way in which committees work and in the discretion enjoyed by their staffs. One safe generalization, however, is that a chairman will rarely invest a lot of his time in the actual drafting of a report: after all, his is a part-time position, it commands no remuneration, and there are many other demands on his time.

Three consequences of conditions just described are of some importance. First, the committees can count on and receive devoted service from their clerks, most of whom develop a considerable commitment to 'their committee'. Secondly, the scale and kind of administrative support enjoyed by committees is such that members who wish to make a contribution still have to do much of the work themselves, and especially chairmen. In other words, members have not so far been willing to become mouthpieces for those who brief them. Finally, it is of some importance for the informative function of committees that the reliance on generalist clerks encourages the maintenance of a fluent and non-technical style in the writing of reports. Most of them display admirable lucidity, and occasionally reveal a salty and even sardonic humour. A delightful example of the latter quality is the opening line of paragraph 130 of the Defence Committee's report on *Westland plc: The Government's Decision-making*: 'The effect of such a letter [from Mr Heseltine, the Defence Minister, to Lloyd's Bank on 3 January 1986] upon the Prime Minister and the Secretary of State for Trade and Industry can have been nothing short of incendiary.'

All in all, the staffing arrangements which have been achieved represent a balance of skills which satisfies most chairmen and members, providing that kind of support which is essential if the political requirements of select committee activity are to be fulfilled. Continuity in the habits of the House has been maintained.

THE CONDUCT OF INQUIRIES: COMMITTEES AND THEIR WITNESSES

For a long time earlier this century it was normal for select committees to concentrate their attention on civil servants in the departments: they were the people expected to provide whatever information was needed. During the past twenty years or so select committees have cast their nets more widely and nowadays regularly call on a wide range of witnesses other than civil servants. Nevertheless, it is the latter who are still in most cases the principal sources of information, at any rate when the subject of inquiry is the direct responsibility of a department of state. If it concerns a public body associated with a department, then it may well be that public employees not in the service of the Crown will be the principal witnesses.

Once a topic has been selected for inquiry the clerk will consider with the chairman what might be the best strategy to adopt in pursuing the investigation. Simultaneously thought will be given to likely sources of information and witnesses. If the topic is clearly within departmental responsibility the clerk will normally have contact with the relevant liaison officer in the department, usually an official of assistant-secretary rank, and from this will emerge suggestions about the most appropriate witnesses. In some instances the committee will know the responsible officials from previous experience, particularly at the top levels of permanent secretary and deputy secretary. Often the department will be asked to submit papers giving an introductory survey of the problem under investigation. This is particularly important for the large number of inquiries which start off as probing investigations, and without any sharp definition at the outset of the problems to be tackled or the direction to be pursued. These then serve as the basis for a more discriminating approach to the subject of inquiry as committee members begin to formulate their priorities and to discern the issues on which it is worth concentrating.

Select committees do now make substantial demands on ministers too. To some extent this is a consequence of the desire of committees to achieve more publicity and to convey the impression that they really are compelling members of the executive to explain their policies to them. But it is equally a logical consequence of the extension of committee remits to include the investigation of policy questions. For if it is policy that is being challenged, the constitutional principle of ministerial responsibility imposes limits on what a civil servant can and will say publicly in front of a select committee. His response is likely to be: 'that is a policy question and if you wish to pursue that you must ask the Minister to come along'. Furthermore, it is ministers, not civil servants, who are answerable to the House. This is why they appear frequently before committees, even though they have the right to refuse to do so. In this way they are acknowledging their accountability before new organs of the House which are often able to submit them to a far closer inquisition than the floor allows. So there has been a steady increase in ministerial appearances before committees which has sharpened the House's control of the political side of the executive.

To illustrate with examples, in 1985–6 the Defence Committee heard two Cabinet ministers on two occasions each, and one other minister once; Foreign Affairs summoned one Cabinet minister twice and two other ministers on two occasions; Treasury and Civil Service heard two Cabinet ministers (one on two occasions, one only once) and two other ministers. These committees are slightly above average in the demands they make on ministers: something like three ministerial appearances in all per session appears to be usual for most committees, occasionally less.

It is hard to resist the conclusion that the summoning of ministers has also become something of a matter of prestige for committees: they like the public attention it promises to secure for them. On the other hand the attention paid to ministers may not add all that much of substance to most inquiries. Ministers too are politicians, and almost by definition have rather more skill and experience in debate than the majority of backbenchers on select committees. So a confident minister can use an appearance before a select committee for his purposes too. Indeed, he may welcome such an appearance and even from time to time prompt it, reckoning to use the committee as a sounding board for gaining reactions to initiatives he wishes to take. And naturally, in this connection it is the members of his own party to whom the minister will pay most attention.

Committees do, in addition, range widely outside departments in the search for advice and witnesses. If the topic of an inquiry concerns an associated public body, then it will be in the firing line, usually in the person of its most senior official. Thus, for example, the chairman of the Manpower Services Commission has regularly appeared before the Employment Committee which annually examines MSC's Corporate Plan. Similarly, when the Education, Science and Arts Committee has inquired into the work of the research councils, it must look to their chairmen or secretaries, and the same applies to the Energy Committee when it tackles problems in the sphere of publicly-owned or -regulated industries like coal or gas.

In the case of associated bodies the committees are still closely concerned with public servants who generally have affinities with civil servants. But committees reach out more widely still. They often turn to pressure groups and a variety of private organizations closely involved in or affected by a particular public service or policy. Often enough the initiative here will come from the organized interests themselves: they hear of an inquiry and will want to put forward views. For some committees (such as Social Services, Environment, or Employment) local authorities and their associations may be important witnesses and there are many other public bodies not connected with the central government (such as universities, charitable foundations, voluntary bodies engaged in social welfare activities) which will from time to time be invited to assist a select committee through an appearance before it. Finally, committees often look to private individuals, people with specialized knowledge and experience, to assist them: this may mean inviting the submission of a paper, sometimes followed by a request to give oral evidence.

It is clear that outside the sphere of the departments the committees must rely very much on the contacts and experience of their clerks and, to some extent, of their specialist advisers. They have the responsibility of identifying sources of information and advice, and in so doing must try to achieve a certain balance of opinions acceptable to committee members. The sessional returns shows that many committees have called upon large numbers of witnesses outside the departmental sphere. For example, in 1985–6 Employment saw two ministers, four civil servants, nineteen other public officials, and sixty other witnesses, most of them not in public positions; Education, Science and the Arts saw two ministers, twenty-four civil servants, six other public officials, and eighty-one other witnesses; Agriculture saw no ministers, eleven civil servants, twenty-five officials from associated public bodies, one peer, and forty-three other witnesses. This high level of attention to non-official witnesses is also paralleled by the large number of memoranda from private persons received and usually published by many committees. It is again noticeable that for some committees these non-official sources are less significant: Defence saw in 1985–6 only thirteen non-official witnesses and Treasury and Civil Service called upon twenty-four.

Until about twenty years ago committees generally conducted all their proceedings at Westminster. This is no longer so, and most of them make visits in the UK and travel abroad too. Indeed, it is remarkable that even committees with strikingly domestic remits manage regularly to identify foreign parts with experience to offer relevant to their subjects of inquiry. At home visits may result in evidence being taken formally and then published in the usual way. Alternatively, such visits may be private, providing members with a chance to gain information informally.

By convention select committees are treated with some deference and the departmental committees are no exception in this regard. This tradition has helped to sustain amicable and co-operative relations between the majority of witnesses and organizations giving evidence on the one hand, and committees on the other. Indeed, it is remarkable how selfless many witnesses are, especially from outside the public service, investing time and effort in work for committees without receiving (or expecting) any payment in return.[22] With the official witnesses, and in particular the civil servants, relations are generally more formal and somewhat wary. Co-operation with select committees has been firmly encouraged by departments, but difficulties do arise. The demand on time, usually of senior officials, is often substantial. Thorough briefs must be written, both for committees and for those appearing before them, and then there is for some officials the strain of appearing in public before the committees. These pressures are for the most part cheerfully accepted, but do sometimes induce in officials a mood of irritation towards committees whose demands often interfere with work more closely related to the solution of practical problems.

More serious difficulties have arisen on account of the relationship of confidential trust between ministers and civil servants. Occasionally a committee has pressed for information or comments which the official has regarded as tempting him to break that trust. Alternatively, a committee has asked for a policy or political view from an official, or sought to find out what has occurred in the transactions between ministers or in Cabinet commitees. A *Memorandum of Guidance for Officials appearing before Select Committees* was reissued in 1980, and contains advice on how to deal with the kind of difficulties just referred to. Naturally, this has to some extent applied restrictions which committees do not like, though the Liaison Committee has recognized that these rules for officials are in general reasonable. In the course of 1986 events following on the Westland plc affair caused the government to issue supplementary advice[23] directed specifically against attempts by a select committee to examine and pass judgement on the conduct of individual officials. The accountability of officials to ministers was stressed and it was made clear that attempts by committees to pin down particular officials would be countered by the assertion of ministerial prerogative to send only a minister or a top-ranking civil servant to answer questions.

Incidents of this kind indicate how sensitive ministers still are about investigations by select committees which threaten to drive a wedge between them and their officials. Nor do civil servants look kindly on such efforts, since they too have an interest in the corporate cover afforded by membership of the Civil Service. Yet in the broad context of select committee work such restrictions on the choice of witnesses and the kind of information that can be provided are of little importance. Over much the greater part of the spectrum of select committee work the flow of information is uninhibited and the willingness of civil servants to help beyond question.

From inside the departments select committees are regarded for the most part with a moderate degree of respect. It is recognized that a favourable and helpful report can assist a department in the pursuit of its policies, and there is also acknowledgement of the fact that criticism may prompt overdue reappraisals of what is being done. Nevertheless, civil servants are all too aware of the limitations of committees: the lack of knowledge of most of their members, the tendency to start from the most elementary position familiar to and usually abandoned long ago by officials, the slow and time-consuming nature of their proceedings, the tendency of members to jump from one topic to another, the desire to gain a dash of publicity even at the expense of pursuing more serious and less glamorous issues. Awareness of such weaknesses induces a kind of amused condescension in some officials: they co-operate cheerfully enough, but they neither fear the committees nor expect all that much from them. Yet if this judgement sounds too cynical, it should be remembered that such attitudes and relationships may still be serving the interests of Parliament and, beyond that, of representative parliamentary government by facilitating links between MPs and the administration. We return to the idea of an explanatory dialogue between experts and representatives of the people in the concluding section.

WHAT COMMITTEES HAVE NOT ACHIEVED

Often very sweeping claims have been made on behalf of select committees and potentialities have been attributed to them which do not seem to have been realized. Here we will briefly consider a few ways in which committees have fallen short of the hopes of their protagonists.

All departmental committees are expected to consider the expenditure of the bodies in their field of oversight. Yet the effort invested in financial scrutinies has been modest and it would be an exaggeration to say that the new select committees have been powerful forces making for more accurate estimating, more efficient expenditure control, and more effective and economical use of resources. One difficulty is technical, that is to say the lack of correspondence between the departmental financial cycle and the parliamentary calendar. As a result committees have too little time for proper scrutiny of estimates, though the Liaison Committee has expressed itself as satisfied that even under these limitations useful scrutiny can be carried out. Indeed, that committee has gone so far as to assert that for the first time in half a century the House is carrying out its historic function of the scrutiny of expenditure on a systematic basis.[24] In reality, however, the concern with financial investigations varies from one committee to another. Some have regularly tried to look at corporate plans or expenditure statements, whilst others have made no such effort and may also have had no comparable financial material on which to work. Behind the relative neglect of finance lies the reluctance of most members to get deeply involved in what soon become complex technical problems. It is policy and specific acts of commission or omission that interest members, and financial scrutiny is usually remote from such matters. This explains why it is not a top priority for most committees. These questions are considered in more detail in chapter 8.

Select committees do, of course, report to the House of Commons and indeed, strictly speaking, this is all that they do. It might be assumed that the flow of reports from committees would excite interest in the House and that attention would be paid to them in the proceedings on the floor. But this happens only intermittently. Until recently there was no formal provision for considering select committee reports on the floor of the House, apart from the annual day devoted to reports of the Public Accounts Committee. In 1982 provision was made for three days to be given over to debates on estimates, the topics to be chosen by the Liaison Committee.[25] This has resulted in a significant increase in the attention paid to committee reports on specific financial issues, chiefly those suggesting misplaced or excessive expenditure. In this respect, even though much remains to be done to achieve comprehensive House of Commons scrutiny of finance, a system at least exists which facilitates detailed scrutiny of estimates and discussion on the floor of the House of matters then highlighted by committees.[26] But the bulk of reports on questions of policy and administration attract no attention on the floor of the House, or at best secure notice in oblique and indirect ways.[27] The reasons for this are first that it is the government that controls time, and it has no inclination to allow debates on select committee reports to interfere with its priorities. But secondly, and perhaps more decisive, is the fact that the addressees of reports are really the departments and it is from them and their ministers that responses are expected. In contrast the House is not directly affected by or interested in most select committee reports, and at best a small band of enthusiasts would turn up for debates on them. Thus the relative neglect of the select committees' findings is an expression of the ruling preoccupations of the House: the rationale of select committee work lies in the process of inquiry itself and in its impact on departments, and is not to be found in regular follow-up action by the House as a whole.

It is convenient to note at this stage that in one respect at least the new select committees have achieved a substantial improvement. This is in the speed with which departmental replies are furnished. The acknowledged aim now is to reply within two months and for the most part this has been achieved. Occasionally there are still delays, but in comparision with practice before 1979 the departments and associated bodies are responding promptly to the recommendations put to them. The forms of response do, however, vary greatly. Some come as a memorandum to the select committee which is then published as a special report; some are issued as command papers by the government; occasionally replies are now given in statements on the floor of the House. Whilst the early provision of government replies to reports is welcome, it should be noted that many recommendations are of a general and unspecific kind. It really does not then require much effort on the part of a department to reply that it shares the concern of the select committee and will continue to keep the problem under review.

It has sometimes been suggested that select committees would develop personalities of their own, becoming the focus of loyalties transcending party. They have also been seen as a new basis for a successful career in politics and as some kind of counter attraction to the lures of service on the front bench. But the committees have hardly moved in this direction or stimulated such developments. On the second aspect, that of committees as the focus of a career, the outcome is still decidedly negative: very few politicians would yet rate a committee chairmanship as in some sense equivalent to ministerial office, and for that reason a natural target of ambition. Nor does committee service yet appear to have become an important factor in preferment to office, and there is little to show that members actually prefer service on committees to real or even shadow office.[28] In other words, as in the past, select committee service remains something distinct and even detached from the other activities of members of the House. It is as politicians on the floor and in their parties that members still chiefly hope to make their careers.

In relation to the first point about the character of committees and what they mean for their members, there is no doubt that the select committee atmosphere and methods enable members to behave differently in committee, shedding much of their partisan commitment. It is clear also that within such a small group as a select committee members get to know each other and friendships may develop even across party boundaries. But it must also be remembered that the opportunities for committees to develop a sense of their own identity and of the shared interests of members are more restricted than it appears at first sight. The committee meetings often taken place under severe time constraints, there is more business to be got through than can easily be coped with, and attendance is often hurried and even desultory with some members coming and going as they attend to other matters simultaneously. Such conditions work against the development of really close ties in committees and, therefore, against the emergence of loyalties which might come into conflict with party commitments. Interestingly, it is when committees travel extensively that members are most likely to get to know each other well and thus acquire some feeling for the group of which they are part. But as a rule members always remember that the role they perform in select committees is slightly artificial, a kind of holiday from the exertions of party conflict on the floor and from the unremitting pressure of demands and grievances flowing in from constituents and organized interests.

Finally, it must be noted that chairmen have not generally become dominating figures in Parliament, shadow ministers, or anything like that. True, many of them are respected senior MPs and a few are former ministers. (The chairman of the Public Accounts Committee is by convention a former Treasury minister.) Some chairmen have received – and indeed sought – publicity for their work and position, becoming known nationally in their particular spheres of interest. To this extent the new committee system has provided for members opportunities not previously available in the House. But the chairman of a select committee should never forget the limitations of his position. He has few powers by virtue of his office, no patronage to dispense, and few, if any, levers to pull. His role is essentially to hold the committee together during its inquiries, to give an impulse towards co-ordination, and cautiously to provide something like a lead in the shaping of committee objectives. With skill and dedication to duty a chairman may influence strongly the character of committee hearings and the thrust of a committee's report. Yet he has to proceed with care. He must remember that overbearing conduct on his part or over-zealous commitment to a particular point of view undermine his own position and weaken the committee. He has to recognize that most members are individualists and want to play their own part in an inquiry. This respect for the basic equality of members, combined with the pressures working in favour of a nonpartisan approach in the final product of a committee's inquiry, suggests that prudent chairmen will remain modest in assessing their own standing and powers. More than anything else it is personal qualities sustaining respect that are the greatest asset a chairman can have.

THE IMPACT OF SELECT COMMITTEES: THE BALANCE SHEET OF REFORM

Without doubt the House of Commons now has a more comprehensive and balanced system for committee scrutiny of the work of the executive than ever before. Most of this is due to the consolidation of the departmental select committees set up in 1979. They signify a continuing, even though selective, oversight of most aspects of government activity, ranging from wide and long-term issues of policy choice through the implementation of numerous services and tasks to the allocation and use of financial resources. Inevitably, much of the scrutiny carried out is impressionistic: it does not penetrate deeply into the conditions of executive activity and, where it is concerned mainly with the identification of accountability, it may not always succeed in achieving final clarity. Nevertheless, the activity of scrutiny itself entails a continuing acknowledgement by ministers, civil servants, and many other public officials that they must be prepared to explain and on occasion justify what they are doing to groups of parliamentarians who, from the point of view of the executive, are laymen.

This process is still best described as the pursuit of 'explanatory dialogues', a judgement made by the author on the work of the Estimates Committee in the twenty years from 1945 to 1965.[29] It was then that the mode of discursive scrutiny now adopted by nearly all select committees engaged in the oversight of administration was firmly established. Clearly there has been structural change since the mid-1960s, quantitative expansion, systematization, and a degree of qualitative development. All this has established select committees as recognized and permanent elements in the parliamentary structure and processes, and has resulted in a strengthening of their powers and enhancement of their reputation. Yet in essentials the notion of explanatory dialogue remains, it is suggested, a valid characterization of the principal purpose met by select committees. They do not make or decisively change policy; they have only a slight influence over finance and levels of expenditure; they do not regularly affect the terms on which services are administered or contribute notably to the improvement of management; they have very little direct impact on legislation, either at the planning stage or when it is before the House, though occasionally a select committee inquiry has prompted or accelerated legislative change as in the case of the Home Affairs Committee's 1980 report on the 'sus' law (police power to stop and search persons found loitering), which was then repealed in the Criminal Attempts Act of 1981; and they do not cause ministers to resign or officials to be disciplined. It must also be added that their impact outwards on the public is muted. Their work receives some benevolent attention from time to time, and there are certainly specialized bodies which look with real gratitude to a committee for the evidence it has assembled and the issues it has highlighted. But in general select committees rate only a short notice on the inside page of the quality newspapers and rarely gain a headline.

Such comments as these may suggest that the whole exercise of scrutiny by select committee embodies more than a touch of charades. Yet this would be to misunderstand what they are doing and the kind of influence they can exert. Notwithstanding great improvements they remain essentially critical bodies dependent solely on their powers of argument and persuasion. They ensure that a significant proportion of Members of Parliament are engaged in a critical dialogue with the government and its agents. Governments respond to the views of select committees in part out of respect for the Commons, in part because they too recognize the benefits to be gained from such a critical explanatory dialogue. Everybody understands that the principal options in public affairs are not resolved through attention to the preferences of select committees; serious political choices are made elsewhere and by other means. Yet this does not render superfluous the inquisitorial and informative functions performed by select committees nor does it weaken the case for maintaining as a vital element in the parliamentary control of the executive the kind of critical dialogue that is possible only in the interaction between the members of select committees and their witnesses.

There is one element in the operation and impact of select committees which may in the longer run have important political consequences, even though at present it is rarely noticed. This is the effect which the multiplication of committee investigations may be having – or may have in the future – on the collective nature of the executive and on its unity. It is a more or less inevitable consequence of committee hearings with the broad, varied, and sometimes nebulous purposes they now have, that the questioning and the search for evidence and information begins to break through the collective personality of this or that department, this or that associated body, and even of the government itself. Ministers appear as individuals, occasionally even in open conflict with each other, civil servants appear and may be tempted into all kinds of pronouncements savouring of policy commitments on their part as individuals, and expert witnesses or representatives of organized interests push their views and suggest ways in which official witnesses may be confused, in error or simply inconsistent. In facilitating this rich and varied exposure of those engaged in the work of government the select committees have also developed an interest of their own in persistently challenging the doctrine of the collective responsibility of ministers and, in so far as it concerns relationships with civil servants, of individual ministerial responsibility too. In other words, select committees often feel an urge to open up the network of government, to expose conflict and inconsistency within it, and to attach responsibility to anyone who can plausibly be regarded as, in Bagehot's sense, an efficient executive agent. And along with the attribution of responsibility there goes often enough a measure of blame.

Some may be in favour of dissolving the collective quality of the government in Britain. It should, however, be recognized that most of those engaged in politics and in the Civil Service oppose such a trend. And if select committees go too enthusiastically down this path, they too are likely to run into increasing opposition. But if eventually governments become less resistant to these efforts to reveal and exploit their internal plurality, then the way may be open to a more profound shift in the role of select committees and indeed in the relationship between the executive and Parliament. Whether Britain would be better governed as a consequence of the loss of coherence and direction which such exploitation of differences within the government would entail must remain more than doubtful.

Meanwhile, the evolution of select committees has proceeded in a manner which maintains the continuity of institutional forms in the House of Commons. It has been a work of cautious adaptation, sensitive to the susceptibilities of those in government, but bringing renewed vitality to the traditional critical functions of Parliament.

Chapter Ten

THE SCRUTINY OF ADMINISTRATION

ST JOHN BATES

The almost complete administrative infallibility of government is an image which is carefully nurtured by governments in many countries. This can never have been more than a fiction in the United Kingdom. Recently various House of Commons committees have discovered that a proposed European Community Trade Marks Office, established to register trade marks that were not in conflict with previously registered trade marks, would not itself be checking previously registered trade marks before registering new ones;[1] that there is no systematic way used to calculate the number of nurses needed in the National Health Service;[2] that the Commissioners of Customs and Excise proposed to use a statutory provision, which empowered them to make regulations authorizing distress to be levied on the goods and chattels of anyone refusing or neglecting to pay tax, to empower themselves to break open in the daytime any house or premises to obtain the goods and chattels;[3] and that a Bangladeshi was removed from Heathrow to Bangladesh before representations made on his behalf by an MP could be properly considered because the Bangladeshi was confused with another Bangladeshi held in detention at the airport who had a similar name.[4]

This brief catalogue of limited administrative competence demonstrates the value of parliamentary scrutiny of the executive. The machinery for this scrutiny has seen an interesting evolution from the establishment of the Public Accounts Committee in the middle of the nineteenth century to the creation of the Commons departmental select committees, which are considered in chapter 9. This chapter is primarily concerned with five committees which scrutinize the activities of government and were thought to be sufficiently useful, either for reasons of utility or politics, to be maintained after the reforms of 1979. They are the Public Accounts Committee, the Select Committee on the Parliamentary Commissioner for Administration (the Ombudsman), the two Select Committees on Statutory Instruments, and that on European Legislation. These committees differ from the departmental select committees in that they are concerned with matters which are not simply associated with a single department and, in the main, within their narrower and more functional terms of reference, they are more comprehensive and systematic in their scrutiny. The underlying question in this chapter is how effective does this type of scrutiny continue to be.

PUBLIC ACCOUNTS

The House of Commons exercises a significant, if sometimes rather formal, supervision of government expenditure. Essentially, no charges may be imposed by government on the citizen without statutory authority, and money raised cannot be spent by government for any purpose other than that for which there is statutory authority. The mechanism for financial supervision which was developed in the middle of the nineteenth century, and continues today albeit in a modified form, enables the Commons to ensure that the government complies with these fundamental constitutional principles. Financial supervision is the responsibility of the Comptroller and Auditor General and the Public Accounts Committee which considers his reports and itself reports to the House of Commons. The government responds to the reports of the committee in published Treasury minutes. The committee's reports, and the government's responses to them, are debated in an annual debate in the Commons and may be raised by Members at other times.

The Public Accounts Committee has a membership of up to fifteen and the Chairman is traditionally a senior member of the opposition. The members of the Committee, which is appointed for the life of the Parliament, are nominated by a motion moved by the government after consultation through the 'usual channels' and not by the Committee of Selection. They are chosen in proportion to party strength in the House itself.

The Committee is appointed 'for the examination of the accounts showing the appropriation of the sums granted by Parliament to meet the public expenditure, and of such other accounts laid before Parliament as the Committee may think fit.'[5] It adopts a non-party political approach to its work. This is facilitated by the fact that it is not concerned with policy. As its chairman, Mr Robert Sheldon, has remarked: 'We do not study the policies – it is not for us to decide that – but once a policy has been announced it is for us to ensure that the money goes for the right purposes and that it is done in an economic, effective and efficient manner.'[6]

The basis for most of the work of the Public Accounts Committee consists of the reports of the Comptroller and Auditor General, although only a very small amount of his work comes before the committee. The Comptroller and Auditor General is appointed by the Crown on a resolution of the House of Commons, which is moved by the Prime Minister and which requires the agreement of the chairman of the Public Accounts Committee.[7] Once appointed, he holds his office during good behaviour and can only be removed by an address of both Houses of Parliament. He is thus able to remain independent of both the government and the Commons, and this is reflected in the limits of his jurisdication and the manner in which he conducts his work. So, although he audits many public-sector accounts, he cannot require the government to impose particular financial and administrative rules to control the use of public funds or to ensure that they are used efficiently,[8] neither, when he is undertaking a value-for-money audit, can he question the merits of the policy objectives of any department or public body.[9] Equally, although he is an officer of the House of Commons and has, by statute, to report to the House on certain matters such as any significant change in the extent or nature of his examinations, he is not a servant of the Public Accounts Committee. However, he maintains a close relationship with the committee and, in respect of some of his work, is subject to its statutory direction.[10]

The audits undertaken by the Comptroller and Auditor General fall into two categories. He audits the accounts of government departments and a wide range of public bodies to satisfy himself that expenditure has been restricted to expenditure authorized by Parliament.[11] For some other bodies, such as universities, he has the right to inspect their books and accounts, although he is not responsible for auditing them.[12] In addition he also conducts a second category of audit, value-for-money audits, in which he examines the economy, efficiency, and effectiveness with which bodies have used their resources to carry out their functions.[13] At present, approximately one-third of the Comptroller and Auditor General's reports are value-for-money audits, and these have become an increasingly important part of his work. The audits are carried out by the staff of the National Audit Office, of which the Comptroller and Auditor General is the head. The office, with a staff of approximately 900, is currently responsible for some 500 public-sector accounts. In the case of each audit, the facts are agreed with the accounting officer of the body with which the audit is concerned; in a government department the accounting officer is usually the permanent secretary.[14] The reports of the Comptroller and Auditor General, which are based on the audits, are factual and do not usually contain explicit critical comment nor the reasons for selecting the topic for report. Once completed, the Comptroller and Auditor General's reports are laid before Parliament.

Although the Comptroller and Auditor General has a wide discretion as to what he will investigate and, as we have seen, is independent of the Public Accounts Committee, he and the Committee work closely together. The concerns of the Comptroller and Auditor General's reports often reflect the recurring interests of the Committee. The reports commonly raise issues such as the need to have the best estimates available before taking a decision, the need for tight cost control of long-term projects, and the desirability of competitive tendering. Increasingly the value-for-money audits have been concerned not only with apparent deficiencies but also with more comprehensive appraisals, over a period of years, of areas where there is substantial public expenditure.[15] The committee plans its schedule of work in the knowledge of forthcoming reports from the Comptroller and Auditor General. In the course of its inquiries the Comptroller and Auditor General gives evidence to the Committee and also attends as a witness, in an advisory capacity, when others give evidence.

It is from the reports of the Comptroller and Auditor General, increasingly those concerned with economy, efficiency, and effectiveness examinations, that the Public Accounts Committee selects its topics for inquiry. Most inquiries are chosen because they are likely to lead to recommendations which will have a wide application in government although they are based on specific instances, rather than because they will simply allow for retrospective criticism. Certainly the emphasis has moved sharply away from simply establishing good accounting practice, which was very much the task of the committee in the nineteenth century. Normally, the committee limits inquiries to matters affecting government departments, rather than the public bodies which are within its jurisdiction.[16] In addition to taking evidence from the Comptroller and Auditor General, most of the evidence is usually taken from the Accounting Officers and other civil servants in the departments concerned.[17] The Committee now normally takes evidence in public, although prior to the 1977–8 parliamentary session the invariable practice was to take evidence in private.

Financial control over projects involving major public expenditure, particularly long-term projects, is of continuing interest to the Public Accounts Committee. Occasionally, these projects may reveal quite serious auditing and financial-control irregularities, for example the serious overcharging by contractors on the Bloodhound missile contracts in the early 1960s.[18] However, a particular concern is the escalation of expenditure on major projects. In 1982, the committee reported on the escalation to £1,000 million of the cost of the Chevaline improvement to the Polaris missile system[19] and, more recently, it has reported on the torpedo programme to the mid-1990s which will involve a total expenditure of £5,000 million.[20] One important result of the Chevaline inquiry was that the Ministry of Defence agreed to supply the committee with an annual statement of major projects, which is currently defined as those in which expenditure will exceed £250 million (although this may be reduced).[21] The agreement was intended to facilitate adequate monitoring of defence expenditure. There is, however, some doubt whether its detailed terms were complied with in respect of the Zircon project, the existence of which became a matter of considerable political controversy in 1987. Although the vast majority of projects involving this level of expenditure are military contracts, the committee is sometimes concerned with civilian contracts where there has been inadequate financial control. Perhaps the most notorious contemporary example of this was the lengthy inquiry into the major public expenditure on the De Lorean Car Company which was carried out by the Committee in 1983–4.[22]

Another area which attracts the attention of the committee is the adequacy of financial decision-making, and these inquiries do not necessarily involve large sums of public money. The committee has, for example, investigated the procedure by which the Ministry of Defence examined whether there should be a single Defence School of Music rather than a number of schools located throughout the country.[23] On the basis of the Comptroller and Auditor General's report, the committee was able to demonstrate that the Ministry was proceeding on miscalculated figures and comparing the costs of operation of existing schools and the projected costs of competing sites for a single school on figures which were not, in fact, comparable. The Treasury minute accepted most of the criticism and a complete reappraisal was undertaken, using accountants from outside the Ministry.[24] Sometimes, of course, the inadequacy of financial decision-making may have greater implications. In a long term survey of NHS manpower, the committee considered the control of nursing manpower and established that there was no central planning of nursing manpower needs in the DHSS because the assessment was devolved to regional health authorities. Unfortunately, nursing manpower needs were assessed in different ways in different authorities and the resulting national picture was, therefore, distorted.[25] Although the Treasury minute reveals that the DHSS holds to the view that nursing manpower requirements should not be determined centrally,[26] the committee's report is a convincing one in this respect.

A third matter of contemporary concern for the committee is the cost-effectiveness of administration. The committee has, for instance, reported on the enforcement procedures against television-licence evaders which were carried out by the Post Office on behalf of the Home Office under 'transitional arrangements' which had been in place for fifteen years.[27] The Home Office calculated that there were some 1.6 million licence evaders which represented an annual revenue loss of £65 million. The committee reported that the payment to the Post Office for carrying out the enforcement procedures was not tied to results or the relative effectiveness of different enforcement procedures and there were no other incentives to improve enforcement. The Home Office measured the costs of enforcement as a percentage of the total licence income rather than of the additional income obtained from enforcement, and there was no mechanism within the ministry for measuring the relative cost-effectiveness of the different forms of enforcement, which ranged from posting licence-renewal reminders to operating TV detector vans. The Treasury minute largely accepted these strictures.[28] More recently the committee has conducted an inquiry into the services provided by government to those wishing to export abroad.[29] The committee reported that there appear to be differences of policy within Whitehall about providing the services and that, contrary to declared general government policy, the Foreign Office tended to give priority to helping the larger firms which were seeking to export. The committee was also critical of the lack of flexibility in staffing these services in the Foreign Office and considered that insufficient attention had been paid to charging for the service as a means of measuring demand and effectiveness as well as providing it with additional funding.

In recent years the Public Accounts Committee has published between thirty-five and fifty-two reports in each parliamentary session, usually devoting each report to a single inquiry. The co-ordinated government response, in the form of a Treasury minute which usually contains responses to a number of reports, is laid some two or three months later and published as a Command Paper. Where the conclusions contained in a report are accepted, the Treasury may issue instructions to Whitehall and other public bodies in order to avoid the repetition of mistakes which have attracted criticism from the committee or to extend the adoption of improved procedures of financial control which the committee has recommended. The more significant of the committee's recommendations to 1969 have been published in two volumes.[30] In this way the work of the committee can be said to have a continuing influence on public-sector financial proceedings which is not limited to the instant case on which it reported.

There is, of course, a political as well as a bureaucratic response to the work of the committee. If the nature of the report merits it, the political response may be sharp and members may use the reports of the committee at question time and in adjournment and other debates.[31] However, the principal occasion on which the reports are considered in the House is in an annual debate for which a day is set aside. The debate is on a 'take note' motion and in recent years the motion has specifically referred to reports which the committee considered to be of particular significance. This does not deprive Members of the opportunity of commenting on other reports but it has given the debates a greater focus. It must be said, however, that the debates on the Public Accounts Committees reports are not popular parliamentary occasions. Attendance is usually limited to frontbench spokesmen, members of the committee, and members with a constituency interest in its reports. As Sir Michael Shaw remarked during the 1986 debate, 'unfortunately, most hon. Members look at the Order Paper, reach for a railway timetable and look up the times of the trains to their constituencies; this has always been so, and I am afraid that it will continue to be so'.[32]

In evaluating the work of the Public Accounts Committee one has to accept that it is effectively limited by the form of the financial information provided by government to Parliament, although this is itself a matter in which it is taking an increasingly close interest.[33] It does not involve itself in matters of policy, although when it is conducting an inquiry based on an economy, efficiency, and effectiveness examination by the Comptroller and Auditor General the distinction between policy and procedure may be a fine one. Certainly it cannot prevent the government making political decisions which are expensive. Even within its terms of reference it has been criticized for reporting *ex post facto* on, relatively speaking, financial trivia. This type of criticism is often overstated, for although in general the committee attracts little attention even in the House and its modern role is not as demonstrably influential as its nineteenth century role of setting good public-sector accountancy practice, its reports do have a pervasive influence on the machinery for public-sector financial decision-making and accountability.

THE PARLIAMENTARY COMMISSIONER FOR ADMINISTRATION

In the 1960s there was a widespread view in the United Kingdom that the remedies available to the citizen to correct inadequate, incompetent, or incorrect decisions taken by government and public agencies were insufficient, and those remedies that did exist were often expensive and cumbersome or ineffective.[34] The main remedies available to the citizen were either a court action seeking judicial review of an administrative decision or, where possible, appeal to a tribunal or making a case before a public inquiry. Failing the adequacy or availability of these methods of redress, the citizen either had simply to request that the decision be reviewed by those who made it or seek the help of an MP who might be prepared to pursue the matter in Parliament. There was also the further consideration that if there was inadequate machinery for correcting poor administrative decisions there would be less incentive to improve the quality of administration.

Encouraged by the experience of the Scandinavian countries and

New Zealand in establishing ombudsmen, a parallel office was established in the United Kingdom in 1967 – the Parliamentary Commissioner for Administration. In the 1970s the concept was extended by the creation of Commissioners for Local Administration for England and Wales and for Scotland[35] and of National Health Service Commissioners for England, Wales, and Scotland.[36] At the time that the office of the Parliamentary Commissioner was created, a Select Committee on the Parliamentary Commissioner was appointed to examine the work of the Commissioner and report to the House. The committee proceeds largely on the basis of the reports which the Commissioner lays before Parliament.[37]

The Parliamentary Commissioner is appointed by the Crown on the advice of the government and, since 1977, the Chairman of the House of Commons Select Committee on the Parliamentary Commissioner is consulted before an appointment is made. Once appointed the Parliamentary Commissioner holds office during good behaviour and can only be removed by addresses from both Houses.[38]

The Parliamentary Commissioner was appointed to investigate complaints from citizens who claim to have suffered an injustice in consequence of maladministration in the exercise of their administrative functions by government departments and other public bodies within his jurisdication.[39] However, he was not given jurisdiction over a number of areas of administrative activity which touch the lives of a large number of citizens, such as the police, local authorities, nationalized industries, and the National Health Service.[40] The position has been ameliorated by the creation of the parallel offices relating to local government and the National Health Service and also by the extension of the jurisdiction of the Parliamentary Commissioner over the years. His jurisdiction now includes some administrative action by consular officials overseas, the Residuary Bodies created under the statutory scheme which abolished the Greater London Council and the six Metropolitan Authorities, and, more recently, a wide range of quangos with executive or administrative functions. The latter jurisdiction came after substantial political pressure, in particular from the select committee. It includes the New Town Corporations, the Commission for Racial Equality, and the Equal Opportunities Commission, but not the Monopolies and Mergers Commission although its inclusion was pressed strongly.[41] However, despite these developments there are areas excluded from the jurisdiction of the Parliamentary Commissioner which have continued to be of concern, principally the exclusion of civil service personnel matters. This particular exclusion accounts for 7–9 per cent of the complaints which the Parliamentary Commissioner had to reject in the four years 1983–6.

There are a number of procedural constraints in bringing a complaint before the Parliamentary Commissioner. He may not normally investigate any matter where the complainant has, or had in the past, a remedy by recourse to a tribunal or by legal proceedings.[42] Furthermore the complainant must direct his complaint in the first instance to his MP and it is for the MP to decide whether or not to refer it to the Parliamentary Commissioner. The difficulties which this appears to pose for the complainant are not so great in practice. By the late 1970s, the Parliamentary Commissioner had adopted a procedure of not simply returning a complaint sent directly to him, but giving the complainant the choice of having the complaint sent to the complainant's MP. If this is acceptable to the complainant, the Parliamentary Commissioner sends the complaint to the MP and formally asks whether or not the case is to be referred to him.[43] A further constraint is that the complainant must refer his complaint to his MP within twelve months of the matter coming to his attention. Only in exceptional circumstances may the Parliamentary Commissioner accept a reference outside this time limit.[44]

There are also problems in determining the extent of the jurisdiction of the Parliamentary Commissioner. He is empowered to investigate 'maladministration' arising out of 'the exercise of administrative functions' of government departments and certain public bodies. 'Maladministration' was deliberately left undefined in the 1967 Act, but during the passage of the bill in the Commons the late Mr Richard Crossman suggested that it included 'neglect, inattention, delay, incompetence, ineptitude, perversity and arbitrariness'.[45] Difficulties can occur where a decision appears harsh but there is no evidence of maladministration. There has been a greater willingness over the years for Commissioners to assume maladministration where the decision which has been reached is harsh, even where the decision may be the result of rigorous application of departmental policy. This has perforce been a cautious development for, by statute, the Parliamentary Commissioner is not permitted to question the merits of a discretionary decision which has been taken by a department, where there has been no maladministration.[46]

What amounts to the exercise of administrative functions of a

195

government department is also a matter which has not been without its difficulties. In some cases it has been argued that while officials are carrying out the functions of the department the functions are not administrative functions. In other cases it has been argued that while officials are carrying out administrative functions they are not carrying them out on behalf of their department. The Parliamentary Commissioner has found his investigations into the administrative work of the courts blocked by the Lord Chancellor's Department because, in the view of that department, their staff who carry out this work are not exercising any departmental functions but are excercising the functions of the courts in administering justice. Consequently, in the view of the Lord Chancellor's Department, the jurisdiction of the Parliamentary Commissioner is excluded.[47]

Where the Parliamentary Commissioner does have jurisdiction he has complete discretion in deciding whether to investigate a complaint referred to him. If he decides to investigate he enjoys wide powers. He has the same powers as a High Court judge to compel any witness to give evidence, and the only papers to which he may be refused access are those which are certified by the Secretary of the Cabinet, with the approval of the Prime Minister, to relate to proceedings of the Cabinet or a Cabinet committee.[48]

The normal investigation procedure is a lengthy and rather slow one. The complaint is first sent to the department which is the subject of the complaint for comment. The average time it takes departments to give their initial comments is eleven weeks; in 1984, it took the DHSS seven months to produce initial comments on one case and the Inland Revenue over a year on another, admittedly complex, case.[49] After the initial comments have been received an investigation officer in the Parliamentary Commissioner's Office will begin what is an entirely private investigation and will eventually produce a draft report. Once this report has been approved in the Office it is sent to the department for the facts in the report to be verified and for comment on such matters as the recommendations in the report, which might include a recommendation for an *ex gratia* payment. The average response time by departments to these draft final reports is just over three months. After the departmental response is received, the report is finalized and presented to the MP who referred the complaint. It can be seen from this outline that the length of time taken to complete an investigation is not entirely attributable to the Parliamentary Commissioner's Office, but it is nevertheless a long time. The Parliamentary Commissioner is hoping to reduce the average time from the receipt of a referred complaint to a completed inquiry from the present eleven and a half months to closer to nine months.[50]

No doubt due to the length of time of inquiries, the complexity of his jurisdiction, and the fact that he has no executive competence to enforce his recommendations, the number of referrals to the Parliamentary Commissioner has remained rather low, although a large percentage of MPs do make referrals. The mean annual number of referrals to the Parliamentary Commissioner since the office was created in 1967 has been 825,[51] and roughly 60 per cent of MPs make one or two referrals each year.[52] Of the referrals made, the Parliamentary Commissioner rejects 75–80 per cent. The grounds of rejection have remained fairly constant in recent years: approximately 50 per cent of referrals are rejected because the complaint is not concerned with administrative actions; approximately 20 per cent are rejected because the authority complained of is outside the jurisdiction of the Parliamentary Commissioner; 7–8 per cent are rejected because the complainant has the right of recourse to a tribunal or a court; and a similar number are rejected because they concern personnel matters of civil servants or members of the armed forces. Although the Parliamentary Commissioner has a discretion whether or not to accept complaints falling within his jurisdiction, the exercise of this discretion only accounts for 12–14 per cent of rejected claims.

In 1986, which was a fairly typical year, only 168 complaints were fully investigated: 49 per cent were found to be wholly justified; 42 per cent were considered to be partly justified; and only 9 per cent were considered on investigation to be unjustified. The DHSS and the Inland Revenue are the departments which consistently generate the most referrals to the Parliamentary Commissioner. In the three years between 1984 and 1986 these two departments generated between 43–50 per cent of all referrals. This is perhaps not surprising given the large numbers of the general public with whom these rather decentralized departments come into contact within any year. Of course, it can be said that in absolute terms, even for these departments, the number of referrals is only a tiny proportion of the annual departmental contacts with the general public. More significantly for the Parliamentary Commissioner they are also only a tiny proportion of complaints about departments handled by MPs.

In 1984, for example, there were 237 referrals of complaints against the DHSS to the Parliamentary Commissioner, of which seventy-one were accepted for investigation, while a senior civil servant in the department estimated that at the headquarters of the department alone they were dealing with about 30,000 complaints a year from MPs.[53]

Of the cases investigated by the Parliamentary Commissioner, some have resulted in political repercussions and others have proved of financial significance to the complainant. The prime example of an inquiry which had a high political profile was the Sachsenhausen case in which the Commissioner found the Foreign Office to be seriously at fault in the procedures which it operated.[54] More recently, there were widespread political and public concern following the Parliamentary Commissioner's criticism of the Home Office for failing to act promptly to review the murder conviction of a man who had been in jail for eight years, although the conviction was based on evidence from a forensic scientist who had been known to have given unreliable and incompetent evidence at other trials.[55] Occasionally, the Parliamentary Commissioner recommends that significant *ex gratia* payments should be paid to a complainant. In 1982, for example, the Department of Industry agreed to pay £57,000 to a company which had been treated in a 'shoddy' manner in respect to an application for industrial assistance[56] and, in 1985, HM Customs and Excise paid a brewer £30,000, having given him the wrong advice on the duty payable on a beer and cider mixture called 'snakebite', as a result of which he had abandoned its production.[57] However, very often there is merely rather mild *ex post facto* criticism of departmental procedures, even where, as in the case of the Bangladeshi deportee mentioned at the beginning of the chapter, the maladministration uncovered is itself quite startling.

The role of the select committee in respect of supervising the work of the Parliamentary Commissioner is not a well-defined one and perhaps reflects the ambivalence which existed in the House about the establishment of the office. Effectively the committee has found itself fulfilling three functions: direct supervision of the work of the Parliamentary Commissioner, reinforcing his recommendations, and acting as a focus for enlarging his jurisdiction and giving his work greater political significance. In supervising the work of the Parliamentary Commissioner the committee has offered constructive criticism. The first three Commissioners all had long and distinguished Whitehall careers and were encouraged by the committee to be more expansionist and outward-looking than they were inclined to be by virtue of their professional experience. The committee was reluctant, for example, for the Parliamentary Commissioner to take too restrictive a view about what amounted to 'maladministration' and was enthusiastic about increased publicity about the role of the Commissioner. More recently, the committee has put some pressure on the Parliamentary Commissioner to reduce the time taken in investigating complaints and as a result the procedures for preparation of reports in the Commissioner's Office have been considerably streamlined. The recommendations of the Parliamentary Commissioner are reinforced by the committee taking regular evidence from civil servants in departments which have been the subject of complaints. The committee usually takes evidence each year from the DHSS and the Inland Revenue and uses these occasions to pursue the types of maladministration on which the Commissioner has reported and to seek assurances that there has been an adequate administrative response. The committee has also long been an advocate for the extension of the jurisdiction of the Parliamentary Commissioner, and it is largely due to pressure from the Committee that the jurisdication has recently been extended to quangos. However, members of the Committee have been, as yet, unsuccessful in their campaign for the Parliamentary Commissioner to be permitted to take inquiries on his own initiative. They have also failed to convince successive governments that there should be an annual debate in the House on the work of the Commissioner.

The value of the committee turns, of course, on the utility of the Parliamentary Commissioner. Although the Commissioner is empowered to obtain a range of evidence which would not be available to an MP pursuing a complaint, the fact is that the Commissioner is relatively little used. This may be because the range of remedies open to the citizen and their effectiveness are both greater than they were in the late 1960s. Certainly the intervening period has seen a dramatic development of judicial review by the courts and review is easier and swifter to obtain. Perhaps also MPs and departments have become more sophisticated in their relations with each other. It is possible that the Parliamentary Commissioner was a creature of his time but that time has now largely passed.

STATUTORY INSTRUMENTS

There is a long history of Parliament delegating to others, by statute, a limited power to legislate. Most commonly it now empowers the government to legislate by statutory instrument. This is sometimes seen as striking a constitutional bargain, and the Select Committee on Procedure has described it in this way: 'The Executive is thereby freed from the necessity of introducing legislative proposals subject to the full parliamentary process; and Parliament is likewise freed from the obligation to subject such proposals to detailed scrutiny.'[58] In reality, the government can take, in primary legislation, the competence to make delegated legislation which it feels is likely to be necessary. If there is any doubt about the competence required, there is a tendency for the government to take wide powers to avoid the tedious necessity of taking wider powers later. It is unlikely that the competence to make delegated legislation contained in a government bill will be amended during its passage through Parliament. Once the bill is enacted the extent of that competence, as opposed to its exercise, cannot be reviewed by the courts.

Despite the democratic and technical advantages of using delegated legislation, and there are a number, it is this combination of the legislative supremacy of Parliament and the dominance by the government of the legislative process which can sometimes make the use of delegated legislation a sensitive parliamentary issue. At one time the concern was that there was an increasing volume of delegated legislation. In fact, over the past thirty years there have been approximately 2,000 statutory instruments made each year.[59] The concern today is rather about the way in which wide powers to make delegated legislation are taken and used. The powers are sometimes surprising. The government has taken powers to make delegated legislation to repeal primary legislation[60] and to give it retrospective effect,[61] and indeed to legislate to virtually the same extent as Parliament.[62] Where wide powers are taken delegated legislation is sometimes used not only for the more traditional purpose of making detailed rules within the broad policy laid down in the primary legislation but also for making the policy itself. As the chairman of the Joint Committee on Statutory Instruments has remarked, 'the trouble is that a lot of statutory instruments today no longer deal with means but with principles'.[63]

It is obviously important that the parliamentary procedures for scrutinizing delegated legislation should respond to these developments. This is particularly so as delegated legislation is almost invariably drafted which each government department and thus lacks the stylistic uniformity of primary legislation which is drafted centrally. The majority of statutory instruments must be laid before Parliament and most instruments that are laid come into force following an affirmative resolution in both Houses, or are subject to annulment by either House. A certain uniformity in these procedures is provided by the Statutory Instruments Act 1946, but the procedure to be applied to a particular statutory instrument is determined by the legislation which grants the competence to make the instrument, the enabling legislation. In effect, the government by its control over the terms of the enabling legislation determines the applicable procedure. Within this procedural framework the Commons plays two roles. It undertakes a technical scrutiny of statutory instruments, primarily in two select committees, and considers the merits of the substance of statutory instruments, either in committee or on the floor of the House.

Since 1973, the technical scrutiny of delegated legislation has been undertaken by the Joint Committee on Statutory Instruments and, for instruments which are only required to be laid before the House of Commons, the Commons Select Committee on Statutory Instruments. Apart from some limited exceptions, these committees consider every instrument which is laid before Parliament and the joint committee also considers all general statutory instruments which do not require to be laid.[64] The joint committee has fourteen members, seven from each House, and the chairman is always an MP; the Commons members of the Joint Committee also serve as the members of the Commons select committee. In examining delegated legislation, the committees have the assistance of Counsel to the Speaker and Counsel to the Lord Chairman of Committees and both committees commonly take written and oral evidence from government departments. In a recent parliamentary session the two committees held seventy-three meetings and considered 1,183 statutory instruments.[65]

The terms of reference of the two committees require them to determine whether special attention of the House should be drawn to a statutory instrument on any one of nine grounds: (i) that it imposes a tax or a charge; (ii) that it is made under enabling legislation which expressly excludes the instrument from challenge in the courts; (iii) that it purports to have retrospective effect where the enabling Act does not expressly provide for such effect; (iv) that there appears to have been unjstifiable delay in the publication of the instrument or in laying it; (v) that the instrument has come into operation before being laid and there appears to have been unjustifiable delay in sending notification of this as required by the Statutory Instruments Act; (vi) that it appears doubtful whether the instrument is *intra vires* the enabling statute, or the instrument appears to make some unusual or unexpected use of the powers in the enabling legislation; (vii) that for any special reason the form or purport of the instrument calls for elucidation; (viii) that the drafting of the legislation appears to be defective; (ix) any other ground which does not impinge on the merits of the instrument or on the policy behind it.

The majority of statutory instruments which are reported to the Commons are reported on the last four of these grounds. The regulations drafted by the Commissioners of Customs and Excise, which were mentioned at the beginning of the chapter, were reported to the House because the Commons committee doubted whether they were *intra vires* the enabling legislation. Criticisms of defective drafting by the committees may range from criticising the draftsman for inadvertently leaving the date of commencement of an order blank[66] through circular definitions such as defining 'work' as including 'the execution of works',[67] to inadequacies in the implementing of EEC directives by statutory instrument.[68] Two other grounds on which the committees have reported instruments to the Commons in recent years are the inadequacy of the explanatory notes attached to statutory instruments, which are intended to inform the reader of the purpose of the provisions in general terms,[69] and delays in making instruments. Sometimes these delays can be considerable and, as a result, leave legal rights unclear. The joint committee has, for instance, reported critically on a five-year delay in implementing an EEC directive and on a two-year delay in replacing a revoked statutory instrument, which laid down rules for formal investigations under the Merchant Shipping Act, with a new instrument.[70]

It has to be said that the two committees labour under some not inconsiderable parliamentary difficulties. They report critically on approximately 2 per cent of all the statutory instruments which they consider. This may be a reflection of the high quality of the drafting of delegated legislation, but equally it may reflect the volume of

202

work which falls to the committees and the very considerable time pressure under which they work. The vast majority of the statutory instruments which they consider are subject to annulment and if a prayer for annulment is to be moved this must be done within forty days (excluding recesses, prorogation or dissolution) of the instrument being laid before Parliament.[71] Within that time span the scrutiny committees must consider the instrument, take any evidence, and report, while leaving sufficient time for a prayer for annulment to be moved.

The scrutiny committees also suffer from other disadvantages. Although the quality of their work is high, there is no procedural requirement in the Commons that votes should not be taken on statutory instruments before they have been considered by the scrutiny committees, even those subject to an affirmative resolution.[72] Neither is there any procedural requirement that once the committees have reported that notice should be taken of their determinations. The joint committee has severely criticized departments for proceeding to make regulations knowing that there is a doubt about their *vires* which has been reported by the committee.[73] Indeed there have been occasions when a scrutiny committee has reported that a statutory instrument subject to affirmative resolution is probably *ultra vires* and the Commons has proceeded to approve the instrument.

Where debates do take place on statutory instruments, they tend to be held at inconvenient times. In the Commons, a debate on the floor of the House on a prayer for annulment must normally be completed by 11.30 p.m. and is usually brought on late. A debate on an affirmative resolution is normally limited to one and a half hours and is also usually brought on late. The level of inconvenience which can arise for Members on politically sensitive statutory instruments subject to affirmative resolution can be illustrated by the debates on two draft orders arising out of the abolition of the Greater London Council and the six Metropolitan Authorities which were debated from 10.52 p.m. on 11 February 1986 until 1.59 a.m. the following day and 250 MPs had to attend for the two votes during that period. Not surprisingly, debates on statutory instruments are unpopular parliamentary occasions. Not only are they at inconvenient times but their immediate utility is limited by the fact that no amendments to statutory instruments may be moved in the House; they have to be either accepted or rejected. Furthermore, it is extremely rare, although not unknown, for the government to be defeated.[74]

However, perhaps the crucial matter is not these difficulties but rather to what extent departments take account of the work of the scrutiny committees. It is said that the real impact of the committees is that their views are taken very seriously in government departments. Certainly, civil servants have a recognized lack of enthusiasm about appearing before parliamentary committees. This is no doubt heightened if, let us say, a departmental lawyer, who has drafted a statutory instrument, has to appear to answer criticism on the adequacy of the drafting, or an administrator has to appear to justify the use of a power in making an instrument. The committee can certainly be quite forthright to witnesses when they consider that their recommendations have essentially been ignored.[75] Nevertheless, to the outsider some of the departmental responses to the committees appear somewhat cavalier. It is perhaps difficult to justify a delay of six years in making amendments to comply with recommendations of a scrutiny committee with which the department itself had agreed.[76] It is also difficult to justify a memorandum from a department which, in response to being asked by a scrutiny committee why, contrary to the committee's recommendations, the department had failed to indicate in the explanatory notes to an instrument the content of instruments which were being revoked, declared, 'it is not clear that [it] would have served any useful purpose. Generally speaking it would seem that those affected by the original orders would have been well aware of their effects, while those not so affected would not be concerned to know what those effects were.'[77] It is true that the recommendations of the committees are reflected in Cabinet Office circulars and in *Statutory Instrument Practice*, however the *Practice* does not contain any detail of the committees' recommendations and there is some evidence that departments do not always comply with the Cabinet Office circulars.[78]

The scrutiny committees are, by their terms of reference, technically excluded from considering the merits of statutory instruments. As time to debate the merits of statutory instruments on the floor of the House will always be limited, standing committees on statutory instruments were introduced in 1973 in order to allow debate off the floor on the merits of instruments. It is generally accepted that this innovation has not been a notable success. A proposal to refer an instrument to a standing committee must be made by a minister; it can be defeated by the objection of twenty MPs in the Chamber. Instruments are debated in standing committees for up to one and a half hours on a neutral motion, which does not permit amendments or encourage constructive and responsible debate. The substantive vote, without further debate, which is subsequently taken on the floor of the House on affirmative resolutions can be brought on by the government at any time once the standing committee has deliberated. Affirmative resolutions are almost always brought on late at night; prayers for annulment are not voted on at all if the instrument has been considered in standing committee. The standing committee procedure has allowed the government to save some time on the floor of the House; in recent parliamentary sessions some ninety to a hundred statutory instruments have been considered in seventy or eighty sittings of the committees.[79] The use of standing committees has enabled a dozen or so instruments subject to the negative procedure to be debated briefly each session, for which no time might have been provided on the floor of the House, but otherwise the procedure is not at all helpful to backbenchers and it has been considered unsatisfactory by successive chairmen of the Joint Committee on Statutory Instruments[80] and by the Select Committee on Procedure.[81] The Procedure Committee proposed a number of changes to the procedure in 1977 but they have not been adopted. Changes have also been proposed by the Procedure Committee in its Second Report of session 1986–7, but these await a government response.

It has been suggested that the House of Commons devotes between four and five hours a week to debating statutory instruments.[82] Much of this time is devoted to debating instruments subject to affirmative resolution and is time that the government has to make available to ensure that such delegated legislation is passed. It may be that greater pressure should be placed on government to provide more parliamentary time for the consideration of delegated legislation. Perhaps proportionally less delegated legislation is now of a detailed technical and uncontroversial nature. The Commons might do well to spend a little more time debating its merits and considering the reports of its scrutiny committees.

EUROPEAN COMMUNITY LEGISLATION

The very considerable differences of opinion in both major political parties about the desirability of membership of the European Community meant that when the United Kingdom joined the Community in 1973 there had been little opportunity in either House to explore the parliamentary implications of membership. Select committees had been appointed in each House to consider the matter and they reported during 1973.[83] They had to contemplate a new constitutional role for Parliament. It is the governments of the member states of the Community that have both the formal and the effective capacity to enact legislative proposals which emanate from the European Commission. National parliaments cannot amend, and it is unnecessary for them to approve, Community legislation. It is true that it may be necessary for national parliaments to legislate at a later date to incorporate some Community legislation into national law. However, national parliaments have no indispensable constitutional role in the Community legislative process. Since the select committees reported in 1973, the European Parliament has acquired an enhanced function in the process but the role of national parliaments has, if anything, declined.

Although not all the recommendations of the select committees were accepted, they did form the basis for the present procedures for dealing with Community legislative and policy proposals in the House of Commons. Forecasts of the agendas of Council of Ministers meetings are presented to the Commons by the government, but these have a limited utility because the agendas are subject to considerable change at a late stage. There are also ministerial statements in the Commons after Council of Ministers meetings. Provision was made for questions on the European Community to be included in the rota for parliamentary questions and for general debates on Community affairs, including debates on the six-monthly reports by the government on the Community. Finally, two committees were appointed, one in each House, to scrutinize draft community legislative and policy proposals. The Commons committee, the Select Committee on European Legislation, is empowered to examine draft legislative proposals of the European Commission, and other documents published by the commission, for submission to the Council of Ministers or the European Council and report to the House on whether they raise questions of legal or political importance.[84]

In fulfilling its task the committee has the considerable advantage of a Commons resolution which effectively ensures that its deliberations are at least considered on the floor of the House. The resolution provides that no minister shall agree to a legislative proposal in the Council of Ministers where the proposal has been recommended by the Select Committee to the House for further consideration and that consideration has not yet taken place. There are only two exceptions to the general terms of the resolution: first, where the commitee has reported that a proposal be considered, but has recommended that agreement to the proposal should not be withheld in the Council of Ministers pending its consideration by the House; secondly, the Minister may decide that, for special reasons, agreement in the Council should not be withheld. In that event, the Minister must explain the reasons for the decision to the House 'at the first opportunity thereafter'.[85] The committee has expressed a strong preference for the minister's explanation being an oral rather than a written explanation, so that Members may have the opportunity to question the minister.[86]

In the early 1980s ministers became somewhat casual about the terms of the resolution. The committee was particularly concerned about the adoption of the European Strategic Programme for Research and Development on Information Technology (ESPRIT) in the Council of Ministers. This proposal had been recommended for debate by the committee some seven months before it was adopted. The Programme had moved to adoption in the Council, in part because the British government dropped its objection to certain elements of it. It was recognized that the failure to hold the debate in advance of dropping the objections, however attractive politically it had become to progress with ESPRIT, was a quite unacceptable way for the government to treat the scrutiny procedure.[87]

Naturally, ministers are responsible for their failure to comply with the resolution. The government has, however, been careful to avoid attracting ministerial responsibility for any frailty in the success of negotiations in Brussels. It has also stoutly resisted any notion that, where a debate takes place on a Community proposal, the terms of the motion impose a mandate on the government and limit its freedom of action in subsequent negotiations.

In an average parliamentary session the committee will consider between 700 and 800 Commission legislative and policy proposals and recommend some 10–15 per cent for debate, although between 25 and 30 per cent of the proposals may be reported as raising questions of legal or political importance.[88] In undertaking this scrutiny the committee faces two areas of particular difficulty. The first of these is obtaining sufficient information on the proposals. There is a government undertaking that parliament will be supplied with a copy of each proposal published by the Commission within forty-eight hours of the English version being received in Whitehall, and also with an explanatory memorandum on the proposal within, in normal circumstances, two weeks thereafter. The explanatory memorandum is produced by the government department with primary responsibility for formulating the British response to the proposal. These explanatory memoranda have caused some concern. Departments are not always prompt in submitting them and often they are in a somewhat laconic and stereotyped form. This is perhaps understandable because the government will not wish to reveal its full position on a proposal at such an early stage of the Community legislative process. For many proposals it may be months, and often years, after they have been published by the Commission before they are adopted in the Council of Ministers. This long gestation period poses an additional problem for the Committee. To do its work adequately the Committee certainly needs further information on proposals while they are before the Council. The proceedings in the Council and its working groups are supposed to be secret, but during this (often protracted) period there may be very major amendments to proposals. Since 1975, the government has agreed to keep Parliament aware of substantial amendments to proposals which are before the Council and are of particular interest to the UK.[89] Unlike the parallel committee in the House of Lords, which reports on fewer Community proposals but in more depth, the Commons committee takes relatively little formal written evidence and rarely takes oral evidence, although it does make periodic visits to Brussels which provide it with further information on proposals.[90]

The second difficulty which the Committee faces is the timing of its inquiries. In some cases this is a matter of trying to ensure that an inquiry on a proposal is completed before it has been adopted in the Council of Ministers. Community legislative proposals move at different speeds and can move unexpectedly. In 1983, of the 672 proposals before the Committee, 141 had been adopted by the Council before they had been considered by the Committee.[91] More commonly the question for the Committee is about the most appropriate stage for conducting an inquiry on a proposal and perhaps encouraging the House to apply pressure on the government in its negotiations in Brussels. If the committee reports on a proposal at an early stage its recommendations may have an enhanced influence because the negotiating positions of the member states will still be relatively flexible. On the other hand, the proposal may undergo such considerable amendment in the Council that the recommendations become otiose. Reporting at a later stage may result in more pertinent but possibly less influential recommendations. A further consideration for the committee is that Community proposals are often developed in stages. The committee may first have before it a policy proposal, perhaps initially one in outline, and later draft framework legislation and thereafter detailed draft legislation. The committee must decide at which stage or stages of this development to devote its time. These various considerations mean that the committee is often involved in repeated scrutiny of Community proposals. So, for example, the committee has reported three times between 1980 and 1986 on the proposed rules relating to credit insurance undertakings,[92] and three times between 1982 and 1986 on proposals relating to tourism in the Community.[93]

The committee may report to the House that a Community proposal raises political or legal questions and make recommendations for its consideration. The manner in which this is done may vary. In the very early years of the committee's existence there was perhaps a tendency to report a rather high percentage of Commission proposals for debate; now the committee reports rather fewer proposals but is more directive in its recommendations. It sometimes simply recommends that a proposal be further considered by the House, but it may recommend that it should be considered with another Commission proposal or in a general debate on the subject matter of the proposal, or it may recommend that the proposal be debated in standing committee.[94]

Debates on Commission proposals take place either on the floor of the House or in a standing committee on European Community documents. Debates on the floor of the House which are simply devoted to Commission proposals are normally late at night and, like statutory instruments debates, are not popular with Members. Until recently, however, relatively little use has been made of the standing committees. This may be, in part, because the select committee has become more selective in reporting proposals for debate and thus an anticipated additional pressure on the time on the floor of the House has not materialized. Reference of Community documents to a standing committee is essentially a matter for the government as is the timing of the debates, both in committee and on the floor of the House. Although successive Leaders of the House have stated that there is an intention wherever possible to bring on the debates as promptly as possible after the committee has recommended a debate, the committee has remained dissatisfied with the timing of debates. The tendency has been to bring on the debate late in the Community legislative process when the opinions expressed by Members are unlikely to be influential because agreement in the Council on the proposal is sufficiently complete that the government would probably be reluctant, or perhaps unable, to disturb it. However, if the government were to bring on a debate early and the Community document were later substantially amended, there is a likelihood that the select committee would recommend a further debate. From the point of view of the Leader of the House it is clearly preferable to bring on a debate late and incur the displeasure of the select committee from time to time than have two debates, particularly if they are to be on the floor of the House.

The Select Committee on European Legislation enjoys a privileged position in the Commons and it does have some influence. There are, however, two factors which may in the future, reduce this influence. The first is that it obtains the preponderance of its information about Commission proposals from government departments. Where it takes written and oral evidence this is largely from ministers and British interest groups. In consequence its conclusions reflect an essentially British perspective on Commission proposals. Although the primary constituency of the committee is the Commons there are dangers in taking too narrow a view in an enlarging Community. The second factor is the adoption of the Single European Act.[95] The Single European Act will make it considerably easier for many proposals to be adopted in the Council of Ministers without the unanimous consent of member states. This will weaken the scrutiny procedures in national parliaments because a government will not necessarily be able to block the adoption of a proposal while awaiting the opinion of its parliament, or indeed when faced with hostility to the proposal within its parliament. In the long term, much more thought will have to be given to the utility of the present scrutiny procedures in Westminster in the light of this constitutional development within the European Community.[96]

POSTSCRIPT

A question posed at the beginning of this chapter was how effective is systematic functional scrutiny of government. However, influence on the executive, or indeed on Members, is notoriously difficult to establish with any precision; and the range and disparate nature of the scrutiny which has been considered in this chapter demonstrate the limitations of generalization. Yet it would seem that the Public Accounts Committee, or at least the Comptroller and Auditor General, does exercise influence; perhaps his influence is enhanced because he is supported by the Committee. The Statutory Instruments Committee also has a degree of influence, which is reflected in *Statutory Instrument Practice* and in Cabinet Office circulars, but perhaps finds it difficult to persuade others to respond to the changing nature and use of delegated legislation. The Parliamentary Commissioner for Administration and his associated committee have been demand-led, and function in such a limited manner, whilst competing with increasingly effective parliamentary and non-parliamentary remedies, that they may find that their recently extended jurisdiction is insufficient to rehabilitate their influence. The European Legislation Committee was the creature of a dramatic constitutional development, to which it owes its special procedural position. The scope of its inquiries and the Single European Act may, however, erode its influence.

The committees which scrutinize the activity of government in a systematic manner do inform Members and underpin other work of the Commons. For instance, some of these committees, in particular the Public Accounts Committee and the European Legislation Committee, will tend to support inquiries by the departmental select committees. Some of the committees have a higher profile in the Chamber than others but this is not perhaps of great moment for their work is not generally that of high politics. More significantly, there is evidence here that systematic scrutiny demands systematic accountability. Forty or more years of technical scrutiny of delegated legislation and 130 years of scrutiny of public accounts bear testimony to the value of such accountability. The challenge is to ensure that there is appropriate systematic scrutiny of areas that continue to matter.

Chapter Eleven

PARLIAMENTARY PRIVILEGE

GEOFFREY MARSHALL

Questions of parliamentary privilege are often raised in the course of political crises and upsets in Britain. The operation of parliamentary privilege raises in fact important issues not only about the proper working of the legislature and the rights of legislators but also about the scope of civil liberties. In the United States and some Commonwealth countries (such as Canada and India) the immunities and punitive powers of legislators are qualified by constitutional provisions that may be enforced by the courts,[1] but in Britain judicial control is limited to interpretation of some relevant statutory enactments and to jurisdictional issues. Moreover, the courts are reluctant to interfere in matters that are regarded as being within the internal concerns of the two Houses. So a great deal in our system rests upon the self-restraint of Parliament and its committees.

Historically, the purpose of the Commons' privileges was the protection of the House from challenges to its authority from the other organs of government, particularly the Crown. Today it could be said that privilege and contempt powers, when properly exercised, are designed to safeguard the House collectively from acts that interefere with its free working and to protect members individually from threats and pressures that may impede them in the exercise of their legitimate functions, whether these impediments come from government or from extra-parliamentary sources.

This proposition leads naturally to a number of questions. What exactly are the functions and activities that deserve the protection of privilege? How are the rights of the House and its members to unimpeded action to be balanced against the rights of the executive to govern and the rights of citizens and constituents to bring to bear legitimate pressures and sanctions on their representatives? How is free speech and debate in Parliament to be measured against free speech and debate about Parliament?

PRIVILEGES AND POWERS

Some of the ancient and undoubted privileges of the House claimed by the Speaker in each new Parliament are of no great significance – for example, those that relate to access to the Crown and the favourable construction of the House's proceedings. The requesting of these is perhaps more in the nature of a courtesy. Indeed if the privileges are undoubted and if they rest, as they seem to, either upon statute or the law and custom of Parliament, there seems no need to seek their confirmation from the Crown at all. Possibly claiming the right to freedom of speech and debate and freedom from arrest can now be considererd more in the nature of a civil reminder to the Crown of selected bits of seventeenth-century parliamentary history.

Amongst powers not listed as heads of privilege in the Speaker's petition are the rights of the Commons to regulate its own composition and to exercise jurisdiction over matters arising within it. There is also the right to punish as contempts acts that impede the exercise of any of its functions. These powers rest upon and are defined by the common law. The courts recognize the penal jurisdiction of each House as an incident of its assumed share in the judicial activity inhering in the High Court of Parliament. For some privilege there is, in addition to recognition by parliamentary custom and the Crown, a statutory basis. Free speech in Parliament is protected by Article 9 of the 1689 Bill of Rights which provides that 'the freedom of speech and debates or proceedings in Parliament ought not to be impeached or questioned in any court or place out of Parliament'. Like some other elements in the English Bill of Rights, that guarantee was imported by the framers of the American Constitution to protect Senators and Representatives. Article 1(6) of the Federal Constitution declares in similar terms that 'for any speech or debate in either House they shall not be questioned in any other place'.

PRIVILEGE AND THE BILL OF RIGHTS

The protection of members and their proceedings is affected by some other statutes in addition to the Bill of Rights, though their exact meaning and implications have caused some argument. Question marks have recently been placed against a number of traditional interpretations of what in the United States is called 'the speech and debate clause'. In 1958 the Privy Council was asked to rule on the effect of the Parliamentary Privilege Act of 1770. A member of Parliament, Mr George Strauss, had been threatened with an action for defamation by the London Electricity Board who were aggrieved by the contents of a letter that he had written about the board's affairs to a minister. The House and its Privileges Committee wished to know whether, if they were to treat the board's threat of legal action against Mr Strauss as a breach of privilege, they would be acting unlawfully under the provisions of the 1770 Act. The terms of that Act were wide. It provided that no action or suit against a Member of Parliament should 'at any time be impeached, stayed or delayed by or under cover of any privilege of Parliament'. The Privy Council advised that these words were intended to prevent abuse of privileges under which the House in earlier times had prevented the bringing of various civil actions against Members and their servants. The Act could not be intended, they said, to allow actions to be brought in respect of words or conduct in the House so as to nullify the protection for free speech given in the Bill of Rights.[2] Lord Denning has recently revealed that the Privy Council opinion was not unanimous and has published his dissenting opinion.[3] In it he argues that the 1770 Act meant what it said, and that Parliament has no privilege to stop citizens from having recourse to the courts. If an action for libel were to be brought in respect of a speech or proceeding in Parliament, the court, if it were satisfied that it was covered by the Bill of Rights, would strike out the action. So there is no inconsistency between abolition of the use of privilege to stay actions and the statutory protection for speech and proceedings. The Privy Council expressed no view however as to whether Mr Strauss's letter *was* a proceeding in Parliament. Lord Denning thought that it was. So did the Commons Privileges Committee. But a majority of the House of Commons thought that it was not.[4]

'PROCEEDINGS IN PARLIAMENT'

Three important issues have been raised about proceedings in Parliament. They relate to their scope, their use, and their relationship with the ordinary law. If Members are not to be called to account for what they do when taking part in the proceedings of the House, the scope of that term is of some importance. It would probably be too wide to extend absolute protection to any act done by a member, whether in or out of the House, that bears some relation to the legislative or supervisory functions of the House. On the other hand, the Committee of Privileges has suggested that communications between members and ministers or officers of the House concerning its business should be absolutely privileged, and proposed a legislative definition of the term 'proceedings' that relates it to all things said, done, or written by members, officers, and witnesses in the course of a sitting and for the purpose of the business being or about to be transacted.[5]

No legislation has as yet been drafted to clarify the issue and clearly a general legislative definition suitable to all purposes is difficult to construct. The desirability of absolute protection depends in many ways on the specific question at issue. Not all conduct that is related to the legislative process should necessarily be absolutely privileged or even privileged at all. In the United States the speech and debate clause has not prevented inquiry into the question of whether a former Senator has accepted a bribe in return for action relative to postal rates legislation. In *US v Brewster*[6] the Supreme Court concluded that the clause only forbade inquiry into acts occurring in the regular course of the legislative process and not into all conduct *relating* to the legislative process. A Member of Parliament who publishes outside the House a libellous speech that he has delivered in the House is not protected by the relationship of his conduct to proceedings in the House.[7] In Canada in 1976 a Minister was found guilty of contempt of court for remarks made in the lobby of the House of Commons[8] although in another case the Canadian Supreme Court held that statements relating to government policy made outside the House could not be the foundation of an action at law if they had also been made in the House.[9]

The British courts have taken what seems a somewhat inflexible line on the use of words spoken in the House in the course of parliamentary debate as evidence in judicial proceedings that relate to events outside Parliament. In *Church of Scientology v Johnson Smith*[10] it was held that what was said or done in the House in the course of proceedings there cannot be examined outside Parliament for the purpose of supporting a cause of action, even though the cause of action arises out of something done outside the House. That was an action against a Member for defamation alleged to have taken place on a television programme and the plaintiffs were seeking to rely on the Member's statement in the House to establish malice. The decision was upheld however in *R* v *Secretary of State for Trade ex parte Anderson Strathclyde*[11] so as to rule out the establishment of a question of fact about the minister's actions that had no relevance to free speech.

The problem is not confined to Westminster. A recent dispute in Australia suggested the possibility of a different interpretation of the Bill of Rights prohibition on the impeachment or questioning of debates or proceedings. The issue arose from a prosecution of a judge (Mr Justice Murphy) on charges of attempting to pervert the course of justice. Mr Justice Murphy's conduct had been the subject of two Senate select committee inquiries and it was argued on behalf of the President of the Senate that Article 9 of the Bill of Rights (as applied to the Australian Parliament by Section 49 of the Constitution) prevented cross-examination in court both of the accused and of other witnesses on the evidence that they had given before the parliamentary committees. In the Supreme Court of New South Wales Hunt J. rejected this contention holding that Article 9 of the Bill of Rights had only the effect of preventing what had been said or done in the course of parliamentary proceedings from being *itself* the subject of criminal or civil action and did not prevent proceedings in Parliament or committee from being used as evidence of an offence committed elsewhere. A witness or a member, in other words, might be examined so as to impeach his credit by reference to the evidence of words spoken in Parliament, provided that there was something other than his participation in the proceedings that was the cause of the action. Adverse parliamentary reaction to this decision however resulted in legislation that now prevents evidence drawn from parliamentary proceedings being used for this purpose.[12]

In Britain even incidental references to the official report of debates in the course of judicial proceedings was formerly thought to require leave of the House. The practice of petitioning for leave seems to have originated in a House resolution of 1818 that required the House's permission for the attendance of its servants to give evidence in respect of evidence taken in the House, but the practice grew of petitioning for leave to make reference to the proceedings in a wider sense. The Privileges Committee considered the position in

1978–9 when a question was raised about the reference made to parliamentary proceedings in an Official Secrets Act case[13] and the House agreed to waive the requirement. That has of course no bearing on the purposes for which the Bill of Rights permits or prevents evidence derived from the report of proceedings to be used.

In 1987 a question of some interest arose as to the type of activity besides debate or committee activities that might qualify for protection from external questioning or intervention. The Attorney General had begun proceedings for injunctions to prevent publication of filmed or written details of a secret defence satellite system (the Zircon satellite project). A number of Labour MPs attempted to hold a showing of the banned film in a committee room of the House of Commons. The Attorney General thereupon applied to the High Court for an injunction against a number of named Members to restrain them from watching the film. Mr Justice Kennedy, without giving reasons, clearly took the view that whether or not the issue involved a proceeding in Parliament it concerned matters internal to the affairs of the House and rejected the application. A request was next made to the Speaker to use his authority to prevent the showing of the film. This the Speaker was reluctant to do but after a briefing by the Attorney-General on Privy Councillor terms he agreed to make an interim order until the House could determine the matter. The Speaker's order was withdrawn when the court injunctions were lifted. Meanwhile the House had referred the order to the Committee of Privileges. In its report the Committee concluded that the Speaker had acted properly, that the showing of the film was not a proceeding in Parliament, that the fact that something was done within the precincts of the House did not in itself confer any privilege or immunity, and that the Courts had jurisdiction in relation to matters not covered by privilege. The Committee thought that, given the difficulties of enforcing an injunction within the Palace of Westminster, the Courts would be unlikely to grant injunctions to prevent disclosures of information within the House.[14]

Ten years earlier a dispute between Members and the Attorney General had raised some related points about the scope of privilege in relation to judicial proceedings, national security, and contempt of court. In the same Official Secrets Act trial that raised the issue of the House's permission for reference to the official report (the so-called ABC prosecution) evidence was given by a security officer whose identity was concealed under the pseudonym 'Colonel B'. After several newspapers had named the officer in defiance of a direction by the court, and contempt proceedings had begun, four Members revealed Colonel B's identity in the House. The name was subsequently published in some newspaper reports and in a radio broadcast. The Members were later held to have breached the House's *sub judice* rule but attention was focused on a different issue by a statement issued for the guidance of the press by the Director of Public Prosecutions. The statement said that it was not accepted that the publishing by the press of Colonel B's name might not be a contempt of court even if it had been made part of a report of proceedings in the House. The Committee of Privileges later conceded that the Director of Public Prosecutions might be right and that his statement was not itself (as some suggested) a contempt of the House.

Though criminal acts committed within the House are not in general protected by privilege, words that might otherwise be criminal contempts or criminal or seditious or blasphemous libels or in breach of the Official Secrets Acts are covered by absolute privilege and protected by the Bill of Rights from prosecution, if used in the course of a debate or a proceeding in Parliament – though cases could be imagined where such words (as perhaps between one Member and another) were not uttered for the purpose of the business being transacted in the House or as part of a parliamentary proceeding.

At the time of the prosecution of Clive Ponting under the Official Secrets Act in 1985 it was suggested that publication of information that would otherwise be in breach of the Act would not be so if it were given to a select committee, since it would thereby be absolutely privileged as a proceeding in Parliament. That would of course protect the committee members from prosecution, and it might have protected Mr Ponting in respect of any evidence given if called and examined by the Committee, but it would not necessarily have prevented his prosecution for supplying the information in breach of the Act. As to members' activities that are not directly connected with the transaction of legislative business, a generous view was taken in *R* v *Graham-Campbell*[15] (in which it was found that freedom from the constraints of the licensing laws was a privilege that was required for the energetic discharge of the duties inherent in the House's role). Lord Hewart added in that case that the bulk of the provisions of the Licensing Acts were quite inapplicable to the

Commons. It was not supposed that use of the bars by Members was a proceeding in Parliament.

The principle adumbrated in this and some other cases is too strongly stated, therefore, if put in the form of a supposition – as it sometimes is – that the general law does not apply to matters internal to Parliament. Admittedly Lord Denman in *Stockdale* v *Hansard* said categorically that 'whatever is done within the walls of either assembly must pass without question in any other place'.[16] But most similar remarks have been concerned with the absence of judicial control over the House's administration of its own membership and its legislative business[17] or with matters closely connected to such business or with the impracticality of law enforcement within both Houses. It is clear that privilege does not oust the operation of the ordinary criminal law within Parliament and it is not denied that a statute passed by Parliament can by specific words override privilege: s.427(7) of the Insolvency Act 1986 provides an example. The matter is perhaps one of parliamentary intention in each case where the general law impinges on Members of Parliament in areas not directly to do with their debates and related proceedings. So it may be (though the matter has not been tested) that the mental health legislation permits the compulsory detention of peers suffering from mental disorders.[18] Possibly also a wide range of other regulatory measures have some application to Members or to the staff of Parliament. If the Insolvency Act, the Trade Descriptions Act, or the Industrial Relations Acts[19] are applicable their effect could be said to purify and protect the role and authority of the House and not to derogate from it.

CHANGES AND REFORM SINCE 1967

On two occasions in recent years the House has reviewed its privilege and contempt powers. In 1967 a select committee[20] was set up to review the law and practice and report whether changes were desirable. A number of proposals were put to the committee, some of them radical – including a redefinition of contempt powers. But few changes were recommended[21] and of those hardly any were implemented. In July 1971 several motions on minor procedural matters were tabled and in the end the House agreed to rescind the resolution passed in 1762 forbidding publication of its debates and also to allow committees to authorize witnesses to publish evidence given by them. Both were steps in the direction of openness and liberality, but small ones. In 1977 the Committee of Privileges recommended some procedural changes for the raising of privilege cases and supported some of the minor recommendations made by its predecessor five years earlier.[22] These latter included abandonment of immunity of members from arrest in civil suits, abolition of the power of impeachment, and encouragement to the House to take into account in contempt proceedings the truth or reasonable belief in the truth of allegations made (if published rationally, appropriately, and proportionately to whatever public interest, if any, might be served by their publication after the making of all such investigations as might be reasonable before the allegations were promulgated). Here were three distinct, though cautious, gestures in the direction of natural justice.

The 1977 Committee added some recommendations of its own. Amongst them were the following:

> that a general statement should be made of the sorts of contempt
> that would be treated as such and that the House's penal
> jurisdiction should be used sparingly and only when essential to
> provide reasonable protection from obstruction likely to cause
> substantial interference with the performance of the House's
> functions or those of its members or officers;
> that 'proceedings in Parliament' should be defined by statute for
> purposes of absolute privilege in defamation;
> that the power to fine should be revived by statute;
> that the existence of a remedy at law for a Member's complaint
> should not exclude it, but the Speaker should take the remedy
> into account when deciding whether to afford precedence to
> debate on that complaint;
> and that complaints should be raised under a new procedure.

On 6 February 1978 the House approved the committee's recommendations for the new complaints procedure and also the suggested qualifications on the exercise of penal jurisdiction in contempt matters. A member wishing to raise a complaint must give written notice to the Speaker as soon as possible after the occasion of the alleged contempt or breach of privilege. The Speaker has discretion to decide if the issue should have the precedence given to privilege matters in the House. If the Speaker informs the House that he will allow precedence the Member is informed and may table a motion for the following day either proposing reference to the Privileges Committee or making some other motion.[23] The recommendations as to legislation on the definition of proceedings and power to fine were not approved.

RECENT COMPLAINTS AND THE PRIVILEGES COMMITTEE

Though the House has declined to codify or distinguish categories of contempts and breaches of privilege they can be seen to fall into several groups. All, if established, have the effect of interfering or having a tendency to interfere with the essential functions of the House, but the inference takes different forms.

One class of contempts consists of misbehaviour in the House or elsewhere by Members themselves. A second group of contempts is made up of acts by outsiders that challenge the authority of the House, or its committees or officers, or obstructs their procedures. The two major groups of alleged contempts that are the subject of members' complaints are however acts that constitute threats, molestation, intimidation, or improper pressures directed towards Members in relation to their Parliamentary duties, and finally contempts committed by speech or writing that reflect on the House or its Members (and thereby indirectly or constructively obstruct the performance of their functions by diminishing respect for them).

Examples in all these categories can be found in cases reported on by the Committee of Privileges since the 1967 Report on Privileges. Since 1967 some thirty-odd complaints have been referred to and reported on by the Committee. Since 1978 the House and the Committee of Privileges have accepted the view that action should be taken only to prevent substantial interference with the House's legitimate functions and that in the case of written or spoken reflection Members should in general pursue legal remedies rather than invoke the House's contempt jurisdiction. So the Committee's recommendations allow some judgement to be made about the extent to which the House's penal jurisdiction has been liberalized. A major effect of the 'substantial interference' rule and the new procedure has been to eliminate complaints – often frivolous – being made on the floor of the House and to halve the number of cases going to the committee.

221

LEAKS AND PREMATURE DISCLOSURES

One increasingly common category of challenge to the House's authority and disobedience to its resolutions has been the publishing by newspapers of reports or evidence being considered by select committees before being reported to the House. Here the committee has been in something of a dilemma, since in every case the disputed material has patently originated in a leak by a member of the relevant committee for political or personal motives and in very few cases has the culprit been discovered. Recent leaks have included draft reports or evidence about biological warfare, the Civil List, wealth tax proposals, the Special Branch, radioactive waste, and a report of proceedings (relating to leakages) of the Privileges Committee itself. After the wealth tax leak the committee recommended that the editor of the *Economist* and its parliamentary reporter should be excluded from the House for six months, but the House overturned the recommendation by 64 votes to 55, perhaps recognizing the inequity of pursuing newspapers while leaving the leaking parliamentary culprits unpunished (though in 1968 an MP, Mr Tam Dalyell, was found guilty of a breach of privilege and reprimanded for leaking information to the *Observer* newspaper). In 1985 the Privileges Committee considered the general problem and concluded that the privilege of dealing with press offenders should be maintained and journalists suspended when necessary in order to deal with the possibility of documents being improperly obtained, or with the contingency of 'substantial interference'. The 1967 Committee on Privileges remarked similarly on the danger that might arise from 'powerful organs of the press' attacking the House not once but persistently. In 1986 the editor of *The Times*, after printing a draft report from the Environment Committee, appeared before the Privileges Committee and defended his action saying that *The Times* had no intention of showing disrespect to the House but had weighed the public interest involved in publication and thought that it was more important than the maintenance in that case of the House's privilege. The committee in its report[25] was not convinced, and alleged that the desire for a scoop may have been involved – a suggestion calculated to diminish respect for *The Times* newspaper and one perhaps best made under the protection of parliamentary privilege. The committee recommended that *The Times*'s lobby correspondent should be suspended for six months, but on a division the House disagreed. Whilst accepting that a contempt had been committed, it was not prepared to exercise its penal jurisdiction.

MEMBER'S BEHAVIOUR AND MISBEHAVIOUR

The privileges enjoyed by Members are capable of being abused and one such opportunity is offered by the absolute protection given to words spoken in the course of debate. Members are of course subject to the discipline of the House itself, but historically privilege has been used to publicize matters that the general law might penalize if spoken or written about outside the chamber. If the justification for that is that reputations should not be slanderously or libellously destroyed or the right to fair trials prejudiced, it is not over-whelmingly evident that defamation and contempt of court become unobjectionable when confined to Westminster. Some Members in recent times have adopted the practice of naming in the House persons who could not be named or attacked outside without legal consequences. It is generally thought – at least by Members – that this may be a necessary facility. It may indeed on occasion benefit a Member's constituents or publicize scandals but the benefit to the general welfare may in some cases be debatable. In March 1986 a question by Mr Geoffrey Dickens was disallowed by order of the Speaker on the ground that it made unnecessary and invidious use of a name in asking for the institution of criminal proceedings. In 1986 complaint was made to the Speaker that some Members were abusing both Question Time and early day motions to make accusations and innuendos against persons outside Parliament. An early day motion by Mr Brian Sedgemore, for example, made reference to allegations that Lord Rothschild was a Soviet agent and Mr Dale Campbell-Savours tabled questions about a long list of former security officers who had allegedly acted in breach of the Official Secrets Acts.

Members who abuse the privileges or rules of order of the House may of course themselves be guilty of contempt and be subject to reprimand, suspension, or expulsion. Mr John Profumo was held in 1963 to have committed a contempt of the House by making a personal statement that was later admitted to be untrue, and in 1947 the House voted to expel a Member (Mr G. Allingham) who in a press article had accused Members of dishonourable conduct, but had himself corruptly accepted payments for disclosing information to the press. Sometimes a collective abuse escapes sanctions as did the action of fifteen Members on 17 January 1985 when they refused to resume their seats after the Speaker had refused to accept further points of order, compelling him to suspend the House for twenty minutes.

THREATS AND PRESSURES: THE PERMISSIBLE LIMITS

One of the recommendations of the 1967 Privilege Committee was that the expression 'freedom from molestation' should be discontinued. It perhaps originated as part of the privilege against the potential harassment of Members by arrest or other legal procedures, but there is undoubtedly a class of contempts punishable by the House that could be called threats, intimidation, or molestation of Members. If we leave aside physical threats, however, it has always been somewhat uncertain what forms of pressure or influence by citizens or constituents might bring them within the ambit of the House's penal jurisdiction.

In the period since the 1967 report a number of such issues have been considered by the Privileges Committee. In 1969 there occurred one of the few cases that have involved actual physical molestation or obstruction of Members, when a sub-committee of the Select Committee on Education and Science visited Essex University and were jostled and manhandled by students. They got little support from the House. Though the committee concluded that the assaults disclosed a contempt[26] – which it would seem beyond question that they did – the committee's report recommended no action and by implication blamed the sub-committee for exposing themselves to the obstruction which they encountered.

Several cases have involved threatened sanctions of various kinds by trade unions. Three such complaints involved a threat to withdraw cash support from pro-Common-Market trade-union-sponsored Members,[27] a National Union of Mineworkers resolution purporting to prohibit such members from speaking against union policy under threat of withdrawal of sponsorship,[28] and a NUPE conference resolution demanding assurances from six NUPE-sponsored members that they would refrain from supporting the government's expenditure policy.[29] Though none of these threats was persisted with, the committee reiterated the view that it had expressed in the case of Mr W. J. Brown[30] in the 1940s, that it is a breach of privilege to take or threaten action that is calculated to affect a Member's freedom of action in Parliament and that members should be free to discharge their duties 'without fear of punishment or hope of reward'. The precise conditions under which freedom, integrity, and independence may be considered to be impaired nevertheless require further elucidation. In the NUPE case the committee conceded that there is nothing improper in an outside body providing financial assistance or reward, provided that this does not betoken any kind of control. But can Members, who presumably hope to continue to be assisted and rewarded, have their reward diminished or removed and still be thought free and unrestrained by hope, fear, or any similar sentiment? A sponsoring body is entitled to terminate its sponsorship – as it did in the case of Mr W. J. Brown – but it must not, the committee has held, use that entitlement so as to seek control over what a member does in the House or to punish him for what he has done. Members who lose their sponsorship stipends without being harangued in relation to any particular measure or measures before the House may perhaps be discouraged but not punished. What of merely political sanctions against Members by outside bodies or constituents? Clearly they can be applied in a democracy but perhaps they cannot be threatened ahead of time if the talk or threat relates to a particular vote or legislative proceeding rather than to a general course of conduct. There is perhaps a distinction between urging voters not to support a Member if he votes in a particular way and using the threat to do so as a way of coercing or influencing the Member's conduct. In 1984 the Committee of Privileges condemned as a breach of privilege remarks by Mr Tony Banks MP in the course of a debate on the Greater London Council (Money) (No. 2) Bill.[31] Mr Banks had said in the debate that he would use his influence at County Hall to restrict new capital projects in the constituencies of Members who voted to make part of the GLC's capital expenditure subject to Treasury control. They should not believe 'that they would get away', he said, 'without some retribution being visited on them'. The Privileges Committee held these words to be a threat to the freedom of action of Members and a breach of privilege. They recommended no further action, on the ground that the threat appeared to have failed to influence the actions of those to whom it was addressed. But the evidence for that seemed to be chiefly the fact that the Member who raised the issue said that it had failed to influence his action.

One form of impediment or restriction on the freedom of action of

Members has been held clearly not to involve any breach of the House's privileges, namely the restriction imposed on a Member who is undergoing a term of imprisonment. In 1971 the Committee of Privileges had little hesitation in reaching that conclusion though they recognized that the constituents of a gaoled MP, 'like the House, are deprived of his services until his release'.[32]

CONTEMPT BY SPEECH OR WRITING

A number of cases about which Members have complained in the past have involved alleged contempt of the House committed by words written to or about Members, or spoken outside the House, that reflect adversely on the performance of their duties. Some examples from the last two decades are as follows. Mr Maxwell complained that an article in the *Sunday Times* had misrepresented his behaviour as Chairman of the Commons Catering Sub-Committee. (No contempt was found by the Privileges Committee.)[33] Mrs Dunwoody complained that the *Travel Trade Gazette*, in criticizing a speech made by her, had surmised that she might have been 'primed' by certain travel trade interests (a 'serious contempt of the House').[34] Mr Ogden complained of a similar article in a Liverpool newspaper that posed the question: 'Eric Ogden MP who does he serve?' (The Committee found it inappropriate to intervene.)[35] Complaint was made of a statement by the National Abortion League that a Select Committee of the House on Abortion was biased (The accusation should not be construed as a contempt the Committee held.)[36]

Further complaints were made about a newspaper allegation that a 'bookies' lobby' existed in the House;[37] about a document issued by the Social Democratic Alliance listing Labour MPs who allegedly had collaborated with Communist Front organizations;[38] and about a remark by a Wolverhampton alderman to the effect that Mrs Renee Short was unwise to visit Wolverhampton as a member of the Estimates Sub-Committee. (The Committee thought this 'could be construed as a contempt of the House but should not in fact be so construed'.)[39]

Sometimes words spoken about Members contain both adverse reflection and implied threats. On 21 August 1983, for example, Mr Harvey Proctor complained of words spoken at a meeting of Women Against Rape to the effect that note would be taken of Members who blocked the Marital Rape Bill and that they would live to regret it.

In several of these cases the committee discussed the principles that should apply to constructive contempt by speech or writing. In general, the committee has suggested, Members should use their legal remedies rather than invoke privilege. On the other hand the House should reserve the use of its powers to punish extreme cases – for example when there is 'constant repetition of an unjustifiable and improper attack . . . upon a group of members'.[40] In a case in 1974, when a Member of the House (Mr Ashton) had alleged in a BBC interview that a number of Members had, for money payments, 'surrendered their freedom of action as Parliamentarians to outside bodies', the committee found this to be a serious contempt, adding that any such conduct as that alleged would amount to a gross contempt of the House.[41] In the case of the complaint made by Mrs Dunwoody, the editor of the newspaper argued boldly that his criticism that the Member had been acting as a 'pawn' of outside interests was justified, leading the committee to note that the House had never definitely decided whether to allow justification. The tradition in fact has been to suppose that contempt of the House is analogous to criminal libel and that justification cannot be pleaded.

PRIVILEGE AND THE TREATMENT OF CONTEMPTS

Survey of the application of privilege and the use made of the House's contempt jurisdiction in recent years suggests that despite the recommendations of the 1967 Committee on Privileges many Members were until 1978 prepared to invoke privilege and to threaten its use in cases that did not merit it. Since 1978 the new procedure for raising complaints has prevented such complaints from being raised publicly. The Select Committee on Privileges, by contrast, has taken a moderate and non-interventionist view and has clearly accepted the injunction that action by the House should be narrowly confined to cases in which there has been substantial interference with the working of the House or the freedom of action of its Members. The House as a whole has also behaved even more circumspectly than the committee – for example in declining to exclude journalists who have printed committee documents leaked by Members and in refraining from extending the ambit of 'proceedings in Parliament'.

A query that arises is whether the House has not been excessively cautious in failing to consider in more detail the kinds of offence against Parliament that should properly fall within its present contempt jurisdiction. There also remains a case for relinquishing the contempt jurisdiction altogether and vesting it in the courts.[42] In particular the courts are a more appropriate forum than the House, both for the weighing of allegations as to contemptuous reflection on the House and of other forms of contemptuous action. Members themselves are unlikely to see the first question in its proper light – namely as one about the survival of a form of seditious libel, and the survival of a contempt jurisdiction without appeal or right of legal representation seems contrary to principle and conceivably may be inconsistent with Article 6 of the European Human Rights Declaration. It remains true that twenty-five years of criticism of the workings of privilege and contempt powers, both by critics and Members themselves, has had an undoubted impact and if the future continues to resemble the immediate past the liberties of Englishmen will not be much threatened by the law, privileges, proceedings, and usage of Parliament.

Chapter Twelve

WHERE HAVE WE GOT TO?

MICHAEL RYLE

I am often asked what have been the main changes in the Commons since I came to work here in 1951. Leaving aside individual personalities, I can point to changes in the types of person who become Members of Parliament, increasing concern with information on every matter, closer contact with the public, greatly increased parliamentary activity by backbenchers (and willingness by those backbenchers to speak and act independently of party guidance), more formal recognition of the role of the opposition, growing difficulty in coming to grips with the details of legislation and of public expenditure, and finally many more staff and consequential demand for accommodation services. These, and many other significant developments, are discussed more fully in the previous chapters of this book. Here I want to pull the threads together and to attempt to weave into an intelligible tapestry a picture of the part the Commons play today in the wider political scene. I will finally speculate on a few areas where further changes may or may not be desirable.

The various strands of the changes listed above are interrelated and self-sustaining. For example, new types of Member, trained in the use of words and figures – teachers and lecturers, advertising and PR men, journalists, social workers, accountants, industrial consultants, and economists – mostly with the benefit of higher education (see Rush, chapter 2) are more likely to be active in tabling motions, questions and amendments, and in using research services or assistants, than were the country gentlemen and retired army officers, on one side, and the former manual workers and trade-union officials on the other, who were the main occupants of their respective backbenches some thirty years ago. Because they are more active, they also take up more constituency cases and they require extra staff, who require accommodation. Because they wish to be active they find scope for interesting backbench work, for example in select committees and in party committees. Because they make the work more interesting, more similarly experienced, interested, and active people are attracted to a parliamentary career. It is a virtuous spiral.

Running through this interweave there is, however, a common theme, and this, I believe, is the central feature of the Commons' function today, namely the acceptance of the Commons as a critical body, concerned, as the Americans put it, with the oversight of government and not, as historically portrayed, as a decision-making body concerned with legislating and controlling government expenditure and taxation. Although the constitutional role of the governing parliamentary party (to which Richards, Norton, and Drewry all draw attention in their chapters), which effectively conditions what measures and policies the government is able to bring before the House, is of great importance, it can nevertheless be argued that the essential role of the Commons was always (except perhaps for a few years in the middle of the last century) the 'critical' one. And the increasing emphasis on this aspect in recent years is reflected, as this book has shown, in the way Members actually use their time and resources, whatever they may claim to be doing or seeking to do.

The extent of this change has, however, not always been recognized, and various commentators (including Walkland in his concluding chapter to *The Commons Today*[1]) have continued to hanker after a concept of the House of Commons as a great old Victorian nanny, keeping the ministerial children in order, deciding what they should be allowed to do, laying down policies, and running the family home. Even the Procedure Committee in its 1978 report could seek for a redress of the 'balance of advantage' between the executive and the legislature, implying that the latter should be able to take some of the decisions taken by the former[2] (their successors in 1987 more realistically concluded that the 'principal objective of parliamentary activity is to put the politics and actions of Government under close scrutiny').[3] This way frustration and disillusion inevitably arise. For, as I argued in the opening chapter of *The Commons Today*, 'much of the criticism of Parliament, and particularly of the House of Commons today, flows . . . from this fundamental mistake in their perceived functions. Parliament is wrongly blamed for bad government, because Parliament does not govern'.[4]

The most helpful – because it reflects reality – concept of the Commons today is simple. The House of Commons is essentially a forum within which the powers of government are exercised; this is where the policies of ministers have to be publicly announced and scrutinized, where the actions of the executive may be publicly discovered, criticized, and defended, where the alternative policies of the opposition are paraded, where the issues of the day are publicly debated, and where the views of the people are articulated by those they have chosen to represent them. We do not have government by Parliament but rather government through Parliament. As Gladstone once argued (even at that Victorian high-tide of the powers of Parliament), the House was convened not to legislate or govern but to be the constant critic of those who do govern.[5]

Whatever may have been the assumptions in earlier years, the experiences of the last thirty must convince any objective observer that the House's influence today (and influence, not power, is the right term), derives from the public nature of its critical proceedings – speaking for and to the people – and not from the powers it formally exercises to approve legislation, expenditure, and taxation (although these formal requirements guarantee the opportunity for the exercises of influential criticism and are essential for giving parliamentary opinion – especially on the government back benches – effective leverage on the government's policies). With one striking exception (the Shops Bill of the 1985–6 session), government bills do not get defeated, although occasionally legislation is withdrawn and more frequently significant changes are made to bills during their passage through Parliament. Nor, today, are the estimates ever directly amended by the Commons which theoretically exercises the 'power of the purse'.

Yet many people, including some MPs and some academics, find it difficult to accept this essentially responsive (as opposed to initiating) and critical (as opposed to decision-taking) parliamentary model. This may be partly because so many of the proceedings of the House are necessarily in a decision-taking form. There are the various stages of bills, there are elaborate financial procedures for sanctioning expenditure (although now largely formal as part of the House's business) and for giving statutory authority for taxation, and there are set piece debates (on the Defence White Paper, for example) when the House's approval is formally sought and given for various aspects of government authority. Many of the codified procedures of the House, especially the standing orders, serve to underline and define these more formal proceedings.

However, there are many areas of government which are unmatched by such formal parliamentary proceedings and where no claim, even theoretical, could be made for seeking parliamentary authority. These include most aspects of foreign affairs, many aspects of economic policy, most decisions in the defence field, including the development of very expensive weapons systems, the allocation of capital expenditure on roads, schools, hospitals etc., and the numbers, levels of pay, and conditions of service in public employment. On all such matters the government does not normally have to seek formal parliamentary authority and, unless there is need for legislation, the initiative for bringing such matters before the House lies not with ministers but with the official opposition or with backbench Members on either side.

Here the procedures – and more formal procedural descriptions of the House – have been largely silent. Until 1985 no time was formally allotted for business initiated by the opposition (although for many years the right of the opposition to choose the topic for debate on the old supply days was generally accepted).[6] The rules are silent on other opportunities that are used by the opposition to bring matters of their choosing before the House. Again, although standing orders make formal provision for private Members' bills and motions to have priority on certain days, they do not specifically set out the numerous other opportunities available for backbenchers.[7] The rules say, for example, that (except for emergency debates under SO No. 20) only ministers may move a motion for the adjournment of the House; the fact that on most such occasions the debate is opened by backbenchers on topics of their choosing is not mentioned.

In general the procedures and many formal analyses of the proceedings of the House tend to emphasize the traditional, decision-taking concept of the House and to play down the critical and overseeing role of the parties and of individual Members. Yet, as this book has shown, increasingly the actual day-to-day work of those parties when in opposition, and of backbenchers on both sides at all times, has been largely concerned with seeking, grasping, improving, and using opportunities for exercising those critical functions.

This comes through clearly from reading the reports of Procedure Committees. Especially since the days when Richard Crossman was leader of the House, the most rewarding route towards parliamentary reform (to which the Study of Parliament Group itself has been to sympathetic) has involved a 'package-deal' approach. Procedure Committees are solely composed of backbench Members and they have naturally and consistently sought to advance and improve (or protect) opportunities for backbenchers, by greater use of select committees, more debating outlets in standing committees, improved scrutiny of delegated legislation and European Community documents, estimates days, use of special standing committees on some bills, provision for emergency debates, additional adjournment debates, etc. But they have placed such changes in the context of an acceptance of the need to protect the government decision-taking processes, especially regarding legislation and the authorization of expenditure. Hence they have accepted or recommended such things as limited debate on guillotine motions, abolition of debate on Consolidated Fund Bills, more timetabling of the committee stages of bills, restricted debate after 10 p.m. on delegated legislation, etc.

The picture that emerges from these reports is of Members generally casting round for opportunities to bring forward business of their choosing and to scrutinize governmental policies and actions at times convenient for them, especially when they can catch media attention.[8] Members on all sides, it may be said, are struggling to free themselves from the limitations imposed on their parliamentary conduct by the traditional framework of the government's legislative programme and its consequent control of the time of the House. This is shown by their increased activity in putting down questions (including private notice questions) and early day motions, in seeking emergency debates under SO No. 20, and in spending much more time on select committee work; it is also shown by the increasing use of less formal opportunities.[9] Most of these activities, it should be emphasized, involve use of procedures which, unlike the legislative process, do not normally involve divisions and are thus far less subject to control by the whips on either side.

The struggle for a platform for more independent criticism is even reflected in the increasing willingness of backbenchers to accept and to participate in the timetabling of debates in various ways, as shown particularly by recent reports of the Procedure Committee.[10] Although on the face of it, this might seem to involve a restriction of critical opportunities, for many Members the greater predictability of business, the curtailment of late sittings in the House and of interminable sittings in standing committees on contentious bills, and the hoped-for consequential release of more time for backbench business, as well as the improved opportunities for looking properly at all clauses of bills, were gains that overweighed the possible loss of influence that oppositions believe they secure by lengthy obstruction of unpopular legislation. Many backbenchers on both sides would prefer to use their time more constructively than in extended fili-busters. It is perhaps noteworthy that neither the government nor the opposition frontbench have appeared sympathetic to these argu-ments. Few of the more important recent Procedure Committee recommendations have been implemented.[11] Both frontbenches, it would seem, prefer to keep control of business firmly in their own hands, rather than that of backbenchers, and this tends to sustain the more formal business of the House rather than the broader oversight role.

However, despite this traditional reluctance to accept the critical role of the House, in practice the work of most Members has in-creasingly been oriented in that direction. Within the framework of a system which serves to sustain an elected majority government in office, while providing a platform for an alternative government party, all three main elements – the government, the official opposition, and backbenchers from both sides – have recognized that the House is not collectively initiating policy (although undoubtedly influencing it) but instead is responding critically to the separate initiatives of those three elements as well as to occasional external impulses. How this has emerged from the studies in the earlier chapters of this book can now be summarized.

Effective parliamentary criticism needs three things: opportunities for the three elements to exercise initiative, appropriate procedures and techniques for critical examination, and information.

The opportunities for the government to initiate business in the House are large and primarily devoted to legislation. As Borthwick shows (chapter 4, table 4.1), the time devoted in recent sessions to all types of business initiated by the government remains more than half the time spent on the floor of the House; nearly 30 per cent of the total time of the House itself is spent on government bills, and between 5 and 10 per cent of the time is also required for delegated legislation, including Northern Ireland legislation. But even when the business is initiated by the government, the main responsibility for its scrutiny – and for the use of time for this purpose – lies with the opposition and backbenchers who table amendments and secure debate on various clauses. The critical processes embrace critical response as well as critical initiative.

The opposition also raise matters of their own choosing. This occurs not only on the twenty allotted opposition days but during Prime Minister's Questions, by amendment to the address in reply to the Queen's Speech, and on other occasions. The varied nature of opposition – which involves consensus as well as conflict – and its complex character is emphasized by Norton (chapter 6). The increasing influence of such criticism – especially when government backbenchers find themselves in temporary alliance with the official opposition – has been notable in the last twenty years.

In chapter 5 Irwin shows the range of opportunities now also available for private Members, and their growing use. She concludes that the limited availability of legitimate opportunities at prime time has prompted more and more Members to use less legitimate opportunities to raise issues that they believe merit attention.

Frustration is naturally felt by backbenchers who have many matters of current concern to them or their constituents that they wish to raise, but only limited opportunities to do so at short notice and at a time when the attention of the House and the media may be caught. Recognizing this frustration, the present Speaker has shown himself particularly sympathetic to backbenchers. So as to enable as many of them as possible to have at least ten seconds of floor time, he calls more supplementaries on selected oral questions of topical interest (as a result fewer original questions get reached, but those lower on the list may still be given a chance to make a point). He allows questioning on ministerial statements to last longer; for example, some 71 hours were devoted to 109 statements (excluding business statements) in 1985–6, compared with 36 hours on 91 statements in 1975–6, giving averages of 39 minutes and 24 minutes, respectively per statement. He calls as many Members as possible on the weekly business questions. And he has been relatively generous, compared with some predecessors, in allowing private notice questions (see Irwin, chapter 5, page 82).

Turning to techniques for critical scrutiny, earlier chapters have shown how these have been significantly extended in recent years. Not all aspects of government can be effectively examined, or new policy ideas efficiently advanced, by the traditional process of debate. Irwin shows the new and extended uses that Members are making of questions, especially written questions, and of early day motions; Robinson (chapter 8) examines new, though as yet not fully used, procedures for scrutinizing public expenditure; and Johnson and Bates (chapters 9 and 10) discuss the increasing use being made of select committees.

The latter development is of the greatest importance. The volume and complexity of government does not shrink, and if Parliament is to match the decision-making processes of government with critical scrutiny there is neither time nor technique for doing all of this on the floor of the House. As far as volume of work is concerned, the solution lies partly in sending matters for debate to standing committees. Drewry (chapter 7) describes how these committees are used for scrutiny of bills and statutory instruments; they are also used for debates on certain more specialized business such as Scottish and Welsh matters and European documents.

Examination of more complex matters, however, requires not only more time but also different techniques than simple debate or questions. Select committees undertake work that the House could not possibly do itself. In my view there is no doubt that the creation of a comprehensive select committee system in 1979, together with further extension of the scope of the committees' inquiries and increasing skills in the last Parliament, constitute the most important, and potentially influential, evolution in the working of the House of Commons for many years. The House has, at last, equipped itself with the machinery and resources to carry out effective criticism over nearly the whole range of government – and, if it wishes, to look over the horizon at problems not yet on the Government's agenda.

The relative success so far of the new select committees gives me great personal satisfaction (I long ago urged their creation, I was in at their birth, and I am now closely involved with their work). I cannot discuss their achievement at length here, but wish to underline one point only. One of the values of the parliamentary question is that every civil servant is aware that if something goes wrong – at any level – he is liable to have to give the facts so that his minister can answer a PQ. Awareness of parliamentary accountability is thus permanently and widely instilled throughout the executive. A similar awareness is created by the Public Accounts Committee and other older scrutiny committees. But these processes of accountability are not usually related to policy. The main achievement of the new departmentally-related select committees has been to extend this awareness of Parliament into the departments of government at the most important, policy-forming, level.

The new committees each carry out up to six or eight inquiries a year – some lengthy and detailed, others short and snappy in response to an issue of immediate concern. Clearly even work of this intensity leaves much of the work of each department unexamined, but the *potential* for examination is now there. In my view the most important aspect of the committee's work is simply this: in each department each section or branch must now know that what they are doing is liable to be examined by the select committee covering the department; and each civil servant advising a minister on a change of policy must have to ask himself, and be prepared for the minister to ask, 'what will the select committee say about this; can we justify it effectively before them?'. This injection of a parliamentary dimension into the policy-forming process, which results from the very conduct of select committee inquiries (quite apart from what they may say in their reports), gives to these committees increasing influence as a now indispensable part of the critical processes of the House.

The third requirement for effective criticism is obvious. The House and its Members must be able to get the information they need about almost all aspects of government, and much besides, and if criticism is to be influential, to publish it. Here again the critical processes of the House have been expanded and developed in recent years. Rush shows in chapter 2 how new types of people are becoming MPs who are more thirsty for information and who are employing more staff to handle it. In chapter 3 Lock describes the growth of research and information services, both personal to Members and more generally through the Library of the House; and he discusses how this information flow could be more effectively provided. Irwin refers to the growth in the use of questions for written answer when seeking information. And the value of select committees in discovering information on complex matters in a systematic way (far more effective than debate or questions) is brought out by Johnson, Robinson, and Bates.

Outward flow of information, not only about the work of the House but about government and the world, as discovered by the House's processes, is essential if Parliament is to be heeded by – and

hence influence – the electorate. Borthwick examines the publication
of debates by Hansard and the press and considers the case for and
against televising the proceedings. Lock describes some of the publications issued by the Library. Irwin emphasizes how some of the
activities of Members, such as tabling early day motions, are concerned with publicizing causes or ideas. And again, Johnson and
Robinson note the educative value of select committee publications.

There is one general point that should be made about the work of
the House as a critical forum. Those who speak in this forum or seek
to gain or give information (including witnesses before committees)
would be severely hampered if they did not have absolute freedom of
speech. The ability of Members to raise controversial issues, or to
criticize the conduct of those who may be doing things detrimental
to their constituents (say in neglecting safety regulations in a factory)
would be greatly impeded if any statement that contained criticism
of a minister, civil servant, or outside body or person was liable to
have to be justified in a court of law, with the rigid requirements of
legal processes. The responsible exercise of the ancient privilege of
freedom of speech remains essential to the effective working of
Parliament. In chapter 11 Marshall examines some of the problems
in sustaining the House's privileges today.

In advancing my main argument for regarding the House of
Commons as a forum for critical scrutiny, I do not claim that that is
its only function. Many Members – perhaps indeed most – enter
Parliament to engage in political warfare, and it would be ludicrous
to pretend that every Member on the government backbenches is
spending all his working hours looking critically at the policies and
actions of his own ministers; he is much more concerned, much of
the time, with attacking the opposition. Nevertheless the overall
impression, which I believe is sustained by the more detailed studies
in this book, is of a House primarily engaged in criticism of parties,
people, policies, and practices – on either side of the divide – rather
than in more detached decision-making or political control. Members
of Parliament do not sit down solemnly to 'make the law'; that is the
function of ministers and their civil servants. The House of Commons
scrutinizes the outcome and requires its explanation and defence.

I believe that this book also shows that the House is performing
this function today more energetically, more efficiently, and in a
more sustained and systematic way, than it did some thirty or forty
years ago. But we must not be complacent. I will conclude with a

few personal comments on certain current problems and possible areas for improvement.

The composition of the House of Commons determines the main parameters of the political scene; and parliamentary processes and the approach of Members to their work are in their turn influenced by that outcome. Parliament creates but also reflects, serves to accommodate and eventually responds to political change. But the response may not be immediate – old ways die hard – and for a time the House may be out of tune with the new melody. Something of this is possibly being experienced today.

The ideological differences between the main parties today are probably as wide as at any time in this century. There is an increasing number of Members on both sides who adopt a militant approach to politics and whose main concern on the floor of the House is to 'put the boot in' to their opponents; some Members on the government backbenches believe that their side will remain in power for many years to come; and some opposition Members act as though they have scant prospect of their party ever becoming a party of government. All of this leads to a noisy and troublesome House – often causing problems for the Speaker and other occupants of the chair.

It may also cause problems for the leaders and whips of both sides. In the past the prospect of power after the next election exercised a moderating influence on an opposition party; it had to be seen as a party fit for government and it had to avoid setting precedents – in use of parliamentary obstruction for example – that could prove awkward when it next came to power. Similarly the governing party had, in the past, to conduct its operations in the House with an awareness that before long it was likely to find itself on the opposition side; it could not afford to behave too arrogantly. Thus we had for most of the 1950s, 1960s, and 1970s a fairly moderate approach to politics with a fair measure of consensus in Parliament. This, among other things, helped the evolution of the select committee system. But the situation today may be rather different. The leaders of the main parties today may find it more difficult – indeed they may not wish – to moderate the behaviour and partisan approach of their own supporters. This raises the question of how far the 'critical forum' theory of the role of the Commons is still tenable.

Certainly it would appear that the cooler, more detached processes, or the use of procedures by backbenchers for cross-party causes, could become less prominent. A weakening of consensus might make it harder to operate select committees; some more militant Members have always shown their contempt for them in any case. There could, therefore, be a move in the next few years away from the critical role towards the purely confrontational.

In my view, however, it may well work out the other way. Government supporters who are confident of remaining in power may get bored with attacking a party which they do not regard as an effective threat and, while they are on the back benches, may prefer to spend their time and make their reputations by being active in careful scrutiny of the conduct of their ministers. For them, work on select committees could be quite rewarding and worthwhile.

Similarly many opposition backbenchers may see that crude slanging of the government will get them nowhere. They may see more advantage in detailed examination of some of the government's policies and actions – for example, by exposure of scandals, attacks on secrecy, and publicity for failures – and generally in calling the Government to account. For this the careful consistent use of questions and persistent inquiry in select committees (as several Members showed in the last Parliament on such issues as the *Belgrano* and Westland) is ideally suited.

Therefore it may well be that the present composition of the House, and the wide divide between the parties, may actually enhance the critical role of the House, just as did, somewhat paradoxically, the narrow majorities of the 1970s. We must wait to see.

Finally there are some aspects in which some change may be needed before the House can perform its critical role as efficiently as possible. First there is the question of the balance of time spent on legislation (some 45 per cent of all stages of bills and related proceedings in recent years) as opposed to other business. While it is important to look carefully and critically at all legislative proposals, time must also be available to consider other major areas of government that do not involve legislation. In other comparable Commonwealth Parliaments – those of Australia and India for example – bills are passed far more speedily (perhaps too hastily), but much more time is spent in debating matters of immediate concern. In the House of Commons, by contrast, many hours were spent in 1981 debating every detail of the Wildlife and Countryside Bill (to take one example) while little time was available on the floor of the

House to debate the Government's decision to proceed with the Trident weapon system and other major projects involving many millions of public money. We should at least question whether we have struck the right balance here, and further consideration may have to be given to the recommendations of the Procedure Committee for timetabling of legislation.

A closely related problem is how to enable the House – especially on backbenchers' initiative – to consider urgent matters or matters of immediate contemporary relevance. Too often issues that are being discussed widely outside Parliament receive little formal attention on the floor of the House. Again the Procedure Committee has made some limited suggestions – possible additional adjournment debates for example[12] – but the problem highlighted by Irwin at the end of her chapter will surely require further attention.

Lastly, as Robinson points out, the House still does not examine systematically the vast canvas of government expenditure. Select committees may be able to look in more depth at the problems of individual departments, but a broader view is also needed. At present there is no occasion when the House is required to match, by any form of parliamentary examination or debate, the central decision of the Cabinet on the overall balance of expenditure between major services, within an accepted total. If Parliament is to scrutinize effectively the central policies of the Government – and hence influence them – it cannot afford to neglect this aspect.

Other challenges may arise. For example, we will soon know whether or not the House is going to accept television on a permanent basis (at present only an experiment has been approved) and, if so, how it will cope with it. A televised House would certainly affect – I would say benefit – the critical process by improving the House's contact with the public. And, quite separately, if, through new voting systems or otherwise, we should ever move into an era of so-called 'hung Parliaments', the role of the Commons would also be fundamentally affected.

These are questions for the future. In the meantime the House of Commons has shown itself capable of performing an increasingly effective critical role. That is why I am optimistic.

241

NOTES

1 THE ROLE OF THE COMMONS

1 A. V. Dicey, *Law of the Constitution* 9th edn, Macmillan, 1939, p. 39.
2 *Considerations on Representative Government*, 1861, ch. 5, OUP, 1948.
3 ibid.
4 See his valuable article, 'The place of Parliament in the legislative process', *Modern Law Review*, vol. 14, 1951, pp. 279–96 and 425–36.
5 *The English Constitution*, 1867, ch. 4, Fontana, 1977.
6 E. A. Foresey, *The Royal Power of Dissolution in the British Commonwealth*, Oxford University Press, 1943; B. S. Markesinis, *The Theory and Practice of Dissolution of Parliament*, Cambridge University Press, 1972; R. Brazier, 'Government formation from a hung parliament', *Public Law*, Autumn 1986, pp. 387–406.
7 *Parliamentary Government in England*, Allen & Unwin, 1938, p. 158.
8 *A Grammar of Politics*, Allen & Unwin, 1925, p. 300.
9 HC Debs, 1951–2, 498, col. 886 ff.
10 *Speeches and Letters on American Affairs*, 1776 p. 73 of the Everyman edition.
11 J. P. Mackintosh (ed.), *Parliament and People*, Saxon House, 1978, paper 13.
12 Discussion of this question was greatly stimulated by Professor Finer's article, 'The individual responsibility of ministers', in *Public Administration*, vol. 34, 1956, p. 377.

2 THE MEMBERS OF PARLIAMENT

1 For an analysis of the general election of 1983 in particular see Anthony Heath, Roger Jowell, and John Curtice, *How Britain Votes*, Pergamon, 1985. For recent longer-term analyses see Richard Rose and Ian McAllister, *Voters Begin to Choose: from Closed Class to Open Elections in Britain*, Sage, 1986, and Mark N. Franklin, *The Decline of Class Voting in Britain: Changes in the Basis of Electoral Choice, 1964–83*, Clarendon, 1985.
2 For a general description and analysis of the selection of parliamentary candidates see Michael Rush, *The Selection of Parliamentary Candidates*, Nelson, 1969, and for more recent developments see Michael Rush, 'The

"selectorate" revisited: selecting parliamentary candidates in the 1980s', *Teaching Politics*, vol. 15, 1986, pp. 99–113.

3 See, for example, Heinz Eulau and Moshe M. Czudnowski (eds), *Elite Recruitment in Democratic Politics: Comparative Studies Across Nations*, Sage, 1976.

4 Unusually, in 1983 of the twenty-three women MPs thirteen were Conservative and ten Labour.

5 See S. E. Finer, H. B. Berrington and D. J. Bartholomew, *Backbench Opinion in the House of Commons, 1955–59*, Pergamon, 1961, and H. B Berrington, *Backbench Opinion in the House of Commons, 1945–55*, Pergamon, 1973.

6 Anthony Barker and Michael Rush, *The Member of Parliament and His Information*, Allen & Unwin, 1970, pp. 380–1.

7 See Philip Norton, *Conservative Dissidents: Dissent Within the Parliamentary Conservative Party, 1970–74*, Temple Smith, 1978, and *Dissension in the House of Commons, 1974–79*, Clarendon, 1980.

8 *Report of the Committee on the Remuneration of Ministers and Members of Parliament* (The Lawrence Report), Cmnd 2516, November 1964.

9 Review Body on Top Salaries, *First Report: Ministers of the Crown and Members of Parliament* (The Boyle Report), Cmnd 4836, December 1971.

10 HC Debs, 1987–8, 120, cols 295–344.

11 HC Debs, 1985–6, 101, cols 1130–42.

12 For more details on pay, allowances, services, and facilities see Michael Rush and Malcolm Shaw (eds), *The House of Commons: Services and Facilities*, Allen & Unwin, 1974, and Michael Rush (ed.), *The House of Commons: Services and Facilities, 1972–1982*, Policy Studies Institute, 1983. For comparative data see Michael Rush, 'The pay, allowances, services and facilities of legislators in fourteen countries – a comparative survey', and Thomas Stark, 'International comparison of the remuneration of Members of Parliament', in Review Body on Top Salaries, *Report No. 20: Review of Parliamentary Pay and Allowances*, Cmnd 8881–II, May 1983, pp. 98–133, and Michael Rush, 'The allowances, services and facilities of legislators in sixteen countries: a comparative survey, 1986', in Review Body on Top Salaries, *Report No. 24: Review of Parliamentary Allowances*, Cm 131–II, April 1987, pp. 89–99.

13 Supply Estimates, 1973–4, Class I, HC 114, 1972–3, and Supply Estimates, 1987–8, Class XIX, Votes 6 and 14, and Classes XX and XXA, HC 227, 1986–7.

14 *Review of the Administrative Services of the House of Commons: Report to Mr Speaker by Sir Edmund Compton*, HC 254, 1974.

15 *House of Commons (Administration) – Report to Mr Speaker* (The Bottomley Report), HC 624, 1974–5.

16 Review Body on Top Salaries, *Report No. 20*, Cmnd 8881–II, May 1983, Section 1, tables 16 and 17.

17 Rush and Shaw, op. cit., pp. 200, 210.

18 Review Body on Top Salaries, *Report No. 24*, Cm 131–II, April 1987, Section 1, tables 1.2, 1.4.

3   INFORMATION FOR PARLIAMENT

1 A. Barker and M. Rush, *The Member of Parliament and his Information*, Allen & Unwin, 1970. The project began in late 1966.
2 Some papers fall into an intermediate category – white papers with green edges. They cover topics on which the government is prepared to accept representations on aspects of its policy, though the broad outlines are settled.
3 Parliamentary questions as an opportunity for backbenchers are dealt with more fully in chapter 5.
4 HC Debs, 1986–7, 115, col. 56w.
5 They are listed in the White Paper on Government Statistical Services, April 1981, Cmnd 8236, pp. 11–12.
6 HC Debs, 1984–5, 79, col. 2w.
7 HC Debs, 1967–8, 769, col. 18w.
8 *Review of Government Statistical Services – Report of the DHSS Study Team*, 1981, para 48.
9 G. Drewry (ed.), *The New Select Committees*, Oxford University Press, 1985, especially chapter 18 by G. F. Lock, 'Resources and operations of select committees – a survey of the statistics', which is the source of the figures quoted in this section unless otherwise stated.
10 If, as sometimes occurs, the reports do not list the evidence in this category, it virtually sinks without trace, except in the case of the very assiduous research worker.
11 *Select Committee Return, 1985–86*, HC 172, 1986–7, especially p. 99.
12 In addition to those that do employ committee assistants, the Defence Committee has been assisted at various times by officials seconded from the National Audit Office.
13 *First Report from the Select Committee on Procedure*, HC 588–I, 1977–8, p. lxxxii.
14 *Sixth Report of the Estimates Committee*, HC 308, 1964–5, p. v.
15 In G. Drewry (ed.), op. cit., p. 380.
16 ibid., p. 389, 391.
17 Review Body on Top Salaries, *Report No. 24: Review of Parliamentary Allowances*, vol. 2, April 1987. Study by Hay Management Consultants Ltd, p. 29. Cm 131–II.
18 In the *Fabian Journal*, November 1957, quoted by Barker and Rush, op. cit., p. 202.
19 G. Alderman, *Pressure Groups and Government in Great Britain*, Longman, 1984, p. 63.
20 Op. cit., pp. 63, 65.
21 Ian Greer, *Right to be Heard*, Ian Greer Associates, 1985, p. 120.
22 *Report of the Committee on Financial Aid to Political Parties* (The Houghton Report), Cmnd 6601, August 1976, p. 20.
23 Op. cit., pp. 241, 249–50.
24 Review Body on Top Salaries, *Report No. 24*, vol. I, paras 54–7 and para. 12 of Appendix B.

25 Sir D. Wass, *Government and the Governed*, Routledge & Kegan Paul, 1984, p. 76. See also P. Hennessy, 'Preparing for power – why the opposition needs more help from the Civil Service', *Listener*, 27 November 1986, p. 4.

26 Op. cit., p. 288–9.

27 Source: reports of the Review Body on Top Salaries.

28 The latter figure no doubt shows the effect – though probably not fully – of the resolution of the House of 16 July 1986 which increased the annual staff allowance by 52.5 per cent from £13,211 per MP to £20,140. Broadly, the result of this increase was that Members could reckon on employing a full-time research assistant as well as a full-time secretary, instead of a part-time (or shared) research assistant in addition to a full-time secretary. The latter mix was thought appropriate by the Review Body on Top Salaries (*Report No. 24*, para 5), but the House thought otherwise.

29 *Second Report from the Select Committee on Assistance to Private Members – Research Assistance*, HC 662, 1974–5, paras 9, 11. The committee gave some examples of what it meant by 'personal assistance': 'For some [Members] the emphasis would be on constituency "welfare" work. For others the emphasis would be placed more on assistance in matters currently before the House. For some the assistance would be concerned with policy matters, for others much more with the research work done in the Library.'

30 *Supply Estimates*, 1974–5, Class XIII, p. 3, and 1987–8, Class XX, p. 26. It is not possible to separate expenditure on secretarial assistance from expenditure on research assistance. The 1987–8 figure includes provision for staff pensions.

31 Op. cit., vol. I, paras 21, 23 and 53.

32 ibid., vol. II, pp. 34–5.

33 Op. cit., p. 264.

34 The staff figure is in terms of full-time equivalent. The figure for the budget excludes some computer costs. On the Library, see D. Englefield, *Parliament and Information*, The Library Association, 1981, pp. 20 ff.; D. Menhennet in M. Rush (ed.), *The House of Commons: Services and Facilities, 1972–1982*, Policy Studies Institute, 1983, pp. 47–69.

35 Cm 131, II, p. 34.

36 Op. cit., pp. 360–1.

37 Op. cit. vol. II, pp. 34–5.

38 Cm 131, I, p. 12.

39 *Report of the Informal Joint Committee on Computers to the Leaders of both Houses*, HC 78, 1976–7, p. 1. In the field of computers there is, unusually, formal co-operation between the two Houses, and the Computer Development Officer works for both the Lords and the Commons.

40 *Fifth Report from the Select Committee on House of Commons (Services)*, HC 377, 1976–7. Debated on 26 January 1978. For an account of the development of POLIS, see *First Report from the House of Commons (Services) Committee, Session 1984–85. Information Technology: Members' Requirements*, vol. II, HC 97–II, pp. 174–9.

41 By mid-December 1985 about a hundred Members had used the office expenses allowance to buy computers and word processors. HC Debs, 1985–6, 89, col. 16.

42 Op. cit., vol. I, para. 10.

43 *Third Report from the Select Committee on House of Commons (Services)*, HC 571, 1983–4, p. xxxvii.

44 HC Debs, 1984–5, 82, col. 1386.

45 Op. cit., vol. I, para. 29.

46 ibid., vol. II, p. 87.

47 A. Likierman and P. Vass, *Structure and Form of Government Expenditure Reports: Proposals for Reform*, Certified Accountant Publications, 1984, p. 26.

48 New Scientist, 3 March 1988, p. 28; The Times, 24 February 1988, p. 2.

49 G. F. Lock, 'The role of the Library', in A. H. Hanson and B. Crick (eds), *The Commons in Transition*, Fontana, 1970.

50 G. F. Lock, 'Statistics for politicians', *Statistical News*, 1971, p. 12.9.

51 *Economist*, 13 September 1986, p. 91.

4 THE FLOOR OF THE HOUSE

1 Some of the points made in this chapter arise from the work of a study group of the Study of Parliament Group on debate in Parliament. I am grateful to the members of that study group and to the MPs and journalists to whom the group talked.

2 For a fuller description of the physical setting of the House see K. Bradshaw and D. Pring, *Parliament and Congress*, Quartet, 1973, pp. 124–6.

3 *First Report from the Select Committee on Procedure 1986–87: A Parliamentary Calendar*, HC 157, 1986–7.

4 For details of the amount of time spent after the 'normal moment of interruption' (10 p.m. on Mondays to Thursdays and 2.30 p.m. on Fridays) see table 1 in *Second Report from the Select Committee on Procedure 1986–87: The Use of Time on the Floor of the House*, HC 350, 1986–7.

5 For details of the length of other recent sessions see HC Debs, 1984–5, 78, written answers, cols 127–8.

6 5 March 1985 on the Water (Fluoridation) Bill.

7 For comparable figures from a decade earlier see S. A. Walkland and M. Ryle (eds), *The Commons Today*, Fontana, 1977, rev. edn 1981, p. 66, table 1.

8 Erskine May, *Parliamentary Practice*, (commonly referred to as 'May's Parliamentary Practice') 20th edn, Butterworth, 1983, pp. 303–4.

9 ibid., p. 304.

10 See also table 5.4 in Helen Irwin's chapter in this volume, p. 97.

11 Under SO No. 10 in 1984–5 and 1985–6; this was renumbered as SO No. 20 in late 1986.

12 The guillotine resolution may also limit time in standing committees.

13 D. Alton, 'A portrait of the Alliance as the Official Opposition', the *Independent*, 6 May 1987.

14 HC Debs, 1984–5, 81, col. 29. The reference to 5 January should read 5 June. I am grateful to Andrew Kennon of the Clerk's Department, House of Commons, for drawing this quotation to my attention.

15 *Third Report from the Select Committee on Procedure, 1985–86: Short Speeches*, HC 592, 1985–6.

16 It is doubtful, for example, whether any modern commentator would go as far as Sidney Low, writing in 1904, when he described the Commons as 'the most remarkable public meeting in the world. . . . Its debates are studied beyond the Channel and beyond the Ocean': S. Low, *The Governance of England*, Fisher Unwin, 1904, p. 55.

17 Mr Francis Pym, quoted in P. Riddell, 'Believer in a balanced House', *Financial Times*, 15 May 1987.

18 See for example, *The Times*, 6 May 1987.

19 One would be unlikely to read today in a newspaper report of the previous day's proceedings: 'The House adjourned at 19 minutes before midnight', *The Times*, 6 May 1947.

20 On this whole topic see *Factsheet No. 40: Broadcasting Proceedings of the House of Commons*, produced by the Public Information Office of the House. These paragraphs draw heavily on this factsheet.

21 *Second Report for the Select Committee on Sound Broadcasting 1986–87*, HC 282, 1986–7.

22 *First Report from the Select Committee on Sound Broadcasting 1986–87*, HC 281, 1986–7.

23 Francis Pym, quoted in the *Financial Times*, 15 May 1987.

24 For a fuller discussion of these arguments see B. Franklin, 'MP's objections to televising Parliament', *Parliamentary Affairs*, vol. 39, 1986, pp. 284–96.

25 Speaking in the House of Commons in March 1901, quoted in Low, op. cit., p. 63.

26 See, for example, the description of the nineteenth-century House in E. Taylor, *The House of Commons at Work*, 5th edn, Penguin, 1963, p. 86.

27 Earl Winterton, *Orders of the Day*, pp. 317–18, quoted in P. G. Richards, *Honourable Members*, Faber & Faber, 1959, pp. 84–5.

28 I. Aitken, 'Labour's absent-minded approach to opposition', The *Guardian*, 22 June 1984.

29 Quoted in *The Times*, 6 December 1984.

30 G. Thomas, *Mr Speaker*, Arrow, 1986, p. 187.

31 See *First Report from the Liaison Committee 1982–83: The Select Committee System*, HC 92, 1982–3 para. 31.

32 A point addressed by the Liaison Committee in HC 92, 1982–3 paras 30–31.

33 A view expressed by N. Shrapnel in *The Performers*, Constable, 1978, p. 139.

34 *Listener*, 1 June 1978; reprinted in D. Marquand (ed.), *John P. Mackintosh on Parliament and Social Democracy*, Longman, 1982, p. 55.

35 Quoted in the *Financial Times*, 15 May 1987.

36 John Watson MP quoted in the *Guardian*, 31 May 1986.

37 22 November 1984. On this incident see, for example, Julian Haviland, *The Times*, 23 November 1984.
38 This point is considered more fully in Appendix 20 to HC 350, 1986–7, cited above.
39 On this see the work of Philip Norton, for example his *The Commons in Perspective*, Martin Robertson, 1981, esp. chapters 9 and 10.

5   OPPORTUNITIES FOR BACKBENCHERS

1 For detailed rules on the content of questions, see Erskine May, 20th edn, ch. 17. These are applied, on behalf of the Speaker, by the clerks in the Table Office.
2 Sir Norman Chester and N. Bowring, *Questions in Parliament*, Oxford University Press, 1982; S. A. Walkland and Michael Ryle (ed.) *The Commons in the Seventies*, Martin Robertson, 1977, ch. 8; S. A. Walkland and Michael Ryle (ed.), *The Commons Today*, Fontana, 1981, ch. 8.
3 HC Debs, 1971–2, 848, col. 1070.
4 See points of order, 16 February 1987, HC Debs, 1986–7, 110, cols 657–8.
5 HC Debs, 1987–8, 1419, col. 6.
6 See for example HC Debs, 1987–8, 118, col. 364.
7 See *Fifth Report from the Select Committee on Procedure*, HC 320, 1976–7, Questions to the Prime Minister, for examples of substantive questions and a discussion of the open question.
8 HC Debs, 1980–1, 997, col. 494*w* and 1979–80, 970, col. 663.
9 See for example HC Debs, 1987–8, 119, cols 508–12, 537–40.
10 In the unusual event of the leader of the opposition tabling a question for oral answer, he would do so by private notice.
11 10 March 1987, HC Debs, 1986–7, 113, col. 160.
12 HC Debs 1987–8, 118, col. 6.
13 See *First Report from the Select Committee on Procedure*, HC 42, 1985–6, The Operation of Standing Order No. 10, para 5.
14 *Third Report from the Procedure Committee*, HC 254, 1986–7, Early Day Motions, Appendix 1.
15 See HC Debs 1986–7, 110, cols 459–60, col. 471, and 1987–8, 119, cols 971–3.
16 See HC Debs, 1987–8, 119, cols 508–12, 537–40.
17 See also 16 February 1987, HC Debs, 1986–7, 110, cols 742–9 and subsequent points of order 17 Feb 1987, HC Deb, 1986–7, 110, cols 776–80, for an instance when a Member sought unsuccessfully to start a third adjournment debate without notice and was asked by the Deputy Speaker not to continue with his speech because he had not given due notice to the minister concerned. In the course of the exchanges that followed, Mr Dalyell made it clear that the reason he had not sought to give notice of his intention to raise a potentially politically embarrassing subject (the police raid on BBC Scotland in Jan./Feb. 1987) was that, if he had done so, government whips would have sought to prolong the

previous debate to prevent there being sufficient time for a further
debate on the motion for the adjournment.

18 See also *Second Report from the Procedure Committee*, HC 350, 1986–7, The
use of time on the floor of the House, paras 66, 72.

19 May, op. cit., p. 337.

20 See J. W. Marsh, 'The constituency MP', in P. Norton (ed.), *Parliament
in the 1980s*, Blackwell, p. 56, and P. Norton, 'Dear Minister', *Papers
presented to the PSA Conference, April 1981*.

21 See *Report from the Select Committee on Parliamentary Questions*, HC 393,
1971–2, para. 28, and HC Debs, 1984–5, 80, cols 1–100w *passim*,
answers to Mr Peter Bruinvels.

22 HC Debs, 1986–7, 113, col. 1250–1.

23 see HC Debs, 1986–7, 110, cols 24–6 and 38–40w.

24 HC Debs, 1984–5, 74, cols 761–3.

25 HC Debs 1986–7, 115, cols 561, 567, 546, 559, 572, 576, respectively.

26 For example, EDM 404 in 1986–7 on the International Year of Shelter
for the Homeless which attracted 256 signatures.

27 *First Special Report from the Committee of Public Accounts*, HC 115, 1980–1.

28 EDM No. 132, session 1981–2.

29 National Audit Act, 1983.

30 Minutes of Evidence of the Procedure Committee, HC 254, 1986–7, Q9.

31 EDM 748, in session 1984–5, tabled by Sir John Biggs-Davison.

32 *Third Report from the Procedure Committee*,. HC 254, 1986–7.

33 ibid., Appendix 1.

34 See HC Debs, 1984–5, 80, cols 545–611 and also Appendices to the
Second Report of the Procedure Committee, HC 350, 1986–7. Use of time on
the floor of the House.

35 HC Debs, 1987–8, 119, col. 169.

36 *Minutes of Evidence of the Procedure Comittee*, 10 March 1987, HC 254,
1986–7, Q34.

37 HC Debs, 1986–7, 115, col. 56.

38 *Second Report from the Procedure Committee*, HC 350, 1986–7, The use of
time on the floor of the House, para. 73.

39 Sessional diary, Journal Office. The figure includes the time taken by
points of order during debates as well as at the commencement of public
business.

6 OPPOSITION TO GOVERNMENT

1 Members of the 'ex-Cabinet' held meetings and these became more
regular towards the end of the century. By the 1880s the term 'Shadow
Cabinet' was being used by some observers.

2 Until the twentieth century, when there was no former premier to lead
the party, separate leaders were chosen in the two Houses.

3 P. Norton, 'The organisation of parliamentary parties', in S. A.
Walkland (ed.), *The House of Commons in the Twentieth Century*, Oxford
University Press, 1979, pp. 10–14.

4 ibid. pp. 21–31. The 1922 Committee was so named because it was

formed by some Conservative Members returned for the first time in 1922 and not, as is sometimes assumed, after the meeting of Conservative MPs at the Carlton Club in 1922 that brought down the Lloyd George Coalition. The Committee was opened up to all Conservative private Members in 1925. See P. Goodhart, *The 1922*, Macmillan, 1973.

5 Erskine May, *Treatise on the Law, Privileges, Proceedings and Usage of Parliament* (commonly referred to as 'May's Parliamentary Practice'), 20th edn, ed. Sir C. Gordon, Butterworth, 1983, p. 252. Under the Ministerial and Other Salaries Act 1975, the Speaker's decision on the identity of the leader of the opposition – a position first recognised by statute in 1937 – is final.

6 D. Van Mechelen and R. Rose, *Patterns of Parliamentary Legislation*, Gower, 1986, p. 57.

7 For the distinction between 'policy' and 'administration' bills, see I. Burton and G. Drewry, *Legislation and Public Policy*, Macmillan, 1981.

8 Van Mechelen and Rose, op. cit., p. 59.

9 ibid. p. 58.

10 I. Jennings, *Cabinet Government*, Cambridge University Press, 1947, p. 15.

11 B. Castle, *The Castle Diaries 1974–76*, Weidenfeld & Nicolson, 1980, p. 79.

12 *First Report from the Select Committee on Procedure* HC 588–1, 1977–8, p. xxiv.

13 *Second Report from the Select Committee on Procedure*, HC 49–1, 1984–5, p. xviii. See especially the memorandum submitted by the study group on legislative procedure of the Study of Parliament Group, HC 49–iv, pp. 72–8.

14 ibid. pp. xxi–xxiv.

15 HC Debs, 1985–6, 92, cols. 1083–1136.

16 See A. Michie and S. Hoggart, *The Pact*, Quartet, 1978.

17 See P. Norton, 'The Liberal Party in Parliament', in V. Bogdanor (ed.), *Liberal Party Politics*, Oxford University Press, 1983, pp. 152–3.

18 The Social Democratic Party has suffered especially given the nature of its creation and its composition (comprising almost exclusively former Labour MPs); Labour MPs sitting below the gangway have made particular efforts to disrupt SDP speeches.

19 J. Grimond, *Memoirs*, Heinemann, 1979, p. 156.

20 See P. Norton, *Dissension in the House of Commons 1945–74*, Macmillan, 1975, pp. 387–9.

21 See P. Norton, *Dissension in the House of Commons 1974–1979*, Oxford University Press, 1980, p. 450.

22 P. Norton, 'Intra-party dissent in the House of Commons. A case study: the immigration rules 1972', *Parliamentary Affairs*, 29 (4), 1976, pp. 404–20.

23 P. Norton, *Conservative Dissidents*, Temple Smith, 1978, ch. 9.

24 P. Norton (ed.), *Parliament in the 1980s*, Blackwell, 1985, ch. 2.

25 *The Times*, 31 July 1987.

26 As one Labour MP pithily put it in conversation: 'I expect the motion to be carried by a small majority – of about 400!' He was not that far out.

The House passed the motion by 407 votes to 34. HC Debs, 1987–8, 120, cols 341–4.

27 Mrs Thatcher was opposed to the creation of the new committees and apparently circulated a paper to this effect. Only two or three members of the Cabinet expressed support for the committees, but given a manifesto commitment to allow a vote on the issue – and not wishing to face similar opposition to that which they had just witnessed from their own supporters on the issue of Members' pay – the Cabinet acquiesced. Confidential source to author.

28 J. Critchley, 'Keeping MPs out of mischief', *The Times*, 20 February 1971.

29 See the *Independent*, 24 July 1987.

30 P. Norton, ' "Dear Minister . . ." The importance of MP-to-minister correspondence', *Parliamentary Affairs*, 35(1), 1982, pp. 59–72; A. Mitchell MP, *Westminster Man*, Thames Methuen, 1982, p. 185.

7   LEGISLATION

1 See Gavin Drewry, 'Public General Acts – now and a hundred years ago', *Statute Law Review*, Autumn 1985, pp. 152–61.

2 See W. H. Greenleaf, *The British Political Tradition*, vol. 1, Methuen, 1983, pp. 40–1; Richard Rose, 'Are laws a cause, a constraint or irrelevant to the growth of government?', *Studies in Public Policy*, no. 124, University of Strathclyde, 1984.

3 Richard Rose, 'Law as a resource of public policy', *Parliamentary Affairs*, vol. 39, pp. 297–314.

4 See G. Ganz, *Quasi-Legislation: Recent Developments in Secondary Legislation*, Sweet & Maxwell, 1987.

5 David Miers and Alan Page, *Legislation*, Sweet & Maxwell, 1982, pp. 1–2.

6 Sir Courtenay Ilbert, *Legislative Methods and Forms*, Clarendon, 1901.

7 See *Report of the Select Committee on Procedure: The Process of Legislation*, HC 538, 1970–1, p. 267. The estimate takes no account of time spent on secondary and private legislation, nor does it include the vast amount of legislative business transacted off the floor of the House.

8 S. A. Walkland, *The Legislative Process in Great Britain*, Allen & Unwin, 1968, p. 20.

9 ibid., p. 71.

10 See John P. Mackintosh, 'The House of Commons and taxation', *Political Quarterly*, vol. 42, 1971, pp. 75–86.

11 G. Drewry, 'The parliamentary response to child abuse', in *After Beckford?*, Social Policy Papers No. 1, Royal Holloway and Bedford New College, 1987.

12 P. Bachrach and M. S. Baratz, 'Two Faces of Power', *American Political Science Review*, vol. 56, 1966, pp. 947–52.

13 Some notable examples from the 1970s can be found in G. Drewry, 'Legislation', in S. A. Walkland and Michael Ryle (eds), *The Commons Today*, Fontana, 1981, pp. 100 ff. For more recent instances, see Donald

14 R. Shell, 'The House of Lords and the Thatcher government', *Parliamentary Affairs*, vol. 38, 1985, pp. 16–32.
15 See T. St John Bates, 'The Procedure Committee and public bills: a seamless robe', *Statute Law Review*, Spring 1987, pp. 44–52, n. 2.
16 *Return of Standing Committees for Session 1984–85*, HC 308, 1985–6.
17 R. H. S. Crossman, *The Diaries of a Cabinet Minister*, vol. 3, Hamish Hamilton and Jonathan Cape, 1977, p. 903.
17 J. A. G. Griffith, *Parliamentary Scrutiny of Government Bills*, Allen & Unwin, 1984.
18 See note 13, above. Also Miers and Page, op. cit., pp. 125–30.
19 *First Report from the Select Committee on Procedure*, HC 588–1, 1977–8, paras 2.19–2.20.
20 See Bates op. cit., n. 8. Also discussion of the Shops Bill 1985–6, below.
21 Bates, op. cit., p. 45.
22 *Second Report from the Select Committee on Procedure*, 'Public Bill Procedure', HC 49–1, 1984–5.
23 ibid., para. 30; and see Bates, op. cit., p. 45.
24 *Second Report from the Select Committee on Procedure*, 'Allocation of time to government bills in standing committee', HC 324, 1985–6.
25 See Study of Parliament Group, 'Private bill procedure: a case for reform', *Public Law*, 1981, pp.206–27; R. J. B. Morris, 'Local legislation since 1974 – the era of Section 262', *Statute Law Review*, 1987, pp. 2–31.
26 Ivor Burton and Gavin Drewry, *Legislation and Public Policy*, Macmillan, 1981, pp. 35–40.
27 Both categories are more fully discussed, ibid., ch. 7.
28 For 'failure rates' in earlier sessions see Drewry, op. cit., table 1.
29 Rt. Hon. Lord Hewart of Bury, *The New Despotism*, Benn, 1929.
30 *Report*, Cmd. 4060, 1932.
31 Alan Beith, 'Prayers unanswered: a jaundiced view of the parliamentary scrutiny of statutory instruments, *Parliamentary Affairs*, vol. 34, 1981, pp. 165–73.
32 See Ganz, op. cit., *passim*.

8   THE HOUSE OF COMMONS AND PUBLIC MONEY

1 *First Report from the Select Committee on Procedure*, HC 410, 1968–9. Memorandum by the Specialist Adviser to the Committee, pp. 263–9. 'With the creation of the Public Accounts Committee in 1861 and the enactment of the Exchequer and Audit Departments Act in 1866, Gladstone was able to say that "the last portion of the circle" of parliamentary control of expenditure was complete' (Parl. Deb., 1866, 181, col. 1373).
2 The new series of national insurance contributions and benefits used to be implemented in the autumn when the annual announcement of changes took place. This set them out of line with changes in tax rates and bands which are announced and take effect in April. Although the announcement of changes will continue to take place in the autumn by a series of stages the implementation dates of the two types of charge and

benefit have been brought into line. By 1987 the transition was complete.

3 *First Report from the Treasury and Civil Service Committee*, HC 44, 1984–5, 'The structure and form of financial documents presented to Parliament', p. v. para. 1.

4 HC Debs, 1986–7, 106, col. 1235.

5 *Second Report from the Treasury and Civil Service Committee*, HC 110, 1984–5, 'The structure and form of financial documents presented to Parliament', p. vi.

6 HC Debs, 1985–6, 92, col. 932.

7 *Fourteenth Report of the Expenditure Committee*, HC 661, 1977–8, 'Budgetary reform in the UK'; Report of the Armstrong Committee, Institute of Fiscal Studies, 1980; *Eighteenth Report from the Public Accounts Committee*, HC 383, 1981–2, 'Publication and content of appropriation accounts'; *Sixth Report from the Treasury and Civil Service Committee*, HC 173, 1981–2, 'Budgetary reform'; Andrew Likierman and Peter Vass, *Structure and Form of Government Expenditure Reports*, Certified Accountants Publications, London, 1984; *Second Report from the Treasury and Civil Service Committee*, HC 110, 1984–5, 'The structure and form of financial documents presented to Parliament'; *Seventh Report from the Treasury and Civil Service Committee*, HC 323, 1984–5, 'Financial documents and Budget papers'; *Tenth Report from the Treasury and Civil Service Committee*, HC 544, 1984–5, 'Financial documents: Treasury proposals'; *First Report from the Treasury and Civil Service Committee*, HC 88, 1985–6, 'The form of the Supply Estimates 1986–7'; *Select Committee on Procedure (Supply)*, HC 118, 1980–1; *Select Committee on Procedure (Finance)*, HC 24, 1982–3. See also *Report by the Comptroller and Auditor General*, 'Financial reporting to Parliament', HC 576, 1985–6.

8 HC 110, 1984–5, p. vii, para. 10.

9 ibid., p. vii, para 15.

10 HC Debs, 1985–6, 92, col. 960.

11 Ann Robinson, 'The financial work of the select committees', in Gavin Drewry (ed.), *The New Select Committees*, Oxford University Press, 1985, ch. 17, pp. 307–18.

12 *Third Report from the Treasury and Civil Service Committee*, HC 158, 1984–85, Special Supplementary Estimates, Class II, Vote 10 (Budget of the European Communities).

13 Other select committees have examined portions of the estimates and a number of debates on their reports have been held on the floor of the House: See Gavin Drewry (ed.), *op. cit.*, p. 307.

14 *First Report from the Treasury and Civil Service Committee*, HC 88, 1985–6, 'The form of the Supply Estimates 1986–87', p. v.

15 ibid., p. 2, Memorandum by HM Treasury.

16 ibid., p. 2, 'Running costs'.

17 Ann Robinson and Cedric Sandford, *Tax Policy Making in the United Kingdom*, Heinemann, 1984, ch. 6.

18 Before 1861 the practice was to introduce several tax bills in a year but when the House of Lords rejected the Paper Duty Repeal Bill in 1860

Gladstone determined to find a means of outwitting the Lords on future occasions. He hit upon the idea of presenting all tax changes in a single Finance Bill. He reasoned that the Lords 'must either accept the whole or try the impossible performance of rejecting the whole' (Morley, *Life of Gladstone*, vol. 1, p. 674). His judgement proved sound until in 1909 the Lords rejected Lloyd George's Budget and thereby invited the reaction of parliamentary reform which effectively stripped them of their financial powers.

19 *Eleventh Report from the Expenditure Committee*, HC 535, 1976–7, 'The Civil Service', especially para. 153. *First Report of the Procedure Committee*, HC 588, 1977–8, paras 8.1–8.2). The Procedure Committee recommended, among other things that the Comptroller and Auditor General should be an officer of the House of Commons and that he should audit all bodies in receipt of public funds including local authorities. See also *First Special Report from the Committee of Public Accounts*, HC 115, 1980–1, 'The role of the Comptroller and Audit General'. Reply by the Treasury, Cmnd. 8323, 1981. For reiteration of the Committee's proposals see *Third Report from the Public Accounts Comittee*, HC 41, 1983–4, and *Eighth Report*, HC 105, 1983–4.

20 Robinson, *The New Select Committees*, p. 307.

21 Tim Eggar, HC Debs, 1982–3, 36, col. 1302.

9 DEPARTMENTAL SELECT COMMITTEES

1 In the 1983–7 Parliament the Liaison Committee issued one full-scale report on the select committee system in 1985 (quoted above); there is a similar, earlier report for the 1979–83 Parliament, published in December 1982.

2 From 1980 to 1987 there were fourteen departmental select committees appointed under 50 no. 130. After the 1987 General Election there were only ten Scottish Conservative members, five of whom held ministerial office. This made it difficult to man the Scottish Affairs Committee. By July 1988 the committee had still not been set up.

3 The Liaison Committee has twice questioned this exclusion but the Government has refused to make any change. Presumably it is felt judicial independence might be endangered if a select committee was established: an interesting application of the separation of powers doctrine.

4 This statement has to be qualified by the special powers of those committees (Foreign Affairs, Home Affairs, and Treasury and Civil Service) to appoint one sub-committee each.

5 1986 SO 130 (1).

6 Some comments on the referral of bills to select committees are to be found in N. Johnson, 'Select committees and administration', in S. A. Walkland (ed.), *The House of Commons in the Twentieth Century*, Oxford University Press, 1979.

7 There is also a Joint Committee on Statutory Instruments not discussed here.

8 For a more detailed account of select committees in the years 1965–80, see N. Johnson, 'Select committees as tools of parliamentary reform', in S. A. Walkland and M. Ryle (eds), *The Commons Today*, Fontana, 1981, ch. 9.

9 *First Report from the Select Committee on Procedure*, HC 410, 1968–9, 'Scrutiny of public expenditure and administration'.

10 On the Expenditure Committee see Ann Robinson, *Parliament and Public Spending: the Expenditure Committee of the House of Commons, 1970–76*, Heinemann, 1978.

11 *First Report of the Select Committee on Procedure*, HC 588–I, 1977–8, para. 1.6.

12 Mr Powell, a member of the 1976–8 Procedure Committee, voted for the select committee proposals.

13 The original recommendation was for twelve committees, but the collapse of devolution schemes for Scotland and Wales made it expedient to add two more, for Scottish and Welsh Affairs.

14 Ed. G. Drewry, Oxford University Press, 1985.

15 *First Report from the Liaison Committee*, HC 92, 1982–3, 'The select committee system', and ditto HC 363, 1985–6.

16 *First Special Report from the Liaison Committee, 1985–6* The government's reply to the committee's first report, HC 225, 1984–5, 'The select committee system'.

17 For comparison it should be noted that the Public Accounts Committee published fifty-two reports in the same period, and the European Legislation Committee twenty-nine. In productivity the 'new' committees have their rivals.

18 The procedural rules governing committees do not permit minority reports, though there are devices for publishing amendments which, though rejected, look like the statements of dissenting minorities. The rules do, however, work in favour of consensus.

19 Sir Robert Armstrong, Cabinet Secretary and head of the Civil Service, gave evidence on 5 February and 5 March 1986 to the Defence Committee on his 'inquiry' into the leaking of a letter concerning Westland plc from the Solicitor General to the Minister of Defence. The record of these hearings covers forty-seven pages.

20 The figure of 195 refers to all those who served on the fourteen departmental committees in 1985–6; it exceeds by thirty-nine the number of members on these committees at any one time.

21 Instances of select-committee members moving quite early to ministerial office can, of course, be found; for example Mrs Edwina Currie, parliamentary secretary at the DHSS since late 1986, had served previously on the Social Services committee. But she had gained notice in other ways too.

22 The sessional returns make clear how 'cheap' are the services secured from many witnesses and writers of memoranda.

23 At the time of writing this additional guidance had not yet been embodied in a revised version of the 1980 *Memorandum of Guidance for Officials*.

24 *First Report from the Liaison Committee*, HC 363, 1984–5, para. 13.
25 Standing Orders of the House of Commons for Public Business, 1986, Nos 52 and 131.
26 Examples such as the financial absurdity of the dog licences then in force are quoted in the *First Report of the Liaison Committee*, HC 363, 1984–5, para. 12.
27 Apart from being named in motions debated in the House, committee reports may be referred to on the order paper as relevant to debate. For a full list of such references see the Appendix to the *First Report of the Liaison Committee* HC 363, 1984–5. In addition, there is scattered evidence suggesting that some debates have been better informed as a result of the publication of a select-committee report.
28 Even service on the opposition front bench takes precedence over serving on a departmental select committee as the record of discharges from select committees in the 1983–7 Parliament shows. Acting as spokesman on a major bill may also require a committee chairman to resign, as illustrated by Mr John Golding's surrender of the chairmanship of the Employment Committee in late 1982.
29 See N. Johnson, *Parliament and Administration, The Estimates Committee 1945–65*, Allen & Unwin, 1966, ch. 6, pp. 167–72.

10 SCRUTINY OF ADMINISTRATION

1 *Twenty-fifth Report from Select Committee on European Legislation*, HC 21–xxv, 1985–6, para. 4.
2 *Fourteenth Report from Committee of Public Accounts*, HC 98, 1985–6.
3 *Second Report from Select Committee on Statutory Instruments*, HC 32–ii, 1985–6.
4 *Third Report from Select Committee on the Parliamentary Commissioner for Administration*, HC 312, 1986–7, pp. 55–65.
5 SO No. 122.
6 HC Debs, 1985–86, 100, col. 1200.
7 National Audit Act 1983, s.1(1). Previously, the appointments were made by the Crown on the advice of the Prime Minister.
8 See the Comptroller and Auditor General's evidence on the nature of his independence to the Expenditure Committee: *Eleventh Report from the Expenditure Committee*, HC 535, 1976–7, Minutes of Evidence, p. 582.
9 National Audit Act 1983, s.6(2).
10 He is required to 'take into account any proposals made by the Committee of Public Accounts' in carrying out any examination into the economy, efficiency, and effectiveness with which any body within his jurisdiction has used its resources in discharging its functions: National Audit Act 1983, s.6(1).
11 Exchequer and Audit Departments Act 1921, s.1.
12 A list of the accounts which the Comptroller and Auditor General either audits or over which he exercises some supervisory function is contained in Cmnd 7845, Annex B.

13 This type of inquiry was given statutory authority in the National Audit Act 1983, pt II.

14 The Treasury appoints accounting officers for each department and public body and they are responsible for ensuring proper financial management. See, with respect to such appointments, the Exchequer and Audit Departments Act 1866 and the Government Trading Funds Act 1973.

15 For the modifications in the approach to the value for money audit see *Third Report of the Comptroller and Auditor General*, HC 41, 1982–3.

16 There are exceptions; the committee has indicated that it will take regular evidence from the chairmen of regional health authorities: *Seventeenth Report*, HC 255, 1980–1.

17 It is very rare for the committee to take evidence from ministers. It could arise if expenditure was incurred on a decision of a minister against the express written advice of the permanent secretary as the accounting officer. The last occasion on which a minister gave evidence was in less dramatic financial circumstances; the Secretary of State for the Environment gave evidence in 1980 during the committee's investigation into the role of the Comptroller and Auditor General: *First Special Report*, HC 115, 1980–1. The committee is empowered to take evidence outside Westminster and it has, for example, paid a visit to the Court of Auditors of the European Community in the course of an inquiry into the work of the Court: *Fifth Report*, HC 92, 1981–2.

18 See HC 183, 1963–4, and the subsequent debate in HC Debs, 1963–4, 693, col. 408.

19 HC 269, 1981–2.

20 HC 406, 1985–6.

21 The Ministry of Defence has agreed to supply the Select Committee on Defence annually with details of current equipment projects estimated to cost £25 million or more for development and £50 million or more for production: *First Report from the Select Committee on Defence*, HC 340, 1986–7. It seems likely that the Public Accounts Committee will be supplied with similar information.

22 HC 127, 1983–4. This inquiry involved Northern Ireland and on most inquiries involving public-sector finance in Northern Ireland the committee is assisted by the reports of the Northern Ireland Audit Office, the head of which is the Comptroller and Auditor General for Northern Ireland.

23 *Eleventh Report*, HC 107, 1985–6.

24 Cmnd 9776.

25 *Fourteenth Report*, HC 98, 1985–6.

26 Cmnd 9808.

27 *Twenty-Seventh Report*, HC 401, 1984–5.

28 Cmnd 9696.

29 *Eighteenth Report*, HC 204, 1986–7.

30 *The Epitome of the Reports of the Public Accounts Committee*, for 1857–1937 and for 1938–69.

31 The Liaison Committee has available to it three 'estimates days' each

year to debate subjects of its choice and it is possible for a report of the Public Accounts Committee to be chosen as a subject for debate.

32 HC Debs, 1985–6, 100, col. 1218.
33 See, for example, *Eighth Report*, HC 98, 1986–87.
34 See, for example, *The Citizen and the Administration*, Justice, 1961.
35 Local Government Act 1973, Pt III; Local Government (Scotland) Act 1975, Pt II.
36 National Health Service Act 1977, Pt V; National Health Service (Scotland) Act 1978, Pt VI.
37 The commission has subsequently acquired a similar role in respect of the Commissioners for the National Health Service.
38 Parliamentary Commissioner Act 1967, s.1.
39 The 1967 Act, s.5(1), (5).
40 See further, the 1967 Act, s.5(3), Sch. 3.
41 Parliamentary and Health Service Commissioners Act 1987; HC Debs, 1986–7 109, cols 1056–83.
42 However, the Commissioner may accept a complaint if he considers that the complainant cannot, for example be reason of cost or complexity, be reasonably expected to pursue such a remedy. See further the 1967 Act, s.5(3).
43 *Annual Report of the Parliamentary Commissioner for Administration for 1978*, HC 205, 1978–9, p. 4.
44 1967 Act, s.6(3).
45 HC Debs, 1966–7, 734, col. 51.
46 1967 Act, s.12(3).
47 *Annual Report of the Parliamentary Commissioner for Administration for 1986*, HC 248, 1986–7, para. 53. The same argument was deployed to deny the Parliamentary Commissioner jurisdiction over a complaint that a Registrar of Marriages had failed to attend a marriage ceremony: HC 490, 1971–2, Case C412/D.
48 1967 Act, s.8.
49 *Second Report, from the Select Committee on the PCA*, HC 312, 1984–5, Mins of Ev. QQ. 174, 176, 177.
50 *Annual Report of the PCA for 1986*, HC 248, 1986–7, para. 21.
51 ibid. In 1986 there were 719 referrals, in 1985, 759, and in 1984, 837. The number of referrals is likely to rise somewhat in consequence of the quangos which are now within the jurisdiction of the PCA.
52 387 MPs referred complaints to the PCA in 1986, 373 in 1985, and 386 in 1984.
53 *Second Report from the Select Committee on the PCA*, HC 312, 1985–6, Mins of Ev. Q.125 (Sir Geoffrey Otton, Second Permanent Secretary, DHSS).
54 For the full story of the investigation and its political aftermath see: *Third Report of the PCA*. HC 54, 1967–8; *First Report from the Select Committee of the PCA*, HC 258, 1967–8; HC Debs, 1967–8, 758 cols 105–17.
55 *Fourth Report of the PCA*, HC 191, 1983–4.
56 *Second Report of the PCA*, HC 150, 1982–3.
57 *First Report of the PCA*, HC 135, 1986–7, p. 1.

58 *First Report from the Select Committee on Procedure*, HC 588–1, 1977–8, para. 3.3

59 HC Debs, 1984–5, 79, col. 89*w*.

60 See, for example, the Transport Act 1985, s.46.

61 See, for example, the Child Abduction and Custody Act 1985, s.2(2).

62 The classic example of such wide powers is perhaps the European Communities Act 1972, s.2(2), which authorizes the executive, subject to the limitations contained in Schedule 2, to implement any European Community obligation of the United Kingdom by statutory instrument. A further sub-section of the Act provides that such a statutory instrument may include 'any such provision (of any such extent) as might be made by Act of Parliament'. Thus, within the terms of the 1972 Act, this delegated legislative competence becomes virtually coterminous with the legislative competence of Parliament.

63 In evidence to the Select Committee on Procedure, HC 257–i, 1985–6, Q. 14; see also *Special Report of the Joint Committee on Statutory Instruments*, HC 31–xxxvii, 1985–6, para. 2.

64 For example, the Safety Zone Orders made by the Department of Energy under the Oil and Gas (Enterprise) Act 1982, s.21, do not require to be laid and are scrutinized by the Joint Committee: see, for instance, *Eleventh Report*, HC 31–xv, 1985–6.

65 *Select Committee Returns for 1983–4*, HC 196, 1984–5; HC Debs, 1984–5, 79, col. 313*w*. In the 1984–5 session they held 58 meetings: *Select Committee Returns for 1984–5*, HC 295, 1985–6.

66 Woolwich Ferry Order, S.I. 1986 No. 330: *Sixteenth Report of Joint Committee on Statutory Instruments*, HC 341–xxi, 1985–6.

67 Building (Prescribed Fees Etc.) Regulations, S.I. 1985 No. 1576; *Fourth Report, of Joint Committee on Statutory Instruments*, HC 31–v 1985–6.

68 See, for example, *Twenty-fifth Report, of Joint Committee on Statutory Instruments*, HC 16–xxxix 1977–8; *Eighth Report of Joint Committee on Statutory Instruments*NC 21–xi 1974–5; *Twentieth Report of Joint Committee on Statutory Instruments*, HC 16–xxxii, 1977–8.

69 *Special Report*, HC 31–xxxvii 1985–6.

70 *Twenty-ninth Report*, HC 41–xxxviii 1983–4; *Thirty-first Report*HC 25–xl, 1984–5; see generally, *Special Report*, HC 31–xxxvii, 1985–6.

71 Statutory Instruments Act 1946, s.5.

72 This is in contrast to the House of Lords Standing Order 68 which provides that no instrument subject to any affirmative resolution may be brought before the House before it has been considered by the Joint Committee on Statutory Instruments.

73 HC 31–xxxvii, 1985–6, para. 15.

74 Government defeats do sometimes occur: the Labour government was defeated in 1978 on regulations made under the Dock Work Regulation Act 1976, and Conservative governments were defeated in both 1972 and 1982 on proposed new immigration rules, although technically they are not statutory instruments.

75 See, for example, *Twenty-sixth Report of Joint Committee on Statutory*

Instruments, HC 31–xxxiii, 1985–6, para. 3; Minutes of Evidence, HC 31–xxxiv, 1985–6.

76 *Twenty-seventh Report of Joint Committee on Statutory Instruments*, HC 41–xxxv, 1983–4.

77 *Fifteenth Report of Joint Committee on Statutory Instruments*, HC 31–xx, 1985–6, para. 4 and App. II.

78 Joint Committee on Statutory Instruments, *Minutes of Evidence*, HC 31–xxxiv, 1985–6, QQ. 2–4.

79 In the 1984–5 parliamentary session, the six standing committees considered 100 instruments at 71 sittings: *Standing Committee Returns for 1984–85*, HC 308, 1985–6; in the previous session they had considered 95 instruments in 80 sittings: *Standing Committee Returns for 1983–84*, HC 107, 1984–5.

80 See, for example, Select Committee on Procedure, *Minutes of Evidence*, HC 257–i, 1985–6.

81 HC 588–I, 1977–8, paras 3.15–3.18.

82 Select Committee on Procedure, *Memorandum of Evidence*, HC 257–i, 1985–6.

83 The Commons Select Committee on European Community Secondary Legislation (the Foster Committee) presented two reports: HC 143; HC 463–I, 463–II, 1972–3. The parallel committee in the House of Lords also presented two reports: HL 67 and 194, 1972–3.

84 For the present terms of reference of the committee, see SO No. 127; for the developments in the terms of reference, see *First Special Report from the Select Committee on European Legislation*, HC 126–iv, 1983–4.

85 For the terms of the resolution, see HC Debs, 1979–80, 991, cols 843–4; previously, there had been a government undertaking in similar terms: HC Debs, 1974, 872, col. 525.

86 *First Special Report from the Select Committee on European Legislation*, HC 126–iv, 1983–4, para. 18.

87 *First Special Report from the Select Committee on European Legislation*, 1983–4, HC 126–iv, paras 8(ii), 19.

88 For the statistics for the Parliamentary sessions 1979–80 to 1983–4, see *First Special Report from the Select Committee on European Legislation*, HC 126–iv, 1983–4.

89 HC Debs 1974–5, 899, cols 36–8, 106–7. This of course leaves the initiative in the hands of the government. The government has also undertaken to inform Parliament, through the Foreign Office, of Commission proposals which have been withdrawn bercause of th e degree of opposition within the Council. Although withdrawal of documents is not common, the system of informing Parliament when it does happen has not always worked well: see, for example, *First Special Report from the Select Committtee on European Legislation*, HC 126–iv, 1983–4.

90 The committee does take oral evidence on some matters from ministers; there is, for instance, evidence taken each year from the Minister of Agriculture on the Community Agricultural Price Proposals. The committee also takes quite extensive evidence on major proposals. When it was considering the Commission proposals for reform of the CAP, it

took evidence from twenty-seven representative bodies in the agricultural sector: *Fifteenth Report from the Select Committee on European Legislation*, HC 21–xv, 1985–6.

91 At that time there was a suggestion that the Commission was submitting documents late to the Council to avoid the political complications of scrutiny by national parliaments and late submission was the subject of a complaint to the Commission by the UK Government: *First Special Report from the Select Committee on European Legislation*, HC 126–iv, 1983–4 paras 8(iii), 12.

92 HC 159–xvi, 1979–80; HC 34–xviii, 1982–3; HC 21–xxix, 1985–6.

93 HC 34–i, 1982–3; HC 21–xxii, 1985–6; HC 22–ii, 1986–7.

94 Where the committee recommends that a document be related in standing committee this has been said by a leader of the House to be the main factor in determining whether the Government moves a motion to refer the document to a standing committee: *First Special Report from the Select Committee on European Legislation*, HC 126–iv, 1983–4 'Minutes of evidence', p. 5. The committee may also report that the document should be further considered by the House but that its adoption should not be delayed pending that consideration, and if circumstances change, for example if the issues raised by the committee have been met by amendments in the Council, the committee can withdraw a recommendation that a document be further considered by the House.

95 The Single European Act (Cmnd 9758), which amends the EEC Treaty, was incorporated into the domestic law of the UK by the European Communities (Amendment) Act 1986.

96 This matter has been considered by the Select Committee on European Legislation: see First *Special Report*, HC 264, 1985–6, and also by the House of Lords Select Committee on the European Communities: see *Twelfth Report*, HL 149, 185–6.

11 PARLIAMENTARY PRIVILEGE

1 Compare for example the Supreme Court's judgement as to the unlawful exclusion of Congressman Adam Clayton Powell (*Powell* v *McCormack* 395 US 486) with the inability of Charles Bradlaugh to secure judicial protection from exclusion by the House of Commons (*Bradlaugh* v *Gossett* [1884] 12 QBD 271).

2 *Re Parliamentary Privilege Act 1770* [1958] A.C. 331.

3 See Lord Denning 'The Strauss case' [1985] *Public Law* 80. In 1958 dissenting opinions were not permitted in the Judicial Committee of the Privy Council, so Lord Denning could not make public his dissent from the majority view at that time. See also Geoffrey Lock, 'Parliamentary privilege and the courts: the avoidance of conflict' [1985] *Public Law* 64.

4 HC Deb 591, 1957–8 col. 334.

5 HC 417, 1976–7, iii. This broadly endorsed the proposals of various earlier committees. See the Clerk of the House's memorandum and supplementary memorandum ('Definition of proceedings in

Parliament'), *First Report from the Committee of Privileges*, HC 365, 1986–7, pp. 4, 49–52.

6 408 US 501 (1972). See also 'Legislative privilege and the separation of powers' 86 *Harvard Law Review* 1113 (1973).

7 *R* v *Lord Abingdon* 1 Esp. 226.

8 *Re Ouellet* (1976) 67 DLR (3rd) 73: (1976)72 DLR (3rd)95.

9 *Roman* v *Hudsons Bay Oil and Gas Company, Trudeau and Greene* [1973] SCR 820.

10 [1972] 1 QB 522.

11 [1983] 2 All ER 233.

12 For an account of the Murphy case and the legislative rejection of the Court's view of the Bill of Rights see H. Evans, *(LXVIII) The Parliamentarian* (1987) p. 17. The Australian Parliamentary Privileges Act 1976 forbids *inter alia* the introduction of evidence based on proceedings in Parliament for the purpose of questioning or establishing the credibility, motive, intention, or good faith of anything forming part of those proceedings in Parliament.

13 HC 102, 1978–9.

14 *First Report from the Committee of Privileges* HC 365, 1986–7. See also HC 222, 1978–9 on the 'Colonel B' case.

15 [1935]1 KB 594. But a narrower view was taken in an earlier case *Williamson* v *Norris* [1899] 1 QB 7.

16 9 A & E 1 at 114.

17 E.g. *Bradlaugh* v *Gossett* (1884) 12 QBD 271 when Stephen J. said that the House of Commons was 'not subject to the control of Her Majesty's Courts in the administration of that part of the Statute Law which has relation to its own internal proceedings'. This view might be particularly applicable to decisions made by organs of the House such as the House of Commons Commission.

18 See HL 254, 1983–4 (Parliamentary Privilege and the Mental Health Legislation) and Patricia Leopold 'The compulsory detention of peers' [1985] *Public Law* 9.

19 These examples are suggested by Mr Geoffrey Lock in [1985] *Public Law* 376, 'The application of the general law to Parliament'. See also his article 'Labour law, parliamentary staff and parliamentary privilege' (1983) 12 *Industrial Law Journal* 28, and 'Parliamentary privilege and the courts: the avoidance of conflict' [1985] *Public Law* 64.

20 HC 34, 1976–7.

21 The 1967 committee's conclusions are discussed in G. Marshall, 'The House of Commons and its privileges', in S. A. Walkland (ed.), *The House of Commons in the Twentieth Century*, Oxford University Press, 1979.

22 HC 417, 1976–7.

23 For full details of the procedure for raising and considering privilege matters see Erskine May, *Parliamentary Practice*, 20th edn., Butterworth, 1983, pp. 169–80, 362.

24 HC 357, 1967–8.

25 HC 376, 1985–6.

26 HC 308, 1968–9. For a case of jostling *by* members themselves in the Lobby of the House see HC 279, 1970–1.
27 HC 50, 1971–2.
28 HC 634, 1974–5.
29 HC 512, 1976–7.
30 HC 118, 1946–7.
31 HC 564, 1983–4.
32 HC 185, 1970–1.
33 HC 185, 1969–70.
34 HC 302, 1974–5.
35 HC 43, 1975–6.
36 HC 275, 1975–6.
37 HC 176, 1976–7.
38 HC 58, 1976–7.
39 HC 197, 1968–9.
40 HC 43, 1975–6.
41 HC 228, 1974.
42 See the discussion of this issue in the Report of the 1967 Select Committee on Parliamentary Privilege and the Memorandum submitted by the Study of Parliament Group, HC 34, 1967–8, at p. 194.

12 WHERE HAVE WE GOT TO?

1 S. A. Walkland and Michael Ryle (eds), *The Commons Today*, Fontana, 1977, rev. edn 1981.
2 HC 588, 1977–8, paras 1.5–1.6.
3 HC 350, 1986–7, para. 74.
4 Pp. 12–13.
5 For a fuller statement of this argument, see my own chapter 1 in *The Commons Today*.
6 There was no such concept as 'opposition time' in the last century. The evolution of such as a major segment of the parliamentary timetable is perhaps the single most important development in the working of the House of Commons in this century. For a full account see M. Ryle, Supply and other financial procedures', S. A. Walkland (ed.), *The House of Commons in the Twentieth Century*, Oxford University Press, 1979, ch. 7.
7 See Irwin, chapter 5.
8 ibid., p. 76.
9 ibid., pp. 85–6, 98.
10 See HC 49, 1984–5 (public bill procedure); HC 324, 1985–6 (allocation of time to government bills in standing committees); HC 592, 1985–6 (shorter speeches; and HC 350, 1986–7 (use of time on the floor of the House).
11 See *Fourth Report from the Select Committee on Procedure*, HC 373 1986–7.
12 HC 350, 1986–7, para. 76.

NOTES ON CONTRIBUTORS

THE STUDY OF PARLIAMENT GROUP

The Study of Parliament Group was established in 1964. Membership is confined to senior members of universities and polytechnics working specifically in the parliamentary field and officers (or ex-officers) of both Houses of Parliament and is restricted to about sixty members. The Group has on several occasions prepared evidence for Select Committees on Procedure. It has undertaken original studies of many parliamentary matters and has published several books and pamphlets in this field. An earlier collection of essays by members of the Group, entitled *The Commons Today*, was published by Fontana Books in 1981

St John Bates is Clerk of Tynwald, Secretary of the House of Keys, and Counsel to the Speaker. He is concurrently Professor of Law at the University of Lancaster and was previously John Millar Professor of Law at the University of Glasgow. He is the co-author of *The Legal System of Scotland* (with Professor A. A. Paterson, 1983 and 1986), co-author of Wade and Bradley: *Constitutional and Administrative Law* (ed. Professor A. W. Bradley, 1985), and deputy editor of the *Statute Law Review*.

Robert Borthwick is Senior Lecturer in Politics at the University of Leicester. He has also taught in the USA. He is the author of various articles on parliamentary organization and joint editor of *British Politics in Perspective*.

Gavin Drewry is Reader in Social Administration at Royal Holloway and Bedford New College. He was the editor of the volume issued by the Study of Parliament Group on *The New Select Committees* (1985). Other publications include *Final Appeal* (co-author, 1972), *Law, Justice and Politics* (1975), and *Law and Morality* (co-editor, 1976).

Helen Irwin is a Deputy Principal Clerk in the House of Commons where she has served in the Clerk's Department from 1970 to 1972 and since 1977. She is currently Clerk of the Social Services Committee.

Nevil Johnson is a Professorial Fellow of Nuffield College, Oxford. Before holding academic posts at the Universities of Nottingham and Warwick he spent some years as an administrator in Whitehall. His publications include *Parliament and Administration: The Estimates Committee 1945–65* (1966), *Government in the Federal Republic of Germany* (1974), and *In Search of the Constitution* (1977). He is former editor of *Public Administration* and a past chairman of the Study of Parliament Group.

Geoffrey Lock is an Assistant Librarian in the House of Commons and Head of the Research Division. He has served in the Library since 1953. He has written articles on parliamentary privilege and has contributed to other publications by the Study of Parliament Group – *The Commons in Transition, 1970, The House of Commons Services and Facilities, 1972–1982, 1983*, and *The New Select Committees*, 1985.

Geoffrey Marshall is Fellow and Tutor in Politics, Queen's College, Oxford. He has published *Parliamentary Sovereignty and the Commonwealth* (1957), *Some Problems of the Constitution* (with G. Moodie, 1959), *Police and Government* (1956), and *Constitutional Theory* (1971). He is also assistant editor of *Public Law*.

Philip Norton is Professor of Government at the University of Hull. His publications include *Dissension in the House of Commons 1945–74* (1975), *Dissension in the House of Commons 1974–1979*(1980), and *The Commons in Perspective* (1981).

Peter Richards was Professor of British Government at the University of Southampton 1969–86. He published *Patronage in British Government* (1963), *Parliament and Foreign Affairs* (1967), *Parliament and Conscience* (1971), *The Backbenchers* (1972). He was a past chairman of the Study of Parliament Group. He died on 23 September 1987.

Ann Robinson is Senior Lecturer in Politics at the University of Wales College of Cardiff; she is the author of *Parliament and Public Spending: The Expenditure Committee of the House of Commons 1970–76* (1986) and many articles in the areas of her main research interests, public expenditure and taxation and the European Economic Community.

Michael Rush is Senior Lecturer in Politics at the University of Exeter and has taught at universities in Canada. He has published *The Selection of Parliamentary Candidates* (1969), *Parliament and the Public* (second edn), and was the co-author of *The Member of Parliament and his Information* (1970). He was also joint editor of the Study of Parliament Group's volume *The House of Commons: Services and Facilities* (1974) and edition of *The House of Commons: Services and Facilities, 1972–82* (1983).

Michael Ryle is Clerk of Committees in the House of Commons having served in the Clerk's Department since 1951. He has written on many aspects of parliamentary practice and procedure and was co-editor (with S. A. Walkland) of two previous volumes of essays in this series, *The Commons in the Seventies* and *The Commons Today*. He is past chairman of the Study of Parliament Group and is currently its President.

INDEX

267